Ha'aha'a Love
Perseverance
Mahalo
Kūlia i ka nu'u
Balance
gether Aloha
Leadership
Ho'omau
Family Alaka'i
i ke kumu
Thankful
Kākou
Humility

Acclaim for Managing with Aloha

Rosa's stories speak to our hearts at a level we understand. For those of us who were there and may have shared in these experiences with Rosa, it is impressive to see how well she is able to put these experiences and the Hawaiian-based values together for all to feel—experiences that seem indescribable come to life from her unique perspective in the pages of this book.

— Christine Bean, *Executive Assistant, Kūki'o*

Born and raised in Hawai'i, I surely appreciate the importance of understanding the values of Hawai'i and the people of "aloha." Rosa Say has been the inspiration and Kumu for my growth and development, as well as for many others. Her new book brings everything into perspective for you as a leader in Hawai'i able to balance your corporate organizational goals while motivating the people of our island and culture. Her philosophy works; I've seen it, and more important, I try to live it everyday at home and at work

— Doreen De Silva, *Director of Human Resources,*
The Fairmont Orchid, Hawai'i

How do I tell people I do not know that Rosa Say is such a great manager, teacher, mentor and guide? And she delivers: the Alaka'i Nalu of Hualalai Resort are a true testimonial to the power and truth contained in these pages. When you read this book, a manual to help create the magic of realized potential, be prepared to see results in your work and life. Be prepared to become a great manager.

— Toni Howard, *Spa Manager, Hualalai Resort*
Manager of the Alaka'i Nalu at historic Ka'ūpūlehu

My experience of working at Hualalai Resort and directly with Rosa Say was without a doubt a defining moment in my personal and professional path. Rosa's passion and her genuine care for her employees and her work was a quality that I admire and respect. Her commitment to the pursuit of excellence is greater than most individuals will ever experience. I cherish the gift I was given by having the opportunity to work with and learn from Rosa.

— Diana Bertsch, *Director, the IronMan Triathlon*

Rosa Say has a commitment to Hawaiian values like no one I have met in the Islands. When I first came to Hualalai on the Big Island, she was the person who really gave me insight on what those values are. Rosa's management style is inspirational to those who have been given the opportunity to work with her. For those of us who are "retailholics" and continue to challenge ourselves, there is much to be learned from Rosa's book.

— Jackie Calkins, *Retail Buyer & Merchandising Manager,*
the Hualalai Resort at historic Ka'ūpūlehu

Rosa emphatically believed that Hawaiian values were as essential to our daily business operations as our policies, procedures and P & Ls. By keeping values such as ha'aha'a (humility) and pono (doing the right thing) at the forefront of our daily focus, we would begin by working on ourselves as managers and leaders and naturally these values would spread throughout our entire departments and the whole organization. Rosa instilled in us that success at the personal and business level could be achieved by remembering our unique Hawaiian heritage and the values possessed of our native culture.

— Erin Lee, *Director of Resort Landscape,*
the Hualalai Resort at historic Ka'ūpūlehu

When I first started working at Hualalai, I felt completely over my head. I mean, I knew all about my industry, but I was relatively new to managing. After working with Rosa Say for just a few weeks, it was obvious to me that I could learn a tremendous amount about managing people. Her solutions were always fair—for the employee and for the company. The most important tool that she has given me is the ability to lead with compassion. We are all people. We all have different jobs. Every job is important, and every person at the company is vital to the operation. I often quote Rosa: "As a working adult, you spend almost one third of your life at your job. But, if you enjoy your job, you will never work another day in your life." As leaders, we can make every employee realize their importance and become truly passionate about their jobs. That's when the payoff really happens—for the manager, for the employees, and for the company.

— Thad Calciolari, *Spa Director,*
the Sports Club & Spa at Hualalai Resort

It's great reading when you know it's coming from the author's heart, and I've experienced it first hand working with her and the Hualalai 'Ohana.

— Max Yarawamai, *Landscape Manager, Kūki'o*

It would be difficult to find a more dedicated and passionate manager than Rosa Say. Her personal commitment to employees of all levels and her faith in their ability to achieve great things is beyond reproach.

— John Freitas, PGA, *Director of Golf,*
the Hualalai Resort at historic Ka'ūpūlehu

Rosa Say's leadership style was an excellent fit for our values driven organization. She is a leader and teacher by example, and inspires others to improve their own leadership skills. She brings out the best in people and I am certain her book will be a recipe for success.

— David K. Chai, *Director of Natural Resources,*
the Hualalai Resort at historic Ka'ūpūlehu

Hawai'i is a unique environment with a sense of Place, Aloha and 'Ohana. Rosa Say has been instrumental in motivating me to another level of management style.

— Earl Sanders, *Director of Golf Maintenance,*
the golf courses at Hualalai at historic Ka'ūpūlehu

The years I spent working with Rosa Say provided daily exposure to the multitude of benefits possible when operating with an uncompromising, values-based management philosophy: deep satisfaction, happiness and an inner peace, while guaranteeing success—in business, relationships and in your personal life. Managing well is an art which can be continuously improved through practice, though never perfected. Rosa's commitment to this art, and to values-based management, are the trademarks she shares with all she meets.

— Jesse Langridge, *Director of Retail,*
the Hualalai Resort at historic Ka'ūpūlehu

Managing

with Aloha

Bringing Hawaii's
Universal Values
to the Art of
Business

Say, Rosa.
Managing with Aloha: Bringing Hawaii's Universal Values to the Art of Business
Rosa Say. -- 1st ed. 3rd printing -- Waikōloa, Hawaii : Ho'ohana Publishing, 2006.

p. ; cm.

Includes bibliographical references and index.
ISBN: 0-9760190-0-0

1. Business--Hawaii. 2. Business ethics. 3. Management.
4. Hawaii--Social life and customs. I. Title.

HF5065.H3 S29 2004
650/.09969--dc22   0411

Published in the United States of America by Ho'ohana Publishing, a division of Say Leadership
Coaching.
Contact us at www.SayLeadershipCoaching.com.

For rights information or to submit requests, please contact:
Jellinek & Murray Literary Agency
2024 Mauna Place
Honolulu, HI 96822
Tel: 808 521 4057
Fax: 808 521 4058
jellinek@lava.net

Jacket photography by Kathleen Fitzgerald
Author photograph by Kris Scanlon, Eye of the Islands Photography

Designed by The Madden Corporation
Distributed by Island Heritage
Printed in Hong Kong by Island Heritage Press

Managing
with *Aloha*

Bringing Hawaii's Universal Values
to the Art of Business

Rosa Say
Founder and Coach
Say Leadership Coaching

Foreword by
Nainoa Thompson

Ho'ohana Publishing
Waikōloa, Hawaii

For Marmee,

From the moment I was born, and you held me in your arms,
you believed I could do this,
and you told me so every chance you had.

You still do.

Treat people as if they were what they ought to be,
and you help them to become what they are capable of being.

— Johann Wolfgang von Goethe (1749-1832),
German writer, scientist and philosopher

Contents

Foreword

By Nainoa Thompson

Those of us who live in Hawai'i know we live in an extraordinary place. There is nothing like this place we call Hawai'i, because it is home. And like any home, Hawai'i has to be cared for.

In *Managing with Aloha*, Rosa explains how our values are about the very identity of Hawai'i. The values we share, as handed down from our ancestors, celebrate our people, our sense of place, and the land that sustains us and inspires us. We grow within these values in the arms of our families. How we thrive and find success in our home is determined by our shared journeys. Spend any time with Rosa discussing these things and she will passionately speak of her belief; that shaped by our values, we create our own destiny. She wants us to prosper in being true to who we are and who we are meant to be.

As Rosa explains, we cannot define wealth simply in financial terms. Money is part of our reality, but wealth is also defined by family, connection to our ancestry, and our best vision of our future. All of these find their inner spirit, their constancy, and their strength in the values that shape our thinking and our actions. And when the needs of our spirit are met, we find any financial wealth is most satisfying when shared in service to the community, which had lifted us toward our greater good.

Rosa says *Managing with Aloha* is a program that will showcase the wealth of talent that exists in Hawai'i, and yet reveals that our home-grown managers embody opportunities that too often are missed. She believes all people are born into goodness, and if managers start from that place of good intent, they will have an opportunity for a profound impact on the people they lead. I share her enthusiasm and hope.

Yet even in Hawai'i there are many who are not thriving and are struggling. Far too many of our children are homeless, living poorly, and are in need of a greater sense of hope. They count on us to work with the assurance that this world holds something better and is worthy of their continued stewardship. We are the caretakers of their hope for a better future and perhaps by tapping into our full potential we can grow to do the most good in that endeavor. Rosa's own story of struggling to find worthwhile work and a job she could be proud of gave me new hope. It's a matter of feeling that you serve rather than that you are a servant.

I am just one of thousands who have had the privilege and opportunity to be a part of the evolution of Hokule'a and to share in her vision. A voyage on Hokule'a is never completely successful unless it is a shared journey, and unless we can share what we have learned with others. Education extends both hands in a farther reach, so all can participate in the experience. It then becomes a voyage of personal knowledge and hope. As Rosa explains so well, learning unlocks doors for us. The more we learn, the more comfortable we become in facing those risks that are before us, and there we find the opportunity to grow and heal.

Two full years of preparation and training can pass before any voyage on Hokule'a. It is the most difficult part of a voyage; when you're continually questioning yourself, anticipating, and planning. The risks are immense, but often the greatest risk is ending that training and preparation.

Fear is a natural part of the process, but you learn to embrace that fear and learn from it as well. It becomes an emotional discipline, another challenge you welcome. Eventually you ask, are you ready to let go of the lines? Are you prepared enough so that the purpose and fulfillment of the voyage is worth taking the risk? If so, then let go and set sail.

This same process happens in different ways in all walks of life, and it is our values that help us make the decisions that are right for us. Rosa's book helps in the appreciation of those values. As Rosa says, "Work is personal." This is a book that helps us tap into the core of who we are and touch the worth of the work that we do. In the end, Managing with Aloha is a personal guide that inspires a future of hope, dignity, and fulfillment.

Prologue

The story of a manager in Hawaii

Every manager has a story. This is mine.

I began my working career on Oʻahu behind Fort Street Mall's F.W. Woolworth lunch counter when I was 15. That was when Woolworth's drugstore design included diner type service, but there were no booths or tables. Customers would sit on red vinyl-topped swivel stools bolted to the floor around these U-shaped bays of counters, one bay with 12 seats for each waitress. The menu was in a laminated card held by this metal grid at the far end of the counter in front of you, a grid curved in at each end to corral your salt and pepper, sugar shaker and ketchup bottle. To your back was the rest of the store, with racks of greeting cards, sewing notions, fishing tackle, or baby food nearly within arm's reach.

There weren't any hostesses. Customers walked right up and sat where there was an empty stool, the counter was wiped clean, and the waitress looked calm and sorta friendly. Job performance was really easy for the boss to measure. Back then your tips went into a locked box, and he'd count them out for you when you clocked out: Good tips meant happy customers. If your bay was usually busy and you were found to be honest, you were an employee he was going to keep. It didn't take me too long to learn my early lessons on satisfying repeat customers, and keeping the balance between making them happy and turning each stool for more money in the till.

1

Fast forward two years, and at 17 I'm boldly lying to the assistant human resources director at a Waikīkī hotel that yes, I'm 18 and can get a blue card to serve liquor. The job I want is opening the Third Floor Restaurant, credited by many as being the granddaddy of fine dining in Hawaii. Because I already know what bosses want to hear, I get the job. Now there are tables and a hostess to deal with, and there are more lessons in the expectations of good customer service. After my first shot, customers will have to remember my name and ask for me. And jeez, fine dining takes way more time; I'll need to get more out of each one of them. The boss will measure my performance in somewhat the same way, right?

As much as I celebrate inside that I got the job, I hesitate to tell most of my friends. This job is in Waikīkī, and it's at a *hotel*. My family will be fine, for they love me unconditionally and have always supported the choices I've made. But with my friends I know what I'll hear, and I do.

"What, you gonna work with *tourists*? Those people don't belong here. Why do you want anything to do with them? You gonna be just another money-hungry local letting those hotel guys commercialize our culture and pretend to know what we're all about. How can you do that? They make a mockery of us, and who we *really* are. How can you be like them? Don't you have any pride?"

Yet along the way, I'd learned that I had to create my own future and not just let it happen to me. Luckily for me, those were lessons that had come from my mom and dad, and they had never steered me wrong. I was sure that not only would it all work out, I could possibly make a difference and prove my friends wrong. And for goodness sake, it was just a job feeding people.

So I take the job. There are new lessons in teamwork, for I have to work with a captain and another waitress. There are new lessons in cooperation, timing, and yes, in manipulation. The hostess I can handle through my customers, but then there's the kitchen and I gotta tell you, the Woolworth fry cooks were sweeties compared to these European chefs. It doesn't take me too long to figure out I'd much prefer being in charge, but there's a glitch in the system here; to be a captain you have to be exotic (translation: Asian, European, or otherwise non-local) and male. One of my friends had said, "You'll see. You're gonna find out they don't care about you, they don't really want you there anyway." Was he right? I shut the thought out of my head and figured out how to get the job done until the time I *was* in charge. It would happen.

Fast forward 19 years, six hotels and two islands. I'm trying to decide between sticking it out though yet another hotel ownership change or joining up with the newest kid on Kona's Gold Coast, the Hualalai Resort at historic Ka'ūpūlehu on the Big Island. I've been managing employees since I hit 18—truthfully 18—and I've sampled that elite group called The Executive Committee in two different international hotel corporations. I still hesitate to tell my local friends where I work, and there's no kidding myself any longer, because I now do way more than just feed people. If anything it's gotten worse, for I still don't feel I've made much of a difference in representing our culture well, and I've moved pretty darn far up the ladder.

I finally choose Hualalai for one significant reason: I meet a man there who I at first dismiss as a hopeless dreamer who needs a reality check. Yet several meetings later, he has achieved something truly amazing to me, and he has done so by talking about a concept that has long been stirring uneasily in my soul: sense of place. Sam Ainslie will be my boss, and he has given me his promise that this time I'll be able to say I work for the Hawaii hospitality industry and hold my head up with pride and dignity. We will manage Hualalai with a respect for her culture and for our employees' sense of place. We will engender an *'Ohana* in business.

In that moment of Sam's promise my path became clear and certain. And it was exhilarating.

It was February 1996, and by this time I'd become a new person: a mother. I was consumed with something vitally important to me—raising my son and daughter with the values that would help them be good people. Warning them about the trappings of life and keeping them safe wasn't enough; I wanted to teach them *how to think*. If there was anything my management career had done for me up to this point, it was grooming the importance I placed in people developing intellectual honesty with themselves. I wanted my kids to make good choices that were steeped in good values that would ground them and place a light in their spirit. They were now 9 and 12 years old, and I was acutely aware that they were smack dab in their formative years; the clock was ticking on the time I had left to shape their lives. They were also the loudest and most influential critics of every decision I made. I could not disregard their opinions as easily as I'd dismissed those of my friends when I'd first decided to work in Waikīkī. My children were the very reason we lived on the Big Island in the first place.

For me, everything connected to good life-shaping values was connected to sense of place. I had no illusions about how growing up in the islands had deeply affected me, giving me my own values, and creating the person I felt I was. Thus far, Hawaii was doing her part in influencing my children as I knew she could. Thus far, my husband and I both felt great about the decisions we'd made for them, and the things we'd taught them. But then there was the matter of my own intellectual honesty with myself in my work; that connection was still incomplete, and it still unsettled me. In my way of thinking, the work someone did defined them—and the work I did defined me. Even the barest hint of hypocrisy was unacceptable.

I loved my work. I loved being a manager. I felt I had a huge responsibility to those I managed, and I took on that responsibility eagerly; I was willing to be held completely accountable. I had learned so much about what I believed it was to manage people well. But were these things—the good things, the *right* things—in practice every day? Was the knowledge I gained through the years used to make a positive difference? I knew there was still more to be done, and it was time. I was primed and ready.

As much as I'd wanted it, and had come to the Big Island hoping to find it, Sam Ainslie's promise was unexpected, and it was truly amazing to me. When it came to nobler, culturally correct pursuits I was accustomed to going it on my own. His promise was bold: *"We will manage Hualalai with a respect for her culture and for our employees' sense of place. We will have an 'Ohana in business."* Woven into his voice, and what actually spoke to me, was his genuinely deep belief and his sincerity, and I could actually feel it. Instinctively I believed him, I had faith in him, and I trusted him, and I began to see how it would be possible—it would happen! I even helped him give orientation to the other local kids. The land beneath my feet seemed to talk to me, and my own belief was nurtured. There was so much hope.

Sam did not know it at the time, but he gave me a new mission. I would define what it meant to be a great manager. Being one would be my new calling.

Over the next seven years I would learn that the search for meaningful work starts within you. I would learn that sense of place is a very powerful and very personal thing, and culture is defined in one's values, one's attitude, and in one's own choices, not in circumstance. I would learn that there is something far worse than "commercializing the culture" and that is ignoring it.

Our culture is alive. It grows and changes every day just as we do. It needs our *Mālama* (our care).

I would learn that to be *Pono*, to feel right within oneself, the answers could only be found within. I would consistently and frequently experience what before had seemed to sporadically occur by happenstance: being someone who manages other people is immensely fulfilling and rewarding when you do it well, with a deliberate and thoughtful plan true to the values you personally believe in, and values you share.

To be a manager is to touch the lives of others in profound ways.

As a manager, you must accept this certainty with responsibility. With care. With *Aloha*.

The day would come when it was time for me to bid farewell to Hualalai. I left the Hualalai Development Company having been vice-president of operations, responsible for a budget in excess of 20 million dollars, and overseeing more than 350 employees in eight diverse disciplines: golf operations, golf maintenance, resort landscape maintenance, sports club and spa operations, retail, food and beverage, natural resource management, ocean recreation and safety. Our canvas included resort hotel operations, club management, land development and real estate sales in the creation of an award winning residential resort community. I had worked with great managers and with a staff who challenged me daily to be a great manager for them, and I loved doing it.

On any given day my employees personally shared their *Aloha* with up to a thousand guests who had come to Hawai'i hoping to find something special within our embrace. Our customers came as visitors and many became residents, unwilling to part with the *Aloha* that had infused their spirit. They had fallen in love with our culture. They had discovered sense of place.

I had discovered that to make that difference I'd always wanted to make, I'd have to share what I'd learned. Mission had become purpose. Managing with *Aloha*, true to the cultural values that drive their employees, had to happen for more managers, and for all those who say, "I run a business, and I hire others to help me." We could bring integrity and nobility to management.

Today I am a management coach, teaching the lessons of *Managing with Aloha* within the services offered by my own consulting company, and I continue to love each and every day doing so. It is immensely rewarding watching great managers emerge because they have deliberately chosen to manage purposefully, with *Aloha*.

E komo mai, come with me.

You can do this: *You* can be a *great* manager.

In so kindly listening to my story, you have already started, so *Mahalo nui*, thank you. Thank you for choosing this book and allowing me to share what I have learned with you.

Introduction

What should managers be?

At some time or another, every child is asked, "What do you want to be when you grow up?" I've never heard one answer, "I'd like to be a manager." I didn't.

Yet I now believe heart and soul that it is a calling to be a great manager. Unfortunately, greatness is rarely achieved, and thus examples are rarely talked about. Children don't hear inspiring stories of managers often enough to want to be one.

Even in Hawaii, where the fanciful romantic concepts of the *Aloha* spirit are marketed and draped like charm bracelets around the hospitality industry, managers are thought of as babysitters. They are not really considered the ambassadors of the *Aloha* spirit, although that spirit is what they seek to peddle, and their profession is not thought of as particularly noble. Why is this?

Process versus people

Early on I was taught that good managers manage good processes. While earning some of my supervisory stripes in the heyday of the Total Quality Management movement I learned how to hunt and destroy variation like a heat-seeking missile, normally sidestepping the people who were a part of the process along the way. I was an open book in my quest to learn my job correctly, and guess what I found? The *Aloha* spirit does not sit streamlined and variation-free within your bulletproof processes; it swims around within your people, surfing the high and low tides of their disposition each day they report to work. Further, there is an *Aloha* approach to managing that brings the very best of what they have to the forefront.

Said another way, I have come to realize that yes, good managers do work with good processes, however the *great* managers are the ones who concentrate on how they manage people. And boy oh boy, high tide, low tide, people are filled to the brim with variation! They have interesting, dynamic, challenging variation, and being a manager who works on valuing those differences as the way to simultaneously improve the process is so much more fun. Yes, fun! And understand this: The fact that processes simply do not and cannot exist for every employee to work variation-free is what makes managers so needed. This intuitive knowledge is the juice that kick-starts truly great managers who seek to make a difference with the people they manage. To execute their jobs well, employees need teachers, coaches, cheerleaders and mentors, and that's what managers need to be for them. Great managers relish the opportunity.

The role of the manager

Instinctively most managers know this. It's probably the reason that one of the earliest traps new supervisors often fall into is trying to be best friend or after-work beer buddy to their employees. Well, take it from someone who has seen this strategy backfire time and again; employees don't really want you to be a father figure, second mother, best friend, soul mate, or even confidant. They want you to be their boss! A strategy-mapping, consistent, objective, organized and predictable boss with an inspiring vision, and a boss who has the same high expectations for everyone they manage—including them-selves. You will seldom, if ever, come across employees who say that to you directly; however, when that's what you deliver, many will thank you for being the kind of leader they wanted. They will recognize in you the manager they needed. They will sing your praises as their best boss ever.

When you hire people they come connected. Your

employees have families and friends. Your role as their manager is a different one, and it is one they come on board expecting you to fill—boss! Your role is to support them in a way that will help them forge good relationships in the branches of the personal network they already have. You do so by keeping them positive and optimistic in their work.

Your place in the continuum is to create a work environment in which they thrive, so that when they return home they are in a great state of mind, ready to openly share the positive energy they had gained at work. You can demonstrate values and character traits such as treating others with honesty and respect, dignity and *Aloha*. In a way you are serving their families and friends, by giving your employees the gift of a good example to follow, and expecting them to do well.

And here's the wondrous thing: Do it right, do it well, and your employee will come back to work the next day at high tide, ready to surf the wave of high productivity with you. Abundance has been created wherein you get back what you have given, and more.

Why focus on management?

Managing with Aloha was written because I fell in love with being a manager. I discovered that my work could be a celebration of the values I had grown up with, values I grew to comprehend more fully within my life in business strongly connected to our culture, and to my sense of place within the islands. Writing the book became voice for my passion about the calling to be a great manager, and for a new sense of purpose. I wanted other managers to fall in love with their work just as I had, by bringing a Hawaiian sensibility to what they do, with love and respect for our culture—or for whatever culture they find they are in. It is a love affair you can have with heart, soul, and complete intellectual honesty, something needed in every business endeavor I know of.

Leadership has been the bigger buzzword for our generation: Aspire to be a leader, and not "just" a manager. This premature and faulty condescension disturbs me, for I see the promise of great integrity and nobility required in being a great manager. Personally I see leadership and management as two different things, something I explore in more depth when we discuss *Alaka'i*, the Hawaiian value of leadership in Chapter 14. It is my belief that managing well comes first, so that emerging leaders can learn the empathy needed to lead effectively when they have found new and better ways, and they will have earned a circle of influence from which to stage their efforts.

It will often require a charismatic leader to create excitement, and lead the way with new and innovative thinking. However it will require a great manager of people to actually inspire employees to get the job done. In choppy seas, the leader may be sitting in front of the canoe with the keenest eye for land, but the manager is the one who is steering. The manager is focused on his paddlers: He is the one who will enable them to bring that canoe to shore.

It is the manager who will touch people directly and affect them more often, and in particular, business managers are the most influential movers and shakers I know. When great management is in place, the ideas of emerging leaders find fertile ground.

Why incorporate values into business?

To manage *with Aloha* is to draw out the best performance of your own management practice from the values that are inherent in your nature *and* a match for the demands of your business. To be a *great* manager is to realize your success depends on the people you manage, and they are driven by their values just as much as you are. You have to respect their culture, and learn to speak the language of their values. In all likelihood, their values will match up with your own much more than you think.

Values are an inseparable part of the fabric of the human race. We have all grown up being shaped by values that are woven into our culture, for values drive the quality of our experiences. These values are layered with the nuances of our parents' life experiences, and those of their parents. I believe we inherit them as surely as we inherit the color of our eyes and the curl in our hair. You learn about them more explicitly when you misbehave, for parents universally have this innate certainty that values = goodness = better behavior.

As far back as I can remember, *Aloha* surrounded me, it was the grandfather of all the other values I'd come to learn, woven into my culture and thus my character. It was a feeling connected to family and community, comforting and familiar but unobtrusive, a sort of color that warmed up the background of everything. *Aloha* was just there, it wasn't something that we talked about much, it was more a way of living that you grew up with—and everyone else assumed you grew up that way. It was good, and it was right.

When I became a manager I quickly figured out I couldn't keep *Aloha* in the background any longer: I had to pay better attention to it and welcome it into my management perform- ance with open arms. Why? Because when I did, it worked, and it worked wonders. I realized that *Aloha* was a statement of personal truths for me, my own source to look inward to. When I released it, *Aloha* made my job easier, and it made me much more effective in delivering the results that were expected of me.

This is a book that shares the stories of how managing with *Aloha* produces a lifetime of productivity that is colored with integrity. Management is about getting things done through other people; it doesn't get any more basic than that. You will best get things done through others by incorporating the values you share with them, values that embrace collabo- ration, and values that also are fundamental good practices in the business environment. And *Aloha* is the most universal value of them all.

The case for managing the Hawaiian way, with Aloha

Who or what is Hawaiian? In my lifetime, this has been a question of debate and controversy. It's a question that stirs passionate emotion, a question capable of creating both unity and division. When I was younger, I'd be hurt and confused by those who claimed you needed to be of Hawaiian blood to *be* Hawaiian, for as far as I knew, Hawaiian was all I was, all I knew how to be. I'd never lived anywhere else, I had no other sense of place; if I wasn't Hawaiian, what was I?

Therefore it came as a great relief to me to hear someone I highly respected give me both his encouragement and his definition: *"These days any resident of this State who considers Hawaii his home and who has a true understanding of the Hawaiian culture ought to consider himself or herself a Hawaiian."* —Dr. George Kanahele.

These words were a gift. In a way I was getting permission to be myself, no matter what anyone else may think. I could *Hoʻomau* (continue) and be true to myself, and that would be enough. For me it would be *Pono*, it would be right.

I first wrote his quote down when I attended classes taught by the late Dr. Kanahele in 1990. A few years later, as my interest grew in his work with the Waiaha Foundation, I would read these same words in the introduction of his book, *Kū Kanaka, Stand Tall, A Search for Hawaiian Values.* When we opened the Hualalai Resort at historic Kaʻūpūlehu, Dr. Kanahele's 1991 essay, *Critical Reflections on Cultural Values & Hotel Management in Hawaii*, was to be our Bible, our ethical scorecard. In his essay, he challenged the leaders of our industry to have the concepts of *Aloha* and *Hoʻokipa* (hospitality) ring true: to give them credibility and validity. To say I have been profoundly—and positively—influenced by Dr. Kanahele would be an understatement. However, Dr. Kanahele also impressed me with his own respect for the *kūpuna* (elders) that he had learned from; in following his example I would continue to seek them out, just as he did.

First one learns. For the learning to stick, be fulfilling and become meaningful, one must apply what they have learned to what they do. They must allow their learning to evolve to personal belief—it becomes their *manaʻo*, the deep and certain belief that drives one's instinctual actions. This is what *Managing with Aloha* represents for me, and this is what I hope to share with you.

Thus from here on, you will read about Hawaiian values, and how *you* can manage with *Aloha*, bringing Hawaii's universal values to the art of conducting business profitably. Trust me, these are *not* contradictory ideas. Part of my goal is to show you how managing with these "soft" concepts are exceptionally good for business. They work better for those hard, gut-wrenching decisions than the exclusionary brutality of the numbers game, because they carry people through the long haul and help you achieve long-term success that can be perpetuated. You will find that the numbers do support and give credibility to values-centered management. My own corporate business experience was but one proving ground, the most recent with over 350 employees driving a multi-million-dollar bottom line. Numbers can be healthy when your success has grown infused with *Aloha*, and perhaps more important, you can feel good about achieving them.

Managing with *Aloha* defines a Hawaiian sensibility for the work we do, and it is the polar opposite of the fear-based management that can weaken and destroy the ethical and humanitarian hopes we have for business today. We live in a very global and increasingly transparent world, and managing with *Aloha* paves the way for managers born and raised with the Hawaiian culture to work in harmony with our "mainland" counterparts for common goals.

Managing with *Aloha* is a program that will showcase the wealth of talent that exists in Hawaii: it reveals that our home-grown managers embody opportunities that too often are missed. Managers who are *keiki o ka ʻāina*, children of this land, have a key advantage: they've grown up with a feel for the place, they have "sense of place." You can manage with *Aloha* and simultaneously find you are in the ranks of the business elite who are innovators, mavericks, and visionaries. Yet you will stand apart, a shining example of how you can achieve business success today and feel absolutely wonderful about it because you have been true to who you are. Not only will you prove that you have what it takes to succeed, you will have defined it.

If you are a manager new to the islands, managing with *Aloha* will help you gain an incredible richness from your experience working within your host culture, while you find comfort in their universal truths, and in values you recognize. *Aloha* is within all of us, it is something we were born with. It is a feeling, a stirring in one's soul that begs to be shared, and a spirit as real as anything you can hold in your hands. And you needn't have been born in Hawaii to have it. You've discovered it within you if you have chosen to live here and work here. Each of us has this choice to make: Do we release our *Aloha* and share it? Do we live it, and do we celebrate it? The arms of *Aloha* are waiting, eager to embrace you.

Whoever you are, it is my fervent wish that you will be a great manager, one who will achieve *Pono* (rightness and balance), that tremendous feeling of satisfaction and contentment when all is good and right for you. It is my dream that a child in your future will recognize his or her own calling, look up to you and say, "I want to be a great manager one day."

How best to read this book

Shall we get started?

I encourage you to initially read this book sequentially, following the order of chapters as they've been placed. I've designed each chapter to be a self-contained primer per value, so that the book can serve you well as a reference guide and source of inspiration once you make the choice to manage with *Aloha*. However upon the first reading you will discover that the values build upon one another: What you have read in previous chapters will frame the concepts you are learning in each new one.

In addition, you will likely find that you develop your own *mana'o* about these values. Your *mana'o* is the whole of those thoughts and beliefs that have become your givens: They are what rings true for you, serving to empower you. Your *mana'o* will help you apply the values of the earlier chapters in a manner that is most natural for you. As you read the later chapters you will find that the meanings of earlier ones have become enriched in your understanding.

Whatever command you may have of the Hawaiian language you must keep in mind that the values I present here have context: They are specifically aimed at improving management practices, and business is a pragmatic affair that seeks its own sensibility and logic.

Chapter 1 is devoted to a discussion of *Aloha* itself.

Chapters 2, 3, and 4 will explore your purpose, mission, goals, and passion for achieving them. With Chapters 5 and 6 we address achievement, and how it is best defined for you, for your company and for your customers.

Chapter 7 reveals my belief that *'Ohana* (family) is a wonderful form for the practice of *Aloha*, especially here in Hawaii. With *'Ohana* in place to sustain your efforts and gain you community support, Chapters 8 through 13 explore the nuts and bolts of day-to-day management: We discuss concepts like teamwork, win-win agreements, responsibility, motivation, training programs, communication and conduct.

Chapter 14 introduces you to *Alaka'i*, the value of leadership, and it contains a discussion of how management and leadership differ. At this point you've learned quite a lot, and in Chapters 15 and 16, *Mālama* and *Mahalo* will address how best to take inventory of your assets and care for them.

I end with *Nānā i ke kumu* (look to your source) and *Pono* (rightness and balance), for these are values that will help you discover your own source of strength and the essentials that keep you grounded. Both of these values help you find balance and contentment as you weave these lessons of *Aloha* together in a way that is most meaningful for you.

I strongly encourage you to mark up this book, allowing it to be a canvas for your own self-expression; The margins have been enlarged specifically for you to do so. In so many ways, management is a hands-on, personal love affair. My suggestion is that you write your first reactions in the margins of the text itself as different values and their concepts speak to you. Write down what you will *do*; spell out the action steps you will take to put the lessons of *Managing with Aloha* into practice. Draw pictures, design whiteboard lessons of your own, or log promises you've made to yourself. Use any blank spaces at the end of chapters to pencil in a windowpane grid and design a storyboard for the future you will create. If you are one of those people who has never marked up a book and just can't bring yourself to do it, use post-it notes. Whatever style you choose to write down your thoughts, *ho'ohiki*: keep those promises you make to yourself, for everything will start or end with you.

Ready?

Read with an open mind, write your thoughts, speak your heart and bring your *Aloha* to life.

This is your call to arms, the arms of *Aloha*. Start a movement with me, and be the one to bring *Aloha* to business today. Your customers are waiting. Your employees, peers, and family are waiting. The very best in your life is waiting.

1

Aloha

Aloha is a value, one of unconditional love
Aloha is the outpouring and receiving of the spirit

The arms of *Aloha* are inclusive, and they seek to serve.
Aloha is an attitude, one that is positive and healthy, for
    Aloha is the value of unconditional love and acceptance.
To be a *great* manager is to share the intent of *Aloha*.
You must give your employees an outpouring of your spirit,
    and you must receive theirs.
This is *Aloha*. This is the calling of great managers.

Managing with Aloha

There is one way I best know how to share with you the management lessons I have learned. It is the same way I now teach and coach emerging leaders to manage their own people, helping them to become value teachers and coaches themselves in the process. In the chapters to follow I will teach you my interpretations of the Hawaiian values I feel best guide great managers. When you weave them together, they define a way to work that I call *Managing with Aloha*. We will explore how this approach can work for you, bringing you success personally and for your business.

The arms of *Aloha* embrace values that perfectly align themselves with the requirements of fundamental business principles. For instance:

- The values of *Ho'ohana* (work with purpose) and *'Imi ola* (seeking your best life) are in perfect alignment with centering one's business with mission and giving it the focus of vision.
- If you are a manager who lives within the value of *Mahalo* (thankfulness), appreciative of what you already have, you are one who constantly takes inventory of the strengths of your team and applies them to the job at hand (*Lōkahi*).
- The most effective managers are the ones who do not foolishly go it alone: They get everyone involved in ways that are stimulating, challenging and inclusive (*Kākou*).
- They trust their people because they know them well (*'Ike loa*), and they dole out very generous portions of meaningful assignments (*Ho'ohana*) and the authority to effectively get them done (*Kuleana*).
- They give advice vs. approval, forgiveness vs. permission, and find that results are achieved faster, in more nimble ways through-out their operations. They are *Alaka'i* (leaders) who excel and innovate, leading with their good example and confident in the trust and respect they have gained from their staff.

We will explore Hawaiian values that are thought of as ancient and very traditional; stories are told of them as taught and practiced with reverence in our islands' history, whatever one's ancestry may be. I am a *kama'āina*, a person who is native born in Hawaii, however not of Hawaiian blood; literally the word *kama'āina* translates to "land child." I am a fourth generation native with the chop-suey of ancestry that makes up the vast majority of Hawaii's present-day population. Yet growing up here, isolated from the cultures of my blood ancestry, gaining my education here and spending my entire working life here, these values are what I know. They are who I am.

Upon becoming a manager I learned to incorporate these values into my language at work and not just at home, finding that the surest way to change your own work behavior for the better is to speak the words that will force you to make it so. You have to walk your talk if you are to internalize new learning, build your confidence and keep your credibility and integrity with others. We *can* change our behavior, and these values helped me change mine in a way that made me a much more effective manager.

My interpretations of these Hawaiian values are offered to you with *Ha'aha'a* (modesty and humility), knowing that they encapsulate only the limited scope of my own learning and management practice. I fully realize that there are many *kumu* (teachers) and *kūpuna* (elders) in Hawaii who know much more than I; as charted by their own life's course, they may tell you of more insightful experiences. I encourage you to listen to the stories that are shared by elders, for their lessons learned can inspire you, and may enrich your own understanding. Values can be as complex as the people who have them, but by their very nature, values will always teach us to be better.

There are more values within the Hawaiian culture than there are within the pages of this book; mine is not an all-inclusive listing.[1] The values we explore here are specifically aimed at improving management practices and our working lives as a whole. I present them to you as modern everyday applications for what I have experienced and still see as today's challenges in business. Businesses seek to please customers through the predictable and consistent actions taken by their employees, whether they are in Hawaii or elsewhere, and those employees are driven by their personal values. I have found that the successful business owners are those who consider their staff to be their partners: they know them, they trust them and they count on them. These things have been made possible through the values they share.

Values are both universal and personal

As we discuss them you will find that the Hawaiian values I've included in the *Managing with Aloha* philosophy are very universal, and you may recognize them by another name in another culture or language. If they call to you in some way, put my book down momentarily: Look to your own history and define your thoughts. For not only are values universal, they

---

[1] The best texts I have read on Hawaiian values from a historical perspective are *Kū Kanaka, Stand Tall* by Dr. George Kanahele, and both volumes of *Nānā I Ke Kumu* published by the Queen Lili'uokalani Children's Center. You will find more information on both within my listing of Recommended Reading.

are highly personalized. They come alive with one's personal *mana'o* (one's thoughts and beliefs) and they are strengthened and continually reinforced with the nuances of their own experiences—a value can have *kaona* (hidden meaning) for someone in a way that is very uniquely meaningful for them. There is a self-awareness that is uncovered for you. When coupled with your mission and with *Ho'ohana* (working with intent and purpose) the result is powerful self-motivation.

Our values drive our beliefs, and often they give our thoughts clarity. When we are true to our beliefs, the decisions and choices we make come to us naturally and easily, especially when we have a goal or objective in mind. It is easier to act on that which you believe. I am a strong advocate for the writing of mission statements, as you will discover when we reach the chapter on *'Imi ola* (to seek life). Our mission defines our goals, and our goals drive our actions. And actions taken, true to clear beliefs that have been borne from good values, give us our integrity. Acting with integrity makes things right for us; it feeds our hunger to be intelligent, ethical and morally just.

Aloha is a value, one of unconditional love

I cringe each time I hear a Hawaii travelogue intone that *Aloha* is simply a greeting, a word the visitor to our islands can use to mean both hello and goodbye. Throughout their visit, that is how most visitors hear the word *Aloha* used, and they will depart believing they understand it, and that they have experienced the *Aloha* spirit because "Alooooooooooha!" was said with such enthusiasm at a *lū'au* (a feast) or by their tour bus driver.

Unfortunately most children growing up in Hawaii today believe this is the only definition of *Aloha* as well, and as much as I hate to admit it now, at one time so did I. To manage with *Aloha*, I first had to learn and understand that *Aloha* is a value I had to choose to believe in, and that when shared with others, my own *Aloha* spirit would be as real and tangible as something you felt you could physically touch.

While a manager for Hualalai Resort at historic Ka'ūpūlehu, a resort community on the Big Island, this definition of *Aloha* was shared with me: "*Aloha is unconditional love, for it is the outpouring and receiving of the spirit. It is an expression of unconditional kindness, hospitality, spirituality, cooperativeness with humility, unity and graciousness that touches the souls of others.*"

I'd read these words over and over, and I found I had a need inside to have this statement of *Aloha* ring true for me. "*Aloha is unconditional love, for it is the outpouring and receiving of the spirit.*"

As you read on, I ask you to keep something in mind whenever I use the words "spirit" or "spirituality." Where I say spirituality, I refer to the spirit within; you could call it the breath of your life, the voice of your soul. For me, the individual religions of the world are merely different expressions people have for their own spirituality within them, and they have made a choice as to who they will honor in their gratefulness. I am not suggesting religiousness; that is your own choice. However I do believe that we should acknowledge our own spirituality and get comfortable with it. One's inner spiritual power is assumed in the Hawaiian culture, and it is celebrated. In many ways *Managing with Aloha* is about tapping into the spirit that is inside you; it embraces your intuition and gut-level feelings.

The purest definition for *Aloha* itself is unconditional love. Love can be an uncomfortable word for many people, for we associate it with sensitivity, raw emotion and other touchy-feely concepts that are not easily discussed openly or with much frequency—certainly not with employees we manage! Ironically love is probably the most universal of all values. Love is a word of complete unselfishness and beauty.

Culturally, our freer use of the word in Hawaii is very much a reason I have intentionally chosen to raise my children here. When we say "I have *Aloha* for you," we are saying we have love and the utmost respect for who you are.

My *Aloha* for you is my unconditional love and acceptance of the spirit that was created within you upon your birth. *Aloha* can be literally defined as the breath of the life within. It is my unwavering belief that the spirit within you is innately good. *Aloha* is the outpouring of my own spirit, freely given to you to receive from me, as well. In doing so, I have faith in you, and I trust you to respect and honor my *Aloha* in return, accepting without question that I have given it to you with nothing but good intent.

Great managers have the intent of Aloha

I am convinced that good management must start with good intent. There simply is no other way. Managers who feel that people inherently need to be worked on and reshaped to their own design are dangerous. They shouldn't be in any aspect of management that affects people at all. To be a great manager is to share the intent of *Aloha*. You must believe that your staff is innately good, worthy of the faith you place in them, and capable of great things. Without this core belief to start with, everything else will just be too difficult, and you will fight battles you cannot win. You cannot win as a manager if your employees cannot succeed working for you because you lack faith and trust in them.

Luckily for me, this understanding was one created in my own value system very early in my management career when I was a restaurant manager at the Hyatt Regency Waikīkī. It was in the late 1970's of flower power, free love and the open experimentation with hallucinatory drugs. Most managers during this time became very good at diagnosing those employees who reported to work high and giddily happy or deeply brooding. One afternoon I had a case of both collide in my restaurant kitchen, when a deeply brooding cook got into an argument with a giddily happy busboy and threw a knife at him. Thankfully he missed, because the groggy busboy didn't have the instinct or reflexes to duck out of harm's way.

At the time, I was too green a manager to know I couldn't—or shouldn't—do so, and I fired both on the spot. I then left the restaurant in the hands of my hostess, grabbed another manager for help, and drove both employees home so they could "come down," delivering them safely to their families, and explaining why. Later my human resources department would have to clean up the legalities for me, conducting the processes of investigation, documentation, and decision by committee that normally precedes actually terminating someone. For my part, I was too obsessed with the question of what these guys would do now, knowing they both needed the jobs I'd so quickly and impulsively stripped away from them. And I'd met their families; wasn't there more *they* expected me to do?

Over the weeks that followed, I ended up checking them both into a rehab program with the agreement that the hotel would pay for it, a commitment well outside the realm of my own authority. Further, I promised they'd get their jobs back if they graduated clean, a promise I had no right to make. My own boss went nuts when he learned I was still involved. He wouldn't tell the HR director what I did—I still don't know who paid the rehab bill—and he made me promise I wouldn't tell her either. Fortunately he still wanted to keep me around in spite of his feeling that I'd suffered some serious lapses in judgment dealing with the entire episode. I believed I'd done the right thing. However, my boss didn't expect them to make it, and he was both amazed and outraged I'd accepted more responsibility for them.

My boss underestimated them: Both would graduate the rehab program. My reward came on the day I got a phone call from one of their mothers. She wanted to say thank you; she felt that my firing her son was the best thing that could have happened to him and for her family. I've never forgotten her words: "We are so very blessed that you gave him your *Aloha*, even on the day you fired him and brought him home to us. That was what he needed most of all, because we didn't know he had this problem. He is fine today only because you gave him your *Aloha*; you knew he wasn't just some terrible person." He was a good person who had made a bad mistake, a mistake *Aloha* allowed me to see beyond so he could get the help he needed.

To be a great manager is to share the intent of *Aloha*. You must believe that your staff is innately good, worthy of the faith you place in them and capable of great things. Their success will lead to your own. Do you have an employee who is disappointing you? Look for the reason, and look for the good within them. They may be in the wrong job at the wrong time in the wrong circumstance. Look for the ways in which they are good and strong, and put them in a position where their goodness and their strengths serve them best. Share your own *Aloha* and you'll more easily figure out how you can get them back on track.

Can you do this with every candidate that walks through the door? Can you believe in the good in everyone? To be realistic about this, probably not. Therefore, as a manager, interview, recruitment, selection and hiring will be the most important things you do. In addition, your employees must have enough open capacity in their lives for the job you offer them. The point I must emphasize is this: When you do hire, select employees you believe in and are willing to create a relationship with. You must be able to give them your *Aloha*, sincerely and completely without reservations. Managers manage through other people—technicians manage systems and processes. Your own belief that the people you manage are innately good is the single most important prerequisite to your own success as their manager. You needn't say the words outright that you love them, but they must feel that you do.

Correcting behavior, preserving self esteem

There is a parenting lesson that can help you be a great manager. When I had my first child I was your typical obsessive new mother, seeking to find the perfect pediatrician for her care. My obstetrician tried to help me identify candidates to interview, but no one was quite good enough. So the day came that my daughter decided to arrive six weeks prematurely, and fragile as she was, she really needed that great pediatrician whom I still had not found for her. From the delivery room she was quickly taken from me to get the care she needed from some mystery man my own doctor summoned.

When I woke up in the recovery room two hours later, the mystery man was standing next to my bed, and he said, "Congratulations, and don't worry, your daughter is fine." Still not fully awake, I asked him, "Are you going to be her doctor?" He answered, "Well, that's up to you, and I understand you give a tough interview. I think she's really beautiful, and I'd like to be her doctor, so you can ask me whatever you'd like to know. Can I share something with you first?" Not feeling much like talking anyway, I silently nodded, and this is what he said.

"I'm sure that the moment she is brought back to you, you will believe there is no possible way you could love another human being more completely. But being her mother will require a lot of you. Days will come that she will misbehave and make you furious, and you'll have to be very careful about what you say to her. No matter what happens, you need to remember how much you love her at this moment, and never ever tell her that she is a bad person. You can tell her that you are disappointed in her behavior, but because you know how great she really is, you know she is capable of wonderful things, and she can behave better from now on. Then you ask her to, for she must choose to. Whether I'm her doctor or not, will you remember to do that for her?" Again, I nodded.

No other question came to mind for me. As far as I was concerned, the interview was over, and Dr. Galen Chock became her doctor. Three years later he'd begin to take care of my son as well, teaching me even more about being a good mom for my children with every well-baby visit, immunization and yearly physical. Over the years I've kept my promise to him, telling my children how great they are whenever I can, and telling them I am positive they are capable of making good choices for themselves. I applaud like crazy when they do.

I'd recall Dr. Chock's advice on a day I was stewing about what to do with a particular problem-child employee: It was one of those "aha!" moments in management for me. I realized that what Dr. Chock had said in the recovery room held the same promise and potential for the staff I managed. Love and respect the person, treating them with the dignity they *will* seek to earn from you, correct and guide their behavior. If there are any variables to be sought out, they are probably lurking in the reasons behind the choices that had been made; talk them out.

My problem child was summoned, and I prepared my thoughts for our meeting. I thought back to when I first hired this employee, remembering why I'd considered him such a great candidate, and why I had been so excited about making him the job offer. I thought about all his successes as he sailed through his introductory period, securing customer compliments, nailing his performance review with honors and graduating probation with flying colors. I thought about some great things he'd done just in the last few days.

When he entered my office, his feet did their duty, shuffling him reluctantly forward as his eyes avoided mine. He was embarrassed and filled with dread. He knew he'd disappointed me, and clearly he was disappointed with himself. This was an employee anticipating a lecture and bracing himself for punishment: He knew he'd done wrong and he expected me to hammer him for it. This was someone who clearly needed the arms of *Aloha* to reach out to him.

His demeanor did not change my resolve to tackle the problem head on, and that afternoon we did speak of why he'd made the wrong choice when he had other options. But I didn't lay into him as he expected me to. Instead I told him I knew he was capable of better, I'd seen it in him on an almost daily basis, and I knew how good he was when he was at the top of his game. So I asked him please, could that be the way he conducted himself at work from here on in? And he did.

We'd come to an agreement that afternoon: If he struggled with a future choice for any reason, he'd raise his hand, and I'd be there to help guide him through it. As I write this today he is known as an informal leader among his peers, for he has learned to carefully evaluate the choices that seem obvious and dig deeper for those that should also be uncovered. His opinion is consistently sought by his co-workers and by his manager. He is no longer a problem child: He is a role model of outstanding performance.

Aloha was in my office that day. As I recall, the word "Aloha" may not have specifically been spoken. It was there as the outpouring of good intent between us. It was a value we shared, one that gave us a comfortable and workable common ground. It centered our purpose for meeting as two human beings, and it gave focus to our conversation, even when there were difficult things to be said. The day was yet another example of what values-centered leadership can successfully do for a manager.

I share this story with you here for another reason as well;

discipline will not be discussed too much more as you read on. It is something that we as managers are called on to handle, probably more often than we care to, and *not* taking action is *not* an option – tacit approval is one of the mortal sins of management. Following up when discipline is necessary is critical within your role as Keeper of High Performance Expectations – for everyone, fair and square. When the need is there, I am confident that Dr. Chock's advice will serve you as well as it has served me. Love and respect the person, treating them with the dignity they will seek to earn from you, correct and guide their behavior. This is the crucial belief managers must have when they seek to manage with *Aloha*.

Customers yearn for the Aloha spirit

Aloha is not just for managers and their employees, your customers long for it, as well. Every single day, somewhere in Hawaii, *Aloha* comes to life. I believe that as it lives and breathes, *Aloha* defines the epitome of sincere, gracious, and intuitively perfect customer service given from one person to another. It is a phenomenon that managers in Hawaii must proactively begin to sustain and perpetuate in a manner designed to help us thrive.

Ultimately, all businesses share the common goal of turning a profit. Long-term success equates to consistent profitability, and we achieve this by pleasing our customers, something that cannot just happen occasionally. It must happen constantly, and we need a way to turn every single customer into a loyal fan. What does it take to secure their loyalty? If you are to be a success in business, you have to take personal responsibility for the determining the answer to this question, and then delivering upon it, giving your customers what they want.

There is a rampant problem in business today that crosses all industries, and Hawaii has not escaped it. Most customers do not feel they consistently get good service from us, whether they seek it at the grocery store, from their utility companies, at their kids' schools, from professionals, or in your business office. "Business as usual" does not mean "business colored with the spirit of *Aloha*," yet it should. You can be the one with loyal and devoted customers who have found *Aloha* in you and everything your company stands for, customers who keep coming back to you for more, happily buying your product or service because they sense it all goes together. You can have customers who become evangelists, telling everyone else about you.

The arms of Aloha are inclusive, and they seek to serve

Think of *Aloha* as an attitude—a *good* attitude. *Aloha* is an attitude that is positive, inclusive, and healthy. In the business environment, *Aloha* is the feeling of good service, given with genuine sincerity for the pure love of it. *Aloha* is a feeling you have because you believe in what you do and in what your business stands for, you feel your work is worthwhile and you are needed to deliver it. *Aloha* permeates your company because all your employees and all your peers feel the same way: They treat each other with openness, honesty, trust, dignity and respect. They freely share the caring and love of *Aloha* with each other, and so naturally, they treat customers that way, too.

And because those customers don't experience *Aloha* too often, they come back to you time and again to get another fix, confident that you will deliver. The actual service or product they pay for becomes icing on the cake, for if *Aloha* is the color of your company, they are equally confident your product will be infused with value, quality and worth: They trust you will not give your customers anything less. They may not be able to specifically give it a name, but they perceive *Aloha* in your character, and it is a discovery that excites them.

There's more! Not only do you keep loyal customers, your staff retention soars. Your peers and your employees stick around because they want to preserve the *Aloha* in their own lives as well. They tell their family and friends they have *Aloha* at work, and you find that recruitment is no longer an issue for you. Everyone wants your business to thrive so it will continue to sustain them, and you find that your staff takes better care of all your assets, same as they have your customers.

As a manager you now have more freedom to learn and to innovate, for with so many invested in the success of your business you no longer need to spend time babysitting. You can work on your business rather than getting stuck *in* it. Because of *Aloha*, you have become an association of business partners where owners, managers and employees are all working cooperatively toward achieving the company's success. Both you and your staff develop a strong belief that it is meant to be that way.

Manage with *Aloha*

The arms of *Aloha* are inclusive, and they seek to serve.
Aloha is an attitude, one that is positive and healthy, for
　　Aloha is the value of unconditional love and acceptance.
To be a great manager is to share the intent of *Aloha*.
You must give your employees an outpouring of your spirit,
　　and you must receive theirs.
This is *Aloha*. This is the calling of great managers.

2

Ho'ohana

Working with intent and with purpose

> Work can and should be a time where you are working to bring meaning, fulfillment and fun to the life you lead.
>
> *Ho'ohana.* Work with intent, work with purpose.
>
> Managers do this for themselves, and they do this for those they manage.
>
> When managers pair employees with meaningful and worthwhile work that is satisfying for them, they will find these employees work with true intention, in sync with the goals of the business.
>
> Be one of those managers.

Hana is the Hawaiian word for work. *Ho'o* is not a word on its own, but a prefix that brings active causation and transition to the Hawaiian base words that follow it. Therefore, the word *Ho'ohana* defines a value in which you work with resolve, focus and determination. You are choosing to work with intent. You are choosing to work with a personal mission in mind. Why does this value hold promise for you? Well, for a moment, let's consider your job itself, and the worth of the time it occupies in your life.

A job or your life?

Once your school days are over and you enter the working

world full-time, you will literally devote a full *third of your life* to the job. There are 24 hours a day. Mindful of your health, you'll spend about 8 hours of that day asleep—that's one third. With a full-time job, you'll spend another 8 hours working—that's another third. That leaves you with only 8 hours left to do what you *want* to do.

Now we both know that you don't really get all of that remaining 8 hours. After all, you have obligations to fulfill, promises to keep, and just, well, stuff to do. You've got to feed the dog, take out the trash, grab some groceries, finish the laundry, service the car, pay the bills, have your teeth cleaned … the list goes on and on, let's call these the "Being a Human Being" hours. So when all is said and done, exactly how much time do you really have to do the things you want to do?

Well, I don't know how you feel about this, but a measly third of my own life left for me and my personal wants and dreams is just not enough – especially when I come to realize I don't even get the full third! So how can I recapture more of it?

I'm not going to mess around too much with the time I should sleep, for making the investment in good health helps fuel the possibilities of those other 16 hours. It's also pretty difficult to cut back on the stuff that fills the time I need to Be a Human Being, especially the things that deal with my connections to other people—those are part of my wants. For instance I freely and happily spend that time I'm on the sidelines rooting for my son at his high school football game, or that I surprise my husband by cooking dinner (lucky me, he's the chef in our family). I also want to keep that time I joyfully do nothing, and the hours I simply play—going shopping, listening to music, reading a book, or watching a movie. So … there's only one place left to rethink, reshape, and redesign—that third of my time on the job, at work.

Redefine the word "work" and make it yours

There are far too many negative connotations being spoken in connection with the word "work," when in practice they should overwhelmingly be positive and energizing instead. There can be, and should be, great fulfillment and

31

pleasure in work. It should feel wonderfully satisfying when you say, "Boy, I really worked hard today." For this to happen, you must work with purpose, and feel that your work is worthwhile.

Work in celebration of your natural strengths, talents, and gifts. Work at something you love doing. Work to fulfill your personal mission. Work to make a difference. Work to serve others well. Work for a cause you deeply care about. Work to leave a legacy. Work to create a better future. Work to deliver a gift to humanity. Do these things, and you *Ho'ohana*. You work passionately and you work intentionally. You work for yourself.

Ho'ohana urges you to indulge in your passion for the pleasures of work by choosing the right work in the first place. You work where and when it enlivens and moves you, and it feels so wonderful to be creative and productive, to celebrate your talent, knowledge and skill. Work becomes that third of your life where you gain meaning, fulfillment and fun. There is absolutely no reason why you cannot work on your own hopes and dreams in sync with the goals and objectives that have been set by your employer. You've just got to take the first essential step, and choose the right job where both can be done. Contrary to popular belief, this is a reality not reserved for entrepreneurs and those who are self-employed: It can be reality for everyone. Why not let it be yours?

What is your passion?

Sit back, try to relax, and see if you can clear your mind for a moment. Now how would you answer this question: What would I want my life's work to be? Or perhaps this is a better question: What would I love to do, often and *intensely*, trusting that I'll somehow get paid for accomplishing it?

I love to teach, and in particular I love coaching managers. I love the science of business and the democracy of free enterprise, where ultimately the customer rules. I love reading, I love the written word and I love the study of how language can influence relationships between people. I love the new global possibilities of networking. I love the notion that we can choose our own destiny and create it. I get passionate about all these things, and by indulging my passions

I gave life to *Managing with Aloha*.

When you choose to live the value of *Hoʻohana*, you choose work that is part of who you are; you enjoy it. You choose meaningful work that is worthwhile and satisfying for you, and thus it can be done with true intention. You choose work that has far greater purpose than punching a clock on time and cashing a paycheck.

You can be a park ranger who just walks his territory routinely, or you can be one who points out wildlife to visitors that they'd miss seeing on their own. You can give them a sense of place—a feel for it, and teach them to respect natural habitats so they may be preserved for future generations. You can flip burgers repetitively at the local fast-food joint, or you can be the next Ray Kroc and study the business opportunity itself. You can figure out how to match your love of great tasting food with production speed, do your own customer research, and learn what it takes to open your own business one day. In my case, I could have been a manager going through the motions of company process, or one determined to discover a better and more noble way, seeking to recognize how people fit into process. In each case both business and employee can win.

These are the teachings to be shared with *Hoʻohana*. Work becomes personal, and it holds personal value, tremendously broadened from the prevalent and frustrating point of view that the work you do on the job is for someone else. The time you are on the job becomes your own again. When you hold a job you love, one that you are convinced will help you realize your personal goals, the paycheck you get every two weeks is icing on the cake, and you join the league of those who say to themselves in wonder, "Imagine, someone is actually paying me to do this!"

The manager as matchmaker

As a manager, you need to let your employees know that this scenario—where they can simultaneously work on their dreams and your business objectives—is entirely possible, and that you are there to support them. They must believe that not

33

only is it okay to work on their own goals while on the job, as their manager you expect them to and will wholeheartedly encourage them to. Your reward will be a self-motivated employee who reports to work each day ready to tackle the job at hand with enthusiasm.

You can start by asking them the same question I asked you: What is the one thing you would love to do, often and *intensely*, trusting that I'll pay you for accomplishing it? Employees need your permission to make their jobs personal. They need to hear you to say, "That's great! I'd love to have you do that for me!"

Once you've matched job to employee, you explain why the performance desired from that job is so vitally important to you and to the success of the company. You create a picture of work with tremendous worth and significance, work that you have faith in them to do, and do well. Work you fully expect them to put their signatures on.

Start from the beginning: the job interview

Therefore, as a manager, this discussion was a part of the hiring process I conducted with every prospective candidate. The concept of *Ho'ohana* was taught to them in their first interview with me, and when I asked them to tell me about their personal goals, I was looking for a connection between their goals and my business objectives.

And there was nothing secretive or manipulative about it. My motives were on the table to be discussed, and we became a task force of two with the same mission: figuring out if their goals and my job offering, including the business objectives inherent within it, were a match. I'd explain that they did have a choice—there were other jobs out there besides the one I happened to have available, and for the sake of their own lives they needed to choose wisely. For if they chose to pursue this job with me, the expectation would be that each and every day they would *Ho'ohana*, they would work with intent, and they would work with purpose.

I clearly remember an interview I conducted for a young man applying for a job as a server attendant in one of our resort restaurants. I was his final hurdle to securing this job, for as his potential division head I conducted final interviews. The finals were designed to dig deeper for any red flags my department managers may have missed in their earlier interviews with candidates, eager as they usually were to get vacancies filled as quickly as possible. I was looking forward to meeting this young man, for my food and beverage director was excited about him, excited enough to prowl the hall outside waiting for me to finish the interview and sign on the dotted line of approval so a job offer could be made.

It was not to be. I was excited about him too, and the young man got a job with us, but not as a server attendant. During the interview, I had uncovered his *Ho'ohana* for the strategic planning of business itself. He valued his independence on the job, feeling he normally worked a quicker pace than most of his peers. He was most proud of his ability to accept responsibility and deliver more than was expected, and he loved coming up with new and different answers to things. He totally enjoyed it when he could have "real conversations" with customers over and above simply serving them. He didn't know too much about us, and food and beverage would've simply been a way for him to pay his bills until he had "got his foot in the door and figured things out." Sound familiar?

I delivered him to another division with my recommendation that he fill a vacancy we had for residential services, a department that had just been established on our growing resort and had been urgently needed. There was much to be accomplished there in a very short amount of time, and this was exactly the kind of person they needed to help them create and build a new department from scratch, one that set its priorities with a highly sensitive ear to what the customer wanted. Today he is one of their success stories; his instinctual performance opened opportunities to serve the customer and helped define the department's future goals. He loves his job.

My food and beverage director was right in his assessment that this young man had depth of character, would be reliable, would be loved by our customers, and "looked the part." However his passion wasn't a fit for the position, and his potential wasn't the best match for any stepping stones possible within food and beverage. He would have been a short term player in our restaurant, just another turnover statistic waiting to happen, and a lost opportunity for the resort.

Early investments for long-term returns

I'd encourage you to stop here and spend some time considering your own interviews for prospective candidates for your business. I can imagine what you're thinking, that it already takes a lot of time for you to interview people, and what I've suggested here are additions that will require even more time. Yes they will. We haven't spoken at all about determining availability, aptitude and basic qualifications, and those character-seeking questions you've learned to ask throughout your own career. And I'm not suggesting those aren't important, or should be overlooked. What I am saying is that if you are going to hire people and manage them well, *uncover their intent* and whether there's a fit within your business goals *before* you waste their time or yours any further. Like my new hire for residential services, you want to get it right the first time.

You can also do it more creatively and effectively than solely investing in long hours of back-to-back interviews. I'll give you an example: My daughter recently got a job with a retail store that schedules prospective candidates for two-hour final interviews actually working unpaid on the shop floor helping customers in whatever way they can. I'll admit that at first I thought it odd and somewhat nervy, but I became intrigued with the idea, sure there was a method to learn about here. When my daughter shared her experience with me, I began to see it as a truly fabulous approach: I wish I'd used the same strategy when I'd hired my own retail clerks!

This is a retail operation that prides itself on sensing what customers need and how they like to be helped, and then delivering these things to them in a highly personal and individual manner. Either my daughter was going to demonstrate she could instinctively initiate quick connections with people, or not. No prior training was needed to test if she really was warm and fuzzy with customers; in those two hours, this genuine ability would prove to be part of her character or it wouldn't. Her own interest in their product they sold and her feelings about it would be readily apparent to the "interviewer" that discreetly watched her engage with both product and customer.

Testing the reliability of their service has since become a game with me, and a validation of sorts that good service *is* out there. I'll visit the White House, Black Market wherever their shops intersect with my travels. They never disappoint me.

Think of your employees as business partners

In my own interviews *Ho'ohana* would be the foundation of an alliance between me and candidate, a collaboration that helped with my match making by uncovering the passion people had for the work they do. With these first conversations our professional relationship began, based on the honesty with which candidates shared personal goals with me, and my honesty on the connection I saw—or truthfully did not see—between their goal and our mutual business success.

Yes, *mutual* success. Not only would we be manager and staff, boss and employee, we would be business partners. There has to be a win in the partnership for both the business and the employee. And do not underestimate the power there is in the simple fact that an employee enjoys what he does every day. When you enjoy something you don't want to give it up. When employees love their role in your company, they nurture a growing interest in your success, understanding that they have much greater job security in a healthy business. They will work with you to ensure that health (translation: the numbers!—the bottom line you need and want). And they will go one step further: When they have passion for what they do, they put up a hand that beckons you to involve them even more. In essence they are saying, "Let me work on the business too, not just in it."

Ho'ohana helps define lifelong passions

Change is inevitable, and the personal and individual meaning of *Ho'ohana* will evolve over time. It will evolve over the future course of an employee's working career in a company, and it will evolve in its link with personal dreams. It's a good thing if their interests grow and change—you've intrigued and engaged them! Thus the hiring process is but one example, and managers need to keep up with staff as their passions grow and their purpose is more clearly defined for them.

My own purpose today is not the same as it was in other stages of my career and my life. For most of my working life, I was content to hold a job in the corporate environment, wanting to be in the thick of things where I could have maximum exposure to my industry network and learn as much as I could from them. The intellectual meanderings of the business mindset fascinate me, and business is complex and diverse; I wanted to play the field and I could travel between different industries. I wanted an experimental playground to work out my theories, and I wholeheartedly shared the business passions of my company's owner, making them my own to actively strengthen my own beliefs. Today my purpose is to remain self-employed and work for myself and my family, giving 100 percent of my energies to my passion for bringing nobility to management by sharing these lessons of *Aloha*. I am thrilled with the effect this decision has had on my personal life.

There were many times I was not articulate about what I wanted, and wondered if my boss really wanted to talk to me about my dreams. The beauty of *Hoʻohana* is that once it is part of the language it makes it easier to talk about: It's not weird or uncomfortable for an employee to hear their manager talk to them about their "passion" and their "purpose" so they can "work with intent." And this match making is not that difficult; I've long lost count of the times an employee said to me, "I've never had a manager who listens to me like you do." Most times having the conversation in the first place and then listening well was all it took. You learn to ask the right questions and stop talking, waiting patiently for *their* answers to fill the silence.

When *Hoʻohana* is incorporated into the vocabulary of your company, it frames the future conversations you'll have. It gets you into people's heads. It helps you make job assignments for projects, and it helps you assign roles on teams and task forces. It helps you counsel someone considering a promotion or transfer. Sometimes it gets you into your own head: It will simply help you get unstuck, when you find you are asking yourself, "Now why was I doing this in the first place?" You look for intent, for reason, for logic, for purpose.

And here's something wonderful: You'll find you're not the Lone Ranger with this. I would hear employees ask each other, "Is this *Ho'ohana* for you? Why?" as a means of wanting to understand how they could help each other work as a team. I'd find that they switched job assignments on their own initiative and with better results, wanting to experiment with a different role or learn a new task. Sometimes their meaning behind the question was, "Do you *hana* (just work), or do you *Ho'ohana* (work with intent)?" It was a wake-up call they gave each other, a subtle way of keeping each other focused and equally committed. The honest employee who told me "this is not *Ho'ohana* for me anymore" did me a favor, diagnosing boredom and complacency that would otherwise turn into a cancer had I missed seeing it for myself.

This has been my experience: When *Ho'ohana* would equate to working on someone's goals and objectives, their job tasks would easily be prioritized – either the task was conducive to the achievement of a goal or it wasn't. Options in decision making were more easily evaluated and assessed— the right decision was the one that brought us closer to our target, our purpose. And these were the decisions that charted action that was clear, purposeful and without hesitation. These were the decisions leading to action that mattered, for with *Ho'ohana* those actions defined intentional work the employee believed was both important to the company and worthwhile for him.

As manager, share your Ho'ohana too

As the saying goes, let your left hand know what the right hand is doing. There was another critical part of the interview process I've described to you. As the prospective candidate's future manager, I would share my own job intent, and describe how my *Ho'ohana* (my purpose) was to be their teacher and coach, not their babysitter. I described the passion I had for my own job, and for the goals of the company. Should I then make the decision to hire them, we'd hit the ground running, and they'd know my intent from the very first day.

Often I had candidates remark, "This has been a really great conversation, not like an interview at all." Those comments were great acknowledgement for me, first that they were receptive and we'd connected, and second that they could now anticipate what our future conversations would be like: They'd be ready to collaborate.

We'd meet again on their first day of work. Now that they were part of my *'Ohana in business* (think team for now) I let them know what they could expect from me on a daily basis. I would purposefully and clearly lay the groundwork for the professional relationship needed for us to both be successful. I told them directly how they'd come to earn my trust, and how I'd work toward earning theirs. I wanted them to discard any prior notions they had of what it was like to "work with the boss" and expect a new and different relationship—a better one. When you hire someone, do they know where you stand, and how they'll be expected to work *with* you?

Ho'ohana gives managers the opportunity to tell their employees where they are coming from. It gives managers a forum to explain why they do what they do, and how their own roles are separate yet complementary. Please, do not be one of those managers with employees who say, "Frankly I'm not really sure what it is my boss does." *Ho'ohana* was spoken with my staff on an ongoing regular basis: They had the right to know what I was doing and why. They counted on me to share my own passion and inspire them—you can't be shy about this when you're the boss! Remember, they are your business partners, and they need to share your purpose if they are to take intentional actions that matter.

The fullness of work that is Ho'ohana

Ho'ohana can open the door to intriguing new conversations for you.

Ask prospective candidates about their true intent. Venture into their passions. Learn to listen well, and establish relationships that will build your collaboration in the future. Ask the questions of Ho'ohana and then stop talking; Wait patiently for answers to fill the silence and lead you.

Ask the employees you have right now: it's never too late. Bring Ho'ohana into the vocabulary of your work day. Have Ho'ohana be your philosophy for giving them meaningful assignments and responsibilities that match up with the things they love to do anyway. Encourage passionate performance.

Ask yourself: do I Ho'ohana? As a manager you affect many others, and you must accept the responsibility inherent in this. You start by taking care of yourself first. If you are in a job you do not love, find the one you *will* love, or figure out how to indulge your passion and be in business for yourself. Your life is far too precious to be mired in the routine of work without purpose, intent or passion.

Work can and should be a time where you are working to bring meaning, fulfillment and fun to the life you lead.

Ho'ohana. Work with intent, work with purpose.

Managers do this for themselves, and they do this for those they manage.

When managers pair employees with meaningful and worthwhile work that is satisfying for them, they will find these employees work with true intention, in sync with the goals of the business.

Be one of those managers.

3

'Imi ola

To seek life
Our purpose in life is to seek its highest form

> With *Ho'ohana*, you have explored your passion and defined your purpose. *'Imi ola* will urge you to seek the highest possible form for that purpose, connecting it to the many possibilities life holds for you.
>
> *'Imi ola* is to seek life. As a value it teaches us that our purpose in life is to seek its highest form for us.
>
> You have choices, and you are able to make the best choice for your own life.
>
> *'Imi ola* is the value that places the ability to achieve your purpose in your own hands, giving you the clear understanding that you have the power to create your own destiny.
>
> The value of *'Imi ola* seeks life at its very best.

'Imi ola celebrates individuality and worth

'Imi ola is the Hawaiian value that causes us to individually ask ourselves the eternal question on the meaning of life – not life as we know it on planet Earth, but our own life. It recognizes that we are all unique, individually blessed with a complex pattern of DNA; it understands that there is no one else like us on the face of the Earth. Therefore our answer to this question is an answer unique to us as well; only we alone

can answer it truthfully and completely, and have it be the right answer, *our* right answer. Best of all we are completely free to answer the question *the way we want it to turn out:* We have the individual power to create our own destiny instead of just letting it happen to us come what may.

This is our wonderful gift as human beings: We have the power and freedom to design and create the destiny we choose. We can seek life in its highest possible form for us. In many ways I think of 'Imi ola as an incredible acknowledgement, for in its generosity it assumes that we deserve the very best that life can offer us, and that we are worthy. We are capable of great things, and the golden ticket to the destiny of our creation is our mission statement.

Your personal mission statement

Over the course of my management career, I have heard countless business gurus tout the great benefits to be reaped from the writing of personal mission statements. Every successful business has a Mission Statement. Looking back over the years, I now realize I lost time and momentum not allowing this certainty to work for me sooner. I sat through seminar after seminar and even did the exercise with true intention, however once class was over I didn't look at that mission statement often enough to have it drive me.

I cannot isolate exactly when all the learning and convincing kicked in, grabbing hold within my belief system to stay, but today I have both a personal mission statement and one for my business, and they are electronically traced on my calendar to be read and reviewed weekly. I read them even more often if ever I struggle with a goal, or simply feel I need a shot of get-up-and-go for the day ahead. I revise and rewrite them with every new journey I take professionally or personally, and with every new belief and conviction that stirs my soul. I give up on looking for any logical or scientific reason why they work, and just happily accept the undeniable fact that they do. When I write down my mission, my purpose in life—written with complete intellectual honesty with myself—I achieve my goals. I just do.

Sometimes it may take awhile, but the reasons for any delays in achieving my goal will come right back to me and my own conviction. You have one example in your hands. I took a journalism class my second semester at the University of Hawaii, and there's a February 1973 entry in my journal that reads, "I will write a book one day." I now know I should have been more specific.

I re-wrote the goal in August of 2003, giving it new life with the purpose of my own Ho'ohana: "I will have my first draft of Managing with Aloha written by Christmas this year. As now designed in my outline, it will teach managers 18 Hawaiian values in my mission to bring nobility, honor, and Aloha to the art of management, with the utmost respect for sense of place." As I set out to do, I completed that first draft on December 21, 2003.

In July of 2002, I had written down my mission to help the Alaka'i Nalu of Hualalai reinvent their reputation, for I believed in them and what they were capable of achieving. The Alaka'i Nalu are incredibly talented watermen; they welcome guests to enjoy the bounty offered by the ocean environment, offering lessons and tours in canoe paddling, sailing, surfing, fishing and swimming. They had shared their passions with me, and as their manager I was bound and determined to help guide them from passion to mission to performance. I felt they had a story that was still to be lived to its fullest potential, a story that would prove to be worthy of the retelling for the benefit of so many others. Today they embody some of my proudest achievements, yet they have also become my teachers. Bear with me, for I'll tell you more of their story soon.

Coach with professional mission statements

As I have shared with you, I fervently believe that to be a manager is to touch another's life in a profound way. I believe that as a manager, you must accept this inescapable certainty with a sense of responsibility, developing yourself to be a teacher, coach and mentor. The most effective way to coach well is with the understanding of your employees' professional mission statements. In teaching employees the value of 'Imi *ola*, we write their mission statements together, and we review them as often as is necessary to keep their conviction alive. We help drive actions that create momentum for them, with a steady eye on the successful achievement of their goals.

As a manager, your role is to mentor your employees on the achievement of their *professional* mission statement. Personal mission statements will often serve to reinforce and add even more momentum to their professional ones, especially if they have learned well the lessons of *Ho'ohana*, working with intent and with purpose. However, personal mission statements come into play for personal interactions and bridge-building goals such as getting married, having children, reinventing friendships and other objectives outside the realm of your professional relationship. Remember your role as a manager: You cannot set yourself up for involvement in an arena you don't belong in. Chances are you have your hands full in your professional arena alone. But here again, this is where *Ho'ohana* and *'Imi ola* make it a lot easier for you.

There is so much you will learn about your staff in coaching them to write their professional mission statements. And as every great coach will tell you: The players they help perform best are those they know best. They know their hot buttons and triggers; they know what will stop them in their tracks. They know the strengths and struggles of their character; they know the play-acting of their personality. They can pick out the light in their eyes and the drag in their step. They know when to move in with support and encouragement, and when to give them some space to work things out on their own.

As for the writing of the professional mission statement itself, I would encourage you to keep it as simple a process as possible. Missions evolve, and by their very nature they beg to be revised and edited often: You cannot allow a lengthy writing process to sabotage the primary objective here. There is immense power in the written word when it is read often by its own author: Your goal is to tap into that power and let it work its magic for you. With most missions, a sentence or two is all you need. This is all the manager needs to do: Get the employee to talk about their dreams and write them down.

From mission to achievable goal-setting

With *Aloha*, *Ho'ohana* and *'Imi ola* you have made considerable deposits in your relationship with your staff. Once they are comfortable with you and they trust you, people can easily tell you what is most important to them, and what purpose and mission in life they aspire to. The difficulty most of us have, and thus the niche great managers shine in, is in writing enabling goals that are the stepping stones we must take toward achieving our purpose and our mission.

Your employees will most likely assume you have more information at your fingertips than they do, and that you have more experience to draw from in advising them. Further, you cannot choose a goal on the merit of the goal alone; it must be judged in the context of the employee who sets the goal and the mission that drove it. The relationship you initiated with *Ho'ohana* is already paying you dividends here. The more you have learned about the employee you coach, the better you'll be equipped to help him or her set goals that are:

- Realistic for them, and realistic within their job environment
- Achievable, while challenging them to stretch
- Meaningful, leading them toward worthwhile work
- Exciting and fun, keeping them enthusiastic while they work on them
- Satisfying and rewarding for them, and conducive to your business success.

One of my Alaka'i Nalu made it his mission to get as many land-bound employees out on the ocean as possible, for he wanted to share his passion for the ocean with "people who live and work here, but never have the chance to experience these things." Let's look at what happened for him in taking mission to goals to achievement:

- We had a weekly promotional program at the time with 16 available seats in canoe, and his goal became to fill those seats up with employees anytime there was a vacancy—*realistic for him and within his job environment.*
- He found that he needed to plan in advance for this,

and he became involved in our reservation process. He set another goal to meet more employees, and he soon got involved in employee networking forums outside the department—*achievable, while challenging him to stretch.*

- Once employees were signed up and arrived, they had to enjoy the experience itself, and employees can have different needs and temperaments than the guests. My Alaka'i Nalu next set a goal to create better communication tools: He created a separate orientation sheet for employees, and a post-trip evaluation form. We enlisted his peers in helping us keep a watchful eye on the experience of our original guests, for we had now expanded our customer base and needed to please both of them simultaneously. Everyone stepped it up—*meaningful, leading them toward worthwhile work.*

- The reactions from these employees was immensely rewarding for him and all of his peers. We found the guests started talking about the opportunity they had to "mix with the locals." An informal cross-training simmered between employee groups, and the Alaka'i Nalu were the biggest beneficiaries. All of the Alaka'i Nalu enthusiastically enlisted in his new program, and he remained its informal leader—*exciting and fun, keeping them enthusiastic while they work on them.*

- We found those post-trip evaluation forms were terrific sources of information, helping us improve the overall customer experience. More and more, resort employees began to promote our programs in their own customer interactions, telling guests what they had experienced themselves. A new goal emerged, to track the referrals and create an incentive program—*satisfying and rewarding for them, and conducive to your business success.*

As manager, all I did was facilitate. The Alaka'i Nalu were the ones who did all the work, satisfying and enjoyable work they had redefined as their Ho'ohana. 'Imi ola and a single sentence mission statement steered intention to action.

Annual performance reviews

When you have worked with an employee to write a professional mission statement, annual performance reviews become the time to assess if their last year was truly one in which they purposefully worked with their professional goals in mind or not. If not, the discussion will revolve around the question why, and it may happen that from that point forward, the time you best spend together is writing a new mission statement—even if it will point the way toward a new and different job for them elsewhere.

I can particularly remember this happening for an assistant manager in our Sports Club and Spa at Hualalai. This is an operation that has repeatedly been named the premiere resort spa in the industry, winning frequent recognition and repeated awards. That made it even tougher for us to eventually realize this manager was in the wrong job for that time in his life, for he had a position to be envied, and one he'd worked exceptionally hard to secure. How could he now walk away from it? But he did, to become a line employee, for what he wanted most in the world was to start a family and be a dad. He felt that the requirements and stress of his management position kept him from a more important dream, and he was open and honest with me about it. His work priorities were always far too pressing for him to concentrate on maintaining personal balance.

His transition into a new role took longer than it should have because I didn't listen well enough—to him. His employees loved and supported him, and in so many other ways it seemed like he was where he belonged. This became a lesson in 'Imi ola for me because in trying to do my part advising him I got stuck on the goals and side-stepped the mission. I was looking in the wrong places for the source of his frustration. He could not write the goals of a fully engaged and effective manager and even hope to achieve them. And worse, he didn't feel all that great about the ones he accomplished. There was no room for those goals in his heart. We both struggled with them in our day-to-day frustrations because the goals themselves were good for the department, and it took an annual review conversation with his department head to turn my focus to the employee where it should have been all along. The light turned on for me. It was time to think '*Imi ola*, seeking life at its very best possible form, and talk mission.

He had started to reveal interests he had in a completely different department, and I'll have to admit to you that I began to help him get there with more resignation than intent, telling myself "Well, he doesn't want to be in the Spa and that's all there is to it." I didn't learn what I fully needed to about this lesson in '*Imi ola* until the good results of this story started to unfold—he was seeking his best possible life. He became a changed person within mere days—or more accurately, he became the person he was intended to be.

He found he could *Ho'ohana*, work purposefully with a real passion for the goals he set for himself, not those we set for him. As his achievements came to fruition he already had new goals in mind that would take him to even greater successes. The rewards he now gets from his work are no longer immortalized in spa magazines, but they are far more priceless. His customers love him, his boss loves him and he loves his work. While on my morning run I recently saw him pull out of our neighborhood post office, and in the backseat sat his son and his daughter. I said to him, "Your children are beautiful!" and his reply was, "Rosa, I'm living my fairy tale."

Great managers don't wait for an annual review to creep up on them; they work with their employees all along the way, referring often to the copies they've kept of each mission statement. They know when to intercept: the energy of commitment falters, daily performance wanders off course, and results are not leading toward achieving the mission written. Great managers make it their practice to schedule periodic reviews with employees to talk through these five sets of questions:

1. Now that a few months have gone by, how do you feel about the goals that you have set for yourself? Do we need to work on any revisions or shall we continue to work on course? Are your goals still a match for your mission? (*Has Ho'ohana and 'Imi ola connected?*)

2. Where do you feel you have made the most progress? Why do you suppose this has happened? How can we duplicate your success? (*Look for the pleasure that*

Ho'ohana, working with intent and purpose delivers.)

3. Were there any unexpected results? What kind of challenges have you encountered? How can I help you? *(Time for more Aloha?)*

4. Are you comfortable with the measurements we've set up to monitor your progress and quantify your achievements? *(Have numbers count success, not failure.)*

5. What is your next step? What kind of timeline are you setting for yourself? *(Keep 'Imi ola at the forefront, seek the best possible form, the best possible life.)*

After each question, be quiet and listen. Let your own light turn on.

Seeking new life

Great managers spot it when goals are achieved, and they take the time to congratulate, reward, and celebrate. The value of *'Imi ola* teaches us that we are never done; if we have reached our target, and we still have time for more life to be lived, it is time to seek again and reach higher, for remember, you are seeking the best possible form for life. It may be that *'Imi ola* has evolved further into seeking *new* life.

This came to be the meaning of *'Imi ola* for the Alaka'i Nalu of Hualalai. They found that the sailing program they initially had offered eventually died, for it was a lesser one of their passions. However when you are an Alaka'i Nalu, the hardest days are those that you cannot enjoy the ocean at all, for conditions do not safely welcome you for the water sports you prefer. Thus came their realization that the sailing canoe was perfect for those days the wind picked up and paddling would be too difficult for the guests. They repainted her, they re-rigged her, they trained to sail her better than they had before. They focused on a mission to be the ultimate watermen; being a paddler was one goal within that mission, and learning to sail a Hawaiian outrigger canoe was another.

The sailing canoe was renamed *Kai'imiola*, holding the meaning for them of new life on the water they loved. For them, *Kai'imiola* also represents a second chance, one they dare not let slip through their grasp again. When her sail is unfurled and she glides over the water, *Kai'imiola* is majestic, proud, and beautiful. The *kaona* (hidden meaning) she now holds for the Alaka'i Nalu, is that they need not give up after a first defeat; they can always strive higher, and breathe new life into the goals they set.

From mission to motivation

Perhaps the most powerful and consistent motivator for the Alaka'i Nalu of Hualalai is the department mission statement they wrote together over the course of several key meetings. As their new manager, my first task was to schedule these meetings and get them to talk. I was looking for their *Ho'ohana*, and with this group in particular, I'd quickly learned this was best done with them as a group. I'd inherited them, there was no interview process with which to begin our relationship, and up to a certain point they were not comfortable in any one-on-one conversations I'd initiate. I caught their not-so-subtle hints that they wanted a level playing field: They defined "level" as just me and my manager role taking them on as a group.

I had to start with their acceptance of my *Aloha* (the outpouring of my spirit); they had to see and believe for themselves that I was going to manage them with good intent. So I started by asking them to explain to me best they could what it was they felt was most important to them. What kind of things did they believe in?

We came to their *Ho'ohana*, the work they *wanted* to do, by talking values. The Alaka'i Nalu are proud of their culture, and they eventually told me just how much with words spoken in fervent passion. Being a waterman is a lifestyle choice that permeates every part of who they are, and they love to simply make the statement of their own identity. The first sentence of their mission statement is emphatic and assertive: "*We are the Alaka'i Nalu of Hualalai at historic Ka'ūpūlehu.*"

No one would be off for the days these meetings were held, for they were all determined to contribute, edit and voice their commitment to the end result. You see, their departmental mission statement was also born out of a strong desire to reinvent their reputation. It was a painful understanding for them to learn that a reputation is something you have earned. Good or bad, it is the recognition that others have for you based on their perceptions of your behavior. At the time I became their manager, the Alaka'i Nalu knew their reputation was not a particularly favorable one, and pure stubborn denial wasn't working to change it. They had to change their behavior and earn a new one. They had to earn it with such vitality and conviction that the old one would never rear its ugly head again.

So those fateful meetings were simply a beginning where they exposed their hearts, openly discussed what was most important to them and wrote their passions on paper. This is the second sentence of their mission statement: *"It is our mission to help our guests and our 'Ohana see what we see and feel what we feel for the ocean and all she is to us, in honor of our deep love and respect for her."*

They define 'Ohana as a family of island residents that includes their personal families, their peers and company associations and the island community as a whole, for they believe all are touched in some way by the ocean. Their sense of place is completely woven into their sense of responsibility and their lifestyle.

My role as manager was purely to facilitate, helping them to articulate the message they could feel but had some difficulty saying out loud and writing down on paper. Once the mission statement was written, my role was one of encouragement, continually assuring them I believed in them, and that I was confident they could do it. I explained why and how what they wanted was also good for our business. My role became that of guide and manager, helping them individually write the realistic and achievable goals that would be their stepping stones to ultimate achievement. Their goal to reinvent their reputation became mine as their manager as well.

The next year would be one where they lived each day with a strong commitment toward living up to the words written in their mission statement. They understood they were being watched and judged, and that they were vying for this coveted award of a new reputation. The story I told you about involving other employees in their programs is but one example of what they have accomplished. Magnify this by the eight of them: Just imagine the empowerment 'Imi ola, seeking the best in life, has brought to them and to the work they do. They created a community paddle that I believe is without equal in the way it shares sense of place with new island residents. They participate in island-wide regattas and paddling events in perhaps the most consistent interaction the Hualalai Resort and Four Seasons Resort, Hualalai have with community cultural spirit and perpetuating Hawaiian traditions. They continue to be one of the vital employee links that bind these two dramatically different corporations, entities that must co-exist in their efforts to work harmoniously for the benefit of the culturally sensitive traveler. There is no question that the Alaka'i Nalu have raised the bar in assuring safety for the guest, and that they provide an unparalleled experience on the water.

Today the reputation of the Alaka'i Nalu has the nobility and honor of their passions, and it pays tribute to the history and integrity of the island watermen. Their joint mission statement is read at every departmental meeting they hold. A moment of quiet reflection time is devoted at the end of that reading so each person may write down for themselves the next action they will take in their individual commitment to the group and the goals they have set. They think of 'Imi ola, and ask themselves, "Do we seek life as an Alaka'i Nalu by seeking its highest possible form?"

Along the way, they have learned to Ho'omau (to persevere), and to constantly question what they must do to perpetuate what they have worked so hard to earn. They question how it can be better, how it can be 'Imi ola: life at its best.

What will be your story?

'Imi ola will guide managers as they seek to reveal the professional mission of those they manage. The most effective way to coach well is with the understanding of how to best connect our employees' Ho'ohana, desire and passion for the work they do, with their 'Imi ola, their mission and goals.

Tap into the power and freedom you have to design and create your destiny in the way you want it to turn out. Be a manager who helps their employees do the same. You may find that you have reinvented your reputation, just as the Alaka'i Nalu did theirs.

'Imi ola is to seek life. As a value it teaches us that our purpose in life is to seek its highest form for us. 'Imi ola celebrates our individuality and worth.

You have choices, and you are able to make the best choice for your own life.

'Imi ola is the value that places the ability to achieve your purpose in your own hands, giving you the clear understanding that you have the power to create your own destiny.

The value of 'Imi ola seeks life at its very best. Choose to make it happen.

4

Hoʻomau

Perseverance
To continue, to perpetuate
Never give up

Anything worth having is worth working for. Persistence is often the defining quality between those who fail and those who succeed.

There is never much satisfaction in giving up, and *Hoʻomau* is the value that will cause you to continue, to persevere in your efforts, and to perpetuate those that have worked well.

Celebrate your strengths in the face of all adversity. The obstacles that test you can actually make you stronger.

Hoʻomau. Persevere. Never give up. Cause the good in your life to last.

In my own personal striving within the business environment the last few years, *Hoʻomau* would be the single word that caused me to focus on what was most important and move forward with resolution, determination and confidence, for *Hoʻomau* encompasses all of these qualities. *Hoʻomau* will always be the value reminding me I can be bigger than my perceived adversity, for anything worth having is worth working for.

Ho'omau means you don't give up easily

In 1990 I uprooted my very young family from O'ahu and made the move to the Big Island of Hawai'i. Mission: to help open the Ritz-Carlton, Mauna Lani as Director of Catering and Conference Services, the first hotel for the Ritz-Carlton Hotel Company in the islands. As happens with all new hotel openings, there came the time for our mass hire, when we would interview and select the majority of the 900+ employees needed to open the 552-room hotel in the manner befitting delivery of the Ritz-Carlton's renowned world-class service.

With the hotel itself in the final stages of construction, we staged our interviews in a nearby fitness complex on the Mauna Lani Resort. We'd soon discover that in the spacious parking lot, other business was being conducted as well: Union representatives approached our arriving candidates as they parked their cars, urging them to sign cards that would be their ballots for union representation. Eager to get to their interview on time, many would sign the cards without reading them, some not wanting to reveal they didn't read English well, others mistaking them for an early step in our own recruitment process. By the time many of the new-to-Hawaii Ritz-Carlton executives inside the buildings discovered what was occurring, many of the cards had already been signed.

Our new employees would never have the opportunity to participate in a final vote. At our first all-staff orientation in our brand-new just-blessed ballroom, the general manager of The Ritz-Carlton, Mauna Lani took the stage to announce that all our hourly employees would have local union representation. The Ritz-Carlton's intention was good: As the newcomer to the Big Island community they did not fear union involvement, and they welcomed their partnership in achieving our ambitious business objectives.

However, many employees wanted to make their own choice: The pained quiet of shocked betrayal hung in the room like a bad omen. Nothing had been mentioned in the recruitment process, and many employees had assumed we'd be a non-union property as were the majority in the Ritz-Carlton chain. So for many it was a complete surprise, including all of the mid-management team in place, those of us charged with owning this new staff and motivating them to deliver upon the promise of sharing their *Aloha* spirit with our new Ritz-Carlton *'Ohana* (family). Greatly underestimating the effect this announcement would have, the executive team chose not to inform the mid-management group in advance of this orientation, and the message interpreted by the majority of these managers was this: The Ritz-Carlton did not trust us to manage our employees ourselves.

It was a dark day for me, for I was among those hearing the wrong message. I was an ex-shop steward for the union myself, and at the time my own personal memories of union negotiations with management were not particularly fond ones: I had visions of adversity and not cooperation, and knowing of the road ahead I felt I didn't have the time to waste on the process. I was also an idealist, one who believed that I could manage my team myself, without the involvement of upper management, a union representative or anyone else. If I had been a younger and single manager at the time, I may have handed Ritz-Carlton my resignation. But that was not an option for me. I had a recently relocated family to take care of, I was to lead a team of six other banquet and catering managers, and in a pre-orientation department meeting of my own I'd just promised more than 70 banquet and convention services employees that together we'd create the premier group and convention operation on the island.

I had to Ho'omau: persevere and continue to go forward—with optimism. I had to remind myself that anything worth having is worth working for, and the vision I had for this operation was a big one. Further, it wasn't just about me: There were a lot of people counting on my leadership—positive, inspiring leadership. Giving up was not an option.

Ho'omau helped me return to my strengths in the face of perceived adversity, and to my truths. Among these truths, *Aloha*: I could and would manage with the good intent a manager needs to share their spirit, and give my trust. *Ho'ohana*: I could and would engage my passion for our business goals, and work with purpose, enlisting my entire team with meaningful job assignments. *'Imi ola*: I could and would lead my staff from mission, to goals, to motivational action, seeking the best possible way. *Ho'omau*: Not only would we persevere, we would perpetuate strength in what we created, causing the good within our creation to last.

Today I am very pleased that I am able to look back at that chapter in my life and tell you we did it. The quick success of our banquet and catering operation infused our just-opened property with the healthy cash flow needed. Our resulting group revenue projections were integral in helping the hotel's executive planning team craft the hotel's business model with the correct mix of groups versus FITs (Free Independent Travelers not associated with banquets and conventions): This mix is a critical assumption in forecasting for such a large hotel in the Hawaii market.

Ho'omau drove us: it had helped us craft a plan and see it through. "We can do this" meant the whole ball of wax, the profitability needed to drive our mutual success. Small obstacles paled in comparison to our bigger objective to be a collaborative team, and those obstacles were easily overcome. *Ho'omau* did not allow us to give up or slow down despite any setback, whether real or imagined. Our plan involved all players, and our union partners would prove to be our business partners as we had asked them to be, not adversaries. We achieved our success together.

Values reveal the correct path to take

Values teach us to seek goodness by their very nature, and the assumption we make is that the best path will also be the right path, a good path.

As it happened in this story, simply speaking the value of *Ho'omau* was a thought-provoking suggestion for me, causing me to look inward at my own choices instead of outward at factors that would have been easy cop-outs. The result was one of true ownership where the interpretation I chose came from inherent personal belief—I could draw from my *Aloha*, from *Ho'ohana*, and from *'Imi ola*, and *Ho'omau* would help me persevere, continuing to strive for what I believed in. I wanted to get the job done; I did not want an excuse not to.

People are more apt to invest in and be committed to

their own decisions than they are to following the marching orders of a leader—even a leader they respect and trust to make decisions for them. I was fully on board with my leadership team at The Ritz-Carlton, Mauna Lani; I believed in their vision for the hotel and I was prepared to give them my very best to help achieve the company's objectives. However, in this particular case I was equally committed to my own vision for our banquet and catering team and much more passionate about it. My own decisions were those that drove me to be the leader needed for our operation.

Fewer words, more meaning

As a manager, I found that the beauty of speaking the Hawaiian values was their promise of more meaning with far less words. Values are textured with hidden meanings for different people, yet these varied and unique interpretations will always circle back to the good intent at the very heart of the value in mind. When you incorporate the language of values into your own management culture, the unspoken message you give your employees is that you have the faith and belief they will come up with the interpretation meaning the most to them. You imply the confidence you have that they will then choose the best path to take moving forward. In doing so, you've taken another step forward yourself toward building trust between you.

Ho'omau is perhaps the best example of this, for in saying *Ho'omau* you encourage others to continue, to persevere, often without even mentioning what it may be you want them to do. What they hear, yet what you need not say, is "You know what to do" and "You are doing well so far—continue." The implication is that you trust them with figuring out the *what* and the *how*, and you have faith that their decisions will be sound ones. You are encouraging them to simply continue on course, to never give up. For that employee to feel that you—their manager—have confidence, trust and faith in them is powerful stuff.

It would be eight years later and at Hualalai that I would take my personal lessons about *Ho'omau* and begin to incorporate them into my every day language on the job. I still had much to learn, and *Ho'omau* would prove to be a good teacher.

Not just again, better

In June of 1998, Hualalai was just three months away from our second anniversary, and there was this pervasive, undeniable feeling among the ranks that we might not make it over the long haul. Sales were good, business was booming, the Big Island community supported us, we'd won awards and even our competitors praised us as "the ones to beat." Ironically that was the problem. We'd worked long and hard to achieve our success, and we didn't know if we could keep it up. Both managers and employees felt beat up; our two years of basking in the glory was pretty demanding, and we were just plain tired. Expectations were huge that we'd continue to deliver *and* that we'd continue to raise the bar even higher. Could we?

A message of support and confidence

Our leadership team was secure in the knowledge our company values had served us well up to that point. Thus they came up with a brilliant strategy: The word *Ho'omau* needed to be incorporated into the daily language of our company. Managers were taught what it meant, they were asked to define it in the context of their departmental goals and they were asked to be teachers of *Ho'omau* themselves. *Ho'omau* became absolutely inspiring, the motivation we all needed. When we'd say "*Ho'omau*," it was like a rallying cry, an encouragement to everyone in earshot to continue, to keep at it, to just do it. We were the right people for the job. There was a tremendous message of confidence given that not only could we do it again, we could do it better.

The leadership team was wise not to set a new goal that explicitly defined for everyone how to in fact "raise the bar" even though that was precisely what we had to do to meet market demands. They knew that everyone already felt over-whelmed, and a new goal would have been seen as unachievable and unrealistic: Our staff would see the management team as clueless and out of touch with the challenges they faced. The word itself, *Ho'omau* was all that needed to be said, for it implied the strong confidence held in our staff, employee and manager alike. People took ownership, and their performance responded, seeming to say, "Yes: I know what to do, and I know how to do it. I will."

Fewer words, more meaning. The other unspoken message in "*Ho'omau!*" was that the speaker knew of the challenge and task at hand, and was there to support you. The company was there to support you; both would be behind your efforts completely. They'd be there helping to lift any burden or move any obstacle with you. If there was to be change, they'd travel the same road and go through it with you, you weren't alone. The leadership at Hualalai astutely looked for how to make this a reality. Managers became more articulate with voicing what they needed to succeed in the best possible way, helping the company deliver the right tools and resources. We learned not to go it alone, and we learned to ask the right questions so that our staff would tell us what *they* needed.

Ho'omau demands managers have a plan

As a manager, *Ho'omau* challenges you to have a carefully crafted plan that makes good business sense. You cannot have a strategy that will both motivate and support your staff without sound business objectives to ground you. Working hard is not good enough, you have to work smart. You need a great plan with evolving dynamics of its own, responsive to the ever-changing needs of your business. It's part of your responsibility as a leader.

The six-man crew in a racing canoe will paddle rough seas with amazing determination, steadfastness and bravery when they have the confidence their steersman knows the ocean, and has a plan by which he will navigate the best course over the water for them. They never stop paddling. With banquets, we crafted plans in the form of event orders that would guide meetings, meals, concerts, and hi-tech displays with a polished and choreographed precision that was amazing. We had trust in the execution we knew our team could deliver, and in turn they felt our event order served as a plan they'd shine with. At Hualalai, operations are as diverse as lodging, property management, food and beverage, retail, sports and recreation, natural resource preservation, landscaping and golf course maintenance, and each manager was required to have a plan in a form we called our operating criteria. Our staff needed to understand the plan itself, and our *Ho'ohana* (how we would work our plans with intent and with purpose), so that they could rally their confidence in us and *Ho'omau*, continue to persevere, never giving up.

Ho'omau compels you from within

Yet *Ho'omau* can be very personal and introspective. For with *Ho'omau* you are doing from within yourself. You are not comparing, not pacing, not following; you are harnessing that which is within you and striving forward on personal power. There is no need to compete with others, and no need to diminish others. Whether you make the effort alone, in partnership or within a team, *Ho'omau* speaks to you, and to the power of your personal perseverance.

Thus *Ho'omau* serves to engender a sense of individual responsibility as well, where one comes to realize that the efforts that count must start and end with themselves. With this realization, this buck-stops-with-me attitude as the jumping off point, *Ho'omau* then serves to cultivate the qualities of tenacity, determination, persistence and resilience.

To *Ho'omau* on a personal level, employees possess vision that is supportive of the company's vision. This is what their self-talk sounds like: "I am talented. I am needed. I am valued. I am recognized. I am growing. I am learning. I am rewarded. I am really enjoying this!" So ask yourself, if you could hear the self-talk of your employees, are those the things you would hear?

When managers do focus on this question of visionary thinking, *Ho'omau* is a value that becomes leadership philosophy for them. They work where their priority should be— with their people. The actions they must take become very clear. They seek to ensure that each one of their employees is fully engaged in achieving the mission at hand, and in doing so they are better engaged themselves. Lesson plans in

Ho'omau compete for attention on their whiteboard, often spiraling into connections with other company values that may need to be fortified and buttressed in the overall battle plan.

Ho'omau battles complacency with renewal

Ho'omau is often the manager's secret weapon that battles complacency and keeps boredom at bay. Complacency and boredom are debilitating enemies in any business, for they weaken momentum and inhibit action, they slow things down. At their worst, they cause your staff to question if they still truly believe in your vision. Employees who are bored are not engaged. They are not challenged, they are not learning, they have stopped growing—and they aren't having fun! Complacency is your warning sign that their vitality has taken some damaging hit, and as manager you need to intercept swiftly and decisively. You need to bring in the artillery; you need to arouse passion for your goals.

Keep in mind that complacency can also be created if you think you have already arrived at your destination, and are far better than everyone else, where any competition is barely seen in the long road behind you. Great leaders understand how their own success can be their worst enemy—and a stealthy one. Once attained, the success you tried so hard and so long to achieve can become the dangerous precursor to apathy and complacency. This is when *Ho'omau* steps forward with a recharged rallying cry that urges us to seek higher. To continue becomes "to perpetuate." To persist becomes to "to renew." The mission is now to perpetuate and cause to last. The good must be a lasting good that renews everyone's commitment and perpetuates the company's vision as the guiding star.

Ho'omau is a journey of continuous improvement

Said another way, *Ho'omau* is the Hawaiian value that can be thought of as the quality of "continuous improvement." *Ho'omau* gives you pause to constantly ask yourself and your staff, "Are we truly there yet, or is there more to do?" "Can we strive higher?" "Is there a larger goal to attain?" "Is there reason to persist in achieving our vision completely and definitively?" You always look for the better way, positive it is out there and that you can still relish and gain much from the journey. Ho'omau is very conducive to the thought that the journey or process can be far more important, rewarding and meaningful than the end result, especially when you Ho'ohana and work passionately.

Clearly this was our lesson at Hualalai when addressing our need for inspiration in 1998: Make the most of the journey. In keeping up with the maddening momentum of success, we had to excel as managers ourselves. We had to challenge ourselves to continually do what was best for our staff and for our operation. When we used the word "Ho'omau!" to encourage our staff we had to first feel assured in their confidence in us as their leaders. It was a journey in which we sought to know our staff and our business exceptionally well, and it was a journey that trained us to be perceptive and proactive instead of reactionary.

An important and meaningful image in Hawaii's culture, the canoe would often lend itself well as an analogy in the lesson. When we were successful and won most of the honors and accolades, we'd speak of being on the crest of the wave while the other canoes in our race were barely ready to launch off the beach. We'd speak of it being time to choose the next destination, embark on the next journey, and Ho'omau, for we weren't pau (finished), we hadn't completed our work nor achieved all we wanted to accomplish. The paddling itself invigorated us and made us feel alive: We sought renewal.

We'd remind ourselves not to diminish the other canoes, and not to focus on simply competing with them for the sake of competition. Far better to "compete" with ourselves to be the best we could be. We'd speak of the power from within that each paddler in our canoe could harness individually, propelling us forward with far greater perpetual motion, far greater reach than we'd previously experienced in the last journey. There were new possibilities. We'd consider the obstacles that may be ahead of us, much as a good steersman focuses on waves as sets, not waiting until the next swell is already upon the canoe. We'd commit to ourselves and to each other that we would *Ho'omau*, continue and cause the good ride we had to last longer. We wouldn't slow down, stopping wasn't an option, and we'd never give up. Best of all, we'd enjoy the paddle.

The lesson of the 'opihi

Obstacles can test you. They can also build you and strengthen you. They build your conviction, your poise, your leadership, your tolerance, your persistence, your self-discipline. Obstacles will shrink when stacked up against the powerhouse of energy in *Ho'omau*, and they magically become catalysts. They make you better.

Every business faces obstacles. What are those you are facing right now? How can you *Ho'omau*? How can you dig in, take stock of who you are and what you have, and persevere? How can those obstacles actually make you better, because they have forced you to rise a notch higher than you would have because things were easy?

One of my favorite whiteboard lessons[2] is a roughly drawn picture of the rock formations common on Hawaii's shoreline. In this simple and easy-to-draw picture, the rocks are dotted with small pyramid shaped shells that are the distinctive homes of *'opihi*—tasty limpets prized at our best Hawaiian *lū'aus* (feasts). Fierce and dominant in the picture are the ocean waves, continually pounding against the rocks, and these little *'opihi* are getting quite a beating. It is the perfect picture of a being that is strengthened and made better by their obstacles.

You see these limpets thrive on the wave action that beats them against the rocks—they need the agitation! The waves cause them to be better; to grow larger; to have more meat and gain the yellow coloring that every island fisherman knows is the mark of the tastiest ones. As the *'opihi* cling to them, they take on the character of the rock that is their anchor; their shells get tougher, and their strength such that the man who is a thousand times their size must employ a knife's blade and the leverage of his back to pry them loose. The *'opihi* never give up.

---

[2] A variation of this whiteboard lesson was first shared with me by Kahu Billy Mitchell at the Hualalai Resort.

Have Ho'omau define the depth of your passion

Place your trust in the certainty that values reveal the correct path to take. Know that *Ho'omau* commits us to our own decisions. Draw from your *Aloha*, from *Ho'ohana*, and from *'Imi ola*, and *Ho'omau* will help you persevere.

With *Ho'omau* you draw strength from within yourself: You need not compete with others, and you do not diminish others. *Ho'omau* will help you cultivate tenacity, endurance, determination, resolution, and resilience. It will help you draw from a deeper well of energy within. Complacency and boredom will not threaten your vitality.

Ho'omau. Continue. Persist. Perpetuate. Renew.

Anything worth having is worth working for. Persistence is often the defining quality between those who fail and those who succeed.

There is never much satisfaction in giving up, and *Ho'omau* is the value that will cause you to continue, to persevere in your efforts, and to perpetuate those that have worked well.

Celebrate your strengths in the face of all adversity. The obstacles that test you can actually make you stronger.

Ho'omau. Persevere. Never give up. Cause the good in your life to last.

5

Kūlia i ka nuʻu

Achievement
Pursue personal excellence
Strive to reach the summit

> *Kūlia i ka nuʻu.* Define what achievement is for you, and
> strive to the highest summit there is.
>
> Pursue personal excellence. Be the best you can possibly be.
>
> Seek achievement that allows you to *Hoʻohana*, work with
> purpose and intent, within *ʻImi ola*, a life lived for its
> highest form.
>
> You will find you *Hoʻomau*; you persist in a way that will
> cause the good to last, for in striving for the best, you
> have become your best. As you grow, your *Aloha* has
> captured more abundance to be shared with others.

Kūlia i ka nuʻu is the Hawaiian value of achievement, and
it promotes personal excellence. Excellence is never an accident: It is always intentional, and it always demands more
than the norm. Excellence in the achievements you set your
sights on will set you apart, for it will color your character
with the destiny of leadership. Therefore it is quite under-
standable that Hawaii's most legendary teacher of *Kūlia i ka
nuʻu* was a queen.

The gift of a Queen

I was a student at the University of Hawaii when I discovered the serene morning pleasures of getting your exercise with a run around Kapiʻolani Park, a verdant oasis between Diamond Head and Waikīkī. So years later, with frequent business trips from the Big Island back to Oʻahu, the promise held for me in staying at Waikīkī hotels was their proximity to the park for my now ritual morning run.

Over the years, the landscape along my run would change as Kapiʻolani Park aged with me, reminding me that nature doesn't stand still: you need to look carefully so you won't miss her surprises. I vividly remember the day I first saw one of those great surprises, completely unexpected and so warmly welcomed. Near the zoo and bandstand, and facing the ocean-side walkway was a newly unveiled bronze statue of Queen Kapiʻolani. I stopped to read the inscription at the base of her pedestal, and read:

Queen Kapiʻolani
Queen of Hawaii 1874 – 1891
Kūlia i ka nuʻu
(Strive for the highest)
Wife of King David Kalakaua and founder of
the Kapiʻolani Medical Center for Women and Children.
"The Queen who loved children" was a woman of
commanding presence, of easy manner and quiet disposition,
ever kind, ever thoughtful of others.
She dedicated her life to the well being of her people.

I was not sure when the statue arrived at the park, for she wasn't there back when I was still in college, yet her timing for me that day of discovery seemed to be perfect. You see I like to imagine she was waiting for me to learn the meaning of her message. Those words—*Kūlia i ka nuʻu*—would not have meant as much to me back then as they do now, and small as she is in her bronze stature there, shaded over by taller and imposing trees, I may even have passed her by completely. Each time I now have a morning's opportunity to visit Kapiʻolani Park, my ritual has changed. I pause at the statue, and silently thank the queen for what she has taught me more than one hundred years later. I soak in the encouragement I imagine she would give me as I think of the summit I am currently facing. I never fail to resume my run with a spurt in energy I didn't have moments earlier. *Kūlia i ka nuʻu* inspires me to be my best, and take actions that matter.

The literal translation of *nuʻu* is summit, or highest place. *Kūlia* is to strive. However *Kūlia i ka nuʻu* is not simply a description the sculptor chose to describe Queen Kapiʻolani; during her lifetime it was widely known by her people as her motto, favorite words she would say often to explain her own beliefs, and to encourage her people to reach constantly, and to reach as high as they could. To act with the spiritual right-ness of actions that stem from being at one's "highest place."

What waits at your highest place?

As a value that inspires us, *Kūlia i ka nuʻu* presents us with some questions to ask ourselves. What is at the top of my mountain? What waits at the summit for me? What will I find there—at my highest place? More importantly, what do you seek there, if you have made the decision to create your own destiny? Have you set your goals high enough, so that their achievement will truly satisfy you?

The images of mountains have always inspired people, and scaling them is considered a monumental feat, whether they be Mt. Everest, Mt. Fuji, or here in Hawaii, the magnificent Mauna Kea (the name means white mountain in Hawaiian, for the snow that often crowns it). They symbolize such vastness in size we are humbled knowing we are just a small part of a world far bigger than ourselves. Ironically, the comfort comes when we realize that we can climb them. In fact, once scaled, we can always climb an even higher mountain, we can always reach further. We will never reach a pinnacle from which we will not be able to set our sights higher. There is always more hope; there is always more promise that waits for us.

Remember those obstacles you stacked up against the more formidable energy of *Hoʻomau*? Well imagine now that you made it: You are celebrating a recent achievement, and enjoying the magnificent view you have up on your summit. When you are soaring at your highest place, your gaze goes across the valleys below toward the next mountain, the higher one you will next set your sights on climbing. Now imagine how small those once-insurmountable obstacles look to you, as they disappear in the refreshing mists that cradle the slopes of your mountain, the mountain you have already conquered. Adversity slips and falls away below you, for the secure footholds are already occupied by your confidence. Once you embark on your next journey and the trek finds you crossing that valley, you need only to look up. The mountain peak you are traveling to always is higher, towering over any obstacle that may be ahead in your path. You can always look up and beyond it, and see your goal.

There's something about mountain climbing that is so progressive and consequential. You don't tackle Mount Everest until you've scaled some smaller peaks first. Back when I was waitressing at The Third Floor Restaurant, I set my next sights on being a captain for better tips and more control. I wasn't ready to be a manager yet, and I surely didn't want to own the place! There was a whole journey to be taken, and being a captain was on top of my next peak. For me it happened in another restaurant, one that held that possibility for me, and I became a captain at the Maile Room of the Kahala Hilton Hotel. Thereafter I'd set my sights on managing a restaurant as my next and higher summit.

Striving holds its own rewards

Then too, there is great pleasure and worth in the act of the striving itself. I absolutely loved being a captain at the Maile Room, and I was very happy working there. While we may be looking for one certain answer as the golden egg or brass ring, we're also gaining tremendous benefit within the exercise of the *doing*. We are doing all of what comes first. We enjoy the striving itself. It moves us, and infuses us with newfound energy and vitality for the peak we'll climb next. It serves to charge our battery.

My running is like that. I am fortunate that my metabolism seems to keep my weight where it should be, and it's an added perk to know that exercise is good for my overall health. However it is the exercise itself that gives me the most satisfaction. So I hit the pavement before the sun does each morning, running way more than the 20 minutes three times per week the doctors recommend to keep you fit, simply feeling it is the best way to start my day. I run alone, for if I can carry on a conversation with someone as I run, I'm not working it enough—I need to push myself harder than that, or it is a social call and not exercise. If I miss a morning to the infrequent island wind and rain, or to catch an early-bird flight or appointment, it takes a lot more willpower to move me out of first gear the rest of the morning: My battery's not fully charged yet.

There's another fringe benefit I love that mystifies me in its frequency, yet I wholeheartedly welcome it—in fact I've begun to expect it. As I run, thinking about nothing, answers magically pop into my head for problems I had been struggling to solve while sitting at my desk or reaching some meeting's impasse the day before. These answers come with amazing clarity and certainty. Many of my first thoughts for the chapters of this book came from my early morning runs. They were the reward of the striving.

Be your best, pursue personal excellence

The message in *Kūlia i ka nuʻu* is a simple and direct one: Be your best. Don't settle for less, for there's no honor and no reward in aiming lower than you are capable of achieving. Once achieved, excellence has a way of permeating every aspect of what you do. And your personal excellence and pursuit of quality is contagious. It affects everyone you touch in an organization, infecting those around you with zest and vitality. Employees love working for managers they feel are hard-working and dynamic. Employees want to work for managers who want the best, and make it known that nothing less will do.

Consider contagiousness for a moment, and the contagiousness of success in particular. Champion teams seem to get renewed when they get in a huddle—everyone is affected, and everyone wants to be a part of it. When I would interview prospective candidates who had specifically sought out our company, I would hear things like this:

"I'm applying here because I want to be associated with the best there is."

"I want to work at a place that understands the difference quality can make, and I want to work with other people who are looking for quality too."

"I want to be proud of what I do, where I am, and who I associate with. I want people to recognize that I'm part of the best there is when I tell them where I work."

Personal pride is important to people. They want to surround themselves with excellence, with environs that will keep them in the flow of the best stream heading toward the biggest ocean. If your company is known for excellence, it will attract quality candidates. If you are a manager known for excellence, you will attract motivated employees and retain them.

Define your personal achievement professionally

When you are someone with a calling to be a great manager, there is a wealth of possibilities out there for you, an entire mountain range of summits. Managers manage people, and this is a common denominator across industry, field and trade.

When I became the director of resort operations at Hualalai, I had specific past experience in lodging, food and beverage, convention and event planning, retail and property management. I knew little to nothing about the other departments I would also manage: golf, the spa business, natural resources, recreation and ocean sports, landscaping and maintenance. Yet I was confident I could apply the knowledge and comfort I had with the common denominator: people. I could *Hoʻomau*: continue to manage my staff well with *Aloha*, *Hoʻohana*, *ʻImi ola*, and my other Hawaiian values. I was confident I could learn what I needed about everything else in their respective disciplines if I let them do the jobs they'd selected for themselves with my support and not interference. I wasn't afraid to ask the managers I led for help, allowing them to shine as my experts in their fields. And I totally enjoyed the journey, being able to satisfy my own hunger for learning new things in the process.

Ask yourself how you can texture more richness into your life's experiences as a manager. And remember that managers are expected to inspire those they manage, something that's hard to do for others when you lack inspiration yourself. If you find your passion waning where you are, ask yourself where else you might ignite a fire of new passion: There's a whole world of mountain summits out there. Management is virtually boundless in its possibilities; any limits are those you place on yourself.

Define what is "best" for the work you do

Within the business pursuits of your company, the message is also "Do what you do best." Do not tolerate dilution or mediocrity, and do not accept anything less than distinction in your field. Focus on whatever your product is, and focus on the quality and essence of that product, don't meander off course and climb lower peaks that only serve to fragment your efforts and sap your strength.

The Hualalai Development Company sells real estate, but they knew that they were building a community, and their product wasn't the land or the buildings. Their product was the "Art of Ho'okipa" (hospitality), a service branding that became synonymous to their customer with what it *felt like* to live in the community called Hualalai. Their service amenities were as varied as property management, retail, golf, spa rejuvenation, fine restaurants and a five-diamond hotel, but the product with which they could "do what they did best" was the art of Ho'okipa. It tied everything else they did together, and their path was clear when they would say "*Kūlia i ka nu'u.*" It was largely felt that Ho'omau described the character of their company as focused determination and persistence, and *Kūlia i ka nu'u* was the epicenter of high quality that connected all the other values incorporated into their mission.

Define the achievement you must deliver as a manager

I've shared with you that I started my management journey with the Alakaʻi Nalu (watermen) of Hualalai with the goal of improving their reputation: This was our highest summit. There would be smaller peaks we'd first have to scale on our journey to prepare us for this achievement, sequentially reaching higher and higher. Let's go mountain climbing, shall we?

- *First peak: plan.*
- *Second peak: communication, relationship, partnership.*

In our first few months together, my own goal was to familiarize myself completely with the validity, feasibility, and dynamics of the department's business plan: We had to work smart with the right plan in place. The Alakaʻi Nalu were given the goal of teaching me what they knew about their field, and helping me understand the *manaʻo* of their *Hoʻohana*: the deeply ingrained beliefs they held about their personal missions. I knew I had to tap into their passion. And this was indeed a summit for them, for they had voiced much frustration about having a manager who understood them: My goal was that they begin to communicate better, taking some responsibility for our relationship. I accepted responsibility for making them business partners: Along the way I taught them business finance, and I sought their agreement on the core assumptions that would help us achieve a consistent profit. I taught them about *Hoʻomau*, for they knew what to do: Fewer words *did* have more meaning for them. I sensed my most important gift to them would be my confidence in them, and their belief I gave it with full trust, sincerely.

- *Third peak: transition plan into action.*

Once we reached agreement on both the common sense and business sense of *what* we were doing, we turned our focus to *how* we would do it. With two peaks behind us, we were buoyed by a new relationship that felt good between us, one infused with *Aloha*: In effect we had built strength and stamina for our next climb. By this time we had written their departmental mission statement, and *'Imi ola* had the Alaka'i Nalu on the path of seeking new life at its fullest. They'd discarded their attitude of "here we go again ... " replacing it with one that asked, "What's next?" We identified any recurrence of "automatic pilot" in their everyday work—after all, the poor reputation that saddled them was hidden there in their actual performance. We looked at everything: the programs themselves, our customer service standards, their performance levels individually and as stimulated by work shifts and assignment dynamics. They now could look at glitches objectively and unemotionally, i.e. in a business context, and they self-corrected with the degree of responsibility a business partner must accept.

- *Fourth peak: the individual responsibility of living up to their name.*

Literally translated, Alaka'i Nalu means "leaders of the waves." As you will learn of more in Chapter 14, *Alaka'i* is one of the Hawaiian values, the value of leadership. The *nalu* is the surf, or the waves of the ocean. I was and would always be their manager. I myself was not an Alaka'i Nalu: It was time for them to write their own goals, and scale their own mountains. They each agreed to write three individual goals for their next year, and put synergy to work in the department. The first goal would have something to do with Ho'okipa (hospitality) so we would be unified in our focus on the all-important guest. The second goal would be on the theme of *'Ike loa* (to know well), for to be Alaka'i Nalu was to be professionals in their own right, and continue the learning in their field. Their third goal would be on leadership, *Alaka'i*. They would *Kūlia i ka nu'u*, pursue personal excellence in their individual leadership potential. They were committed to being the best, individually and as a group.

Competition itself is not a goal

The Alakaʻi Nalu became extremely committed to supporting each other as they pursued excellence. *Kūlia i ka nuʻu* is a reminder that competition serves no purpose if its only goal is to leave someone else behind. *Kūlia i ka nuʻu* reminds you to strive to be *your* best, not just better than someone else. It calls for some introspection, being sure that you are not your biggest obstacle. If you must compete, compete against your previous self; improve.

This same perspective can be of great value when applied to your business as a whole. Today there are frequent laments as to the lack of plain old good service across the spectrum of business offerings. Businesses seem to blend together in their mediocrity and in their sameness. However it is not enough to ask how you can be different, competing on uniqueness or novelty; you must ascertain how you can be the best. Determine what you can deliver to customers, and how you can do it in the way they want it most. If you are truly the best—even for yourself and your own professionalism—the customer will seek you out, and they will be faithful to you. They are thirsting for what you can offer them; they are hungry to be satisfied customers, and they will remain your customers if excellence is what you offer.

A higher peak in the Competition Mountains

In Hawaii's resort community and visitor industry, there is a higher peak everyone strives to scale in the realm of competition. While we recognize that our island neighbors can capture some business that potentially had been ours, our greater calling is to promote all of Hawaii, and celebrate the success of the industry as we continue to work toward our own. We want the entire island and the entire state to be a successful destination, and at times our neighbors are not those we should compete against. Their success will feed into our success, and ours will help stimulate theirs. This is a mountain we climb together, and sometimes it proves wise to join forces with those you at first were inclined to compete with. In climbing our mountain, where at the summit we find Hawaii is the travel destination of choice, we all strive to create a place of comfort, escape and *Aloha* that prospective visitors will flock to.

I believe it was this value of *Kūlia i ka nuʻu*, held by so many here, that helped us realize our strength together in the aftermath of the terrorist attacks of September 11, 2001, on the United States. The travel industry took severely damaging hits in those uncertain months that followed, yet in a relatively short time, we were successful in reminding travelers that Hawaii offered U.S. soil to them, and could be a safe haven to visit. This was a period of time in which the warmth and beauty of the islands were secondary in what a traveler wanted.

Those formerly in competition throughout Hawaii eagerly joined forces to tell our story together. In Hawaii, we seek to dish up a feeling that is very real. It is a vibrant tangible energy force connected to our spirit of *Aloha* that is called *Hoʻokipa* (hospitality), something we'll visit in the next chapter. It called out to many visitors, and they came to experience it for themselves. The perceived risk in traveling to Hawaii began to lessen. The September 11 tragedy had far-reaching economic effects to the detriment of our country: In Hawaii we rebounded much more quickly than most, and *Kūlia i ka nuʻu* enabled us to do so.

I would later learn that the statue of Queen Kapiʻolani was unveiled at Kapiʻolani Park on December 31 of that year as we all looked forward to the promise of more prosperity in 2002. In part, the news release done by the City and County of Honolulu gave this description of what sculptor Holly Young had captured: "Her bronze statue, which is mounted on a pedestal faced with black granite, depicts the Queen in 'street costume' at about the age of 40. Her face has a warm, subtle smile and one of her arms is slightly extended, palm open, as if to welcome someone into her home." In those final months of 2001, Hawaii's entire travel industry extended our own arms as well, and I like to think the Queen would be proud of us.

Kūlia i ka nuʻu will circle back to Aloha

Kūlia i ka nuʻu is a value of hope and of promise. There *is* more out there for you. Reach high. Remember that excellence is never an accident: It is always intentional, and it always demands more than the norm.

> *Kūlia i ka nuʻu.* Define what achievement is for you, and strive to the highest summit there is.
>
> Pursue personal excellence. Be the best you can possibly be.
>
> Seek achievement that allows you to *Hoʻohana*, work with purpose and intent, within *ʻImi ola*, a life lived for its highest form.
>
> You will find you *Hoʻomau*; you persist in a way that will cause the good to last, for in striving for the best, you have become your best. As you grow, your *Aloha* has captured more abundance to be shared with others.

6

Hoʻokipa

The hospitality of complete giving
Welcome guests and strangers with your spirit of Aloha

Hoʻokipa is the Hawaiian value of hospitality.
Hoʻokipa is to welcome guests, customers and even strangers with your spirit of *Aloha*, transcending the norm in serving others.
Hoʻokipa is the hospitality of complete giving. It defines a true art of unselfishly extending to others the best that we have to give.
In sharing our Hoʻokipa with others, we gain our own joy and we invest in our own well-being.

Kūlia i ka nuʻu (strive to reach the summit) helps us define achievement for ourselves, and for our business. Hoʻokipa will help us define the achievement we must attain to satisfy our guests and our customers. When we serve others unselfishly, in a way that is genuine, gracious and satisfying, our guests will return often for the experience we offer; they will feel they have discovered the true art of Hoʻokipa, an unequalled hospitality that is infused with *Aloha*. Our business will thrive, for it will be known as a place that delivers on the promise of exceptional service. We will thrive, for we experience the joy in giving.

Ho'okipa is the summit of our product and service

Working in Hawaii's "hospitality industry," *Ho'okipa* was one of the first Hawaiian words taught to me as a new employee starting my first job in Waikīkī. However, it was taught to me simply as the "word that means hospitality," and I'd come to define it as a value many years later. Even as a value, *Ho'okipa* may be one that is more easily translated and explained, yet rare is its complete delivery. Sadly, this is true throughout our Hawaii today, and I'm one of those crusaders who believe we can—and must—turn this around. Practicing the art of *Ho'okipa* is not difficult, but it takes true intent, the intent of *Aloha*.

In our study of *Kūlia i ka nu'u*, we spoke of pursuing excellence in the achievement we seek for ourselves, and for our business. *Ho'okipa* is the very definition of excellence in service, and thus *Ho'okipa* will help us define the achievement we must attain to satisfy our guests and customers, the people who pay us. Business 101 teaches us to give customers what they want: Choose the right product or service, one that the market demands, with enough regularity to reward you with profits if you become the supplier of choice. Assuming you've done that, managing with *Aloha* incorporates the art of *Ho'okipa* to achieve a service and product *delivery* that is unparalleled in the dreams of your customers, turning them into loyal customers for life. When people feel they have experienced the ultimate in good service, they return for more of it time and again.

Mea Ho'okipa as service provider

I have been taught that if you were called Mea Ho'okipa in old Hawaii, it was a compliment of the highest possible order. It meant that the person who accorded you that recognition felt that you embodied a nature of absolute unselfishness. With the compliment they were also saying *"Mahalo"* (thank you), appreciative of the hospitality you extended to them with complete and unconditional *Aloha* (the outpouring of your spirit). In acknowledging you as "Mea Ho'okipa," they were actually saying, "Your arms of *Aloha* have embraced me; I accept your graciousness, and I am exceptionally thankful for the outpouring of your generous spirit." Fewer words, more meaning.

The Mea Ho'okipa were those who always seemed to radiate well-being, with an inner peace and joy that came from the total satisfaction they received from their acts of giving. They were those who truly gave of themselves freely, and gave often, never trading favors or silently hoping for anything in return. Their own pleasure and satisfaction came from the act of giving itself. Giving was their inner source of joy and contentment.

Now wouldn't that be a compliment you'd like to receive from someone, especially from your customer? Isn't that a feeling you'd want to experience? I wrote down this quote from a *Successories* poster I had seen once, for I'd immediately thought to myself, they're referring to Ho'okipa;

"Never underestimate the power of giving.
It shines like a beacon throughout humanity.
It cuts through the oceans that divide us and
brightens the lives of all it touches.
One of life's greatest laws is that you cannot hold a torch to light
another's path without brightening your own as well."

This "brightening of your own [path] as well" is the abundance of *Aloha* we've already talked about.

Ho'okipa defines the art of true service

As a manager, I offer you this very teachable point of view: *Ho'okipa* defines the art of true service. You see, the Mea Ho'okipa do not experience their inner peace and joy unless they have given to another person. Their spirit is conveyed through the equation of warm and beneficial human interaction. To a customer, *Ho'okipa* is unparalleled service—it is the epitome of service! —for it was given to them completely unconditionally, something that is exceptionally rare.

Customer service. Great customer service. No one in business will challenge the inevitability that they will struggle and eventually fail if they cannot deliver it. Further, my own belief is this: To deliver great customer service, you have to select and hire the people who were born to be Mea Ho'okipa. You cannot train people to be Mea Ho'okipa if they do not genuinely and unselfishly care about being of service to other people, possessing this innate generosity and graciousness of spirit. You are wasting your time if you try, for their insincerity will reveal itself to your guests and customers.

Mea Ho'okipa were born that way

Personally, I do not believe that you can teach someone to be Mea Ho'okipa: Either they are or they aren't. You can't fake a genuine sincerity for giving that you simply don't have in you. The good news is that many people have it.

Learn to interview in a way that reveals those naturally born Mea Ho'okipa. Hire them on the spot. You can then better devote your time toward creating the best possible environment for them to deliver their art of *Ho'okipa* without shackles, boundaries, or inhibitions. You discard any rules that get in the way of them doing what they feel the guest needs— not always what that customer may think they want, but what they really need to be satisfied. When it comes to their guest— your customer—Mea Ho'okipa are extremely intuitive: They inherently possess the instinct to know the difference and they proceed accordingly, giving them perfect delivery of service. Mea Ho'okipa are dripping with caring, that marvelous ability to instinctively know what their guest needs to be happy; they can feel it.

As their manager, you simply build a stage for your stars and keep them in the spotlight. You say *"Ho'omau!"* and demonstrate your complete confidence, faith, and trust in them. Once your customers have experienced the giving of your staff, their *Ho'okipa* and their *Aloha*, those customers will return again and again to get more of it, to feel that experience. It's just too good to be true. And the cash registers in your box office will be singing.

Now think about this for a second. As rare as the experience, you probably have been the recipient of terrific customer service at some time or another. Try to remember it. I am certain the person who gave it to you radiated behind their smile, and you thought to yourself, "Wow, she's in a great mood today." You couldn't help smiling back, and she made you feel good, too. You didn't feel you bothered or interrupted her, for she seemed to get a kick out of helping you. *Ho'okipa* was a tangible energy force; it was something you could *feel*. She was Mea *Ho'okipa*, and she had all the natural-born qualities you need to uncover when you hire anyone you will put on stage for your customers. You know what these qualities look like, you can interview for them with very little difficulty. But do you?

I'll give you another hiring hint. If you would, read back over this section again and notice the subtle difference in language, for "fewer words, more meaning" can apply to the English language too, and your choice of the *right* words. I have learned that true Mea Ho'okipa have a strong preference for the word "guest" over "customer" —it's an interview giveaway. "Customer" implies that payment of some kind is given in exchange for a service, whereas you would never expect anything in return from a "guest." Mea Ho'okipa seek to turn all prospective customers into their guests.

Caring by nature, empathy with practice

So what about that teachable point of view? If you nail down the proper hiring, what are you teaching? You already have the strength and character of the service provider, the inborn graciousness and unselfishness that is innately there. You nurture it by sharing the manager's good intent of *Aloha* so that the strengths of the Mea Ho'okipa will surface and continue to grow.

What you teach are things like anticipation of specific needs that will surely arise from the dynamics of your business. You talk about how empathy helps make guest connections. You continually seek to define what your particular customer needs from you, and you develop a product that your Mea Ho'okipa will take exceptional pride and joy in being able to give to them. Mea Ho'okipa are true "people persons" who dwell in the kinesthetic land of feelings; They are not product technicians although they may need some technical tools to deliver what the guest needs. All these efforts require a great manager who aspires to be teacher, coach and mentor, especially when it comes to empathy.

Caring and empathy are not the same thing. Mea Ho'okipa are caring by nature, however they may need to practice empathy; Think of empathy as wearing the shoes of the customer. Do you sell hotel rooms? Real estate? Aircraft engines? Stocks and bonds? It may be that your employees will never have the need for the product for themselves, and they may have no desire for it. You have to coach them to empathize with that need as one your customer does have, a desire that they need fulfilled.

For example in Hawaii many of our employees are very unfamiliar with the lifestyle of our customers; They have not grown up the same way, and they do not live the same way. So we look for the common ground between them, in teaching them to practice the empathy they need to better anticipate the needs of our customer. Pace is different. Many visitors will comment that life seems to slow down for them in Hawaii, and they've come for that very reason, feeling the need to step back, relax and rejuvenate. It is how our employees live. Yet when the visitor becomes customer, our "Hawaiian time" is not fast enough to please them thus, our training efforts will concentrate on anticipating needs with better timing.

My home is your home

The notions of hospitality within Ho'okipa lend themselves well to the analogy of welcoming guests to your home. This is the common ground we will often speak of. Culturally, the Mea Ho'okipa of Hawaii take exceptional pride in their homes as places of comfort for their guests, and places that instill all who enter with a sense of well-being. Their homes had to be made worthy of the visit, and they were constantly putting things in order.

In Hawaii we don't refer to "the customer" as much as we use the words "guest" and "visitor." This is a cultural distinction within our sense of place, hence a second (albeit secondary) factor that has found its way into the language of the Mea Ho'okipa. You may have noticed the word "stranger" used in the definition of *Ho'okipa* crowning this chapter. For the Mea Ho'okipa of old Hawaii, the stranger was the one who had the most need for their unconditional love and *Aloha*; if they were strangers to our land they were the ones who most needed to find a place of refuge and comfort. They could offer this to them best within their own homes, and they did.

Care for the workplace

Since the workplace is the home to which we welcome our visitors and guests, *Ho'okipa* helps us promote the utmost care and respect for that workplace. When you know that guests are coming over, you clean your house from top to bottom, hide the chipped china and hang the guest towels; If your guests are going to see the way you live, you want to make a good impression. Within the teachings of *Ho'okipa*, we are able to promote the same care and respect for our business assets. Employees are expected to treat the workplace and everything within it as well as they treat their own homes, with the same pride of the Mea Ho'okipa. For my Alaka'i Nalu, their workplace asset was the canoe. For my golf staff, it was the golf course. For my retail clerks, it was inventory and the shop itself. *Ho'okipa* is a seemingly intangible value about a "soft concept" that helps you take exceptionally good care of "hard" assets associated with significant dollar value.

Visualize Ho'okipa on a summit: Kūlia i ka nu'u

Once again, *Kūlia i ka nu'u* (strive to reach the summit) helps us define achievement for ourselves, and for our business. *Ho'okipa* will help us define the achievement we must attain to satisfy our guest and our customer.

How do you apply this in your own company, and within your own management style? Practicing the art of *Ho'okipa* is not difficult, but you must first realize that you can't go it alone if it's to be perpetuated: It has to permeate your operation. *Ho'okipa* is a vibrant and tangible energy force connected to our spirit of *Aloha*. In very simple terms, it is a feels-good feeling, and one that everyone wants. Employees throughout a company need to feel like they are *internal* customers, treated just as well as your external paying ones—*Aloha* is inclusive; It's for everyone. We've got several chapters to go here, and we'll soon deal with the employee side of the equation. For now, let's keep our focus on customers, and what you must achieve for them to be successful in your business.

Find a way to determine what *feeling* your customers associate with your company—just ask them. Then name the feels-good feeling, the spirit, that you *want* your company to give to your customers, and seek to make it happen. The unfortunate state of affairs here is, in fact, your opportunity: *Ho'okipa* is largely thought of as a lost art in business, and one you can be known for reviving.

I'd suggest you start by identifying the Mea Ho'okipa you already have in your company—trust me, you do have them—and enlisting their help. Put them in a forum to speak directly with your customers—their guests—and let them find out what your customers define as the achievement you must attain to satisfy them. They can listen with less emotional baggage than you can, and they intuitively will make the right call for you.

One good example of this is in retail. When you are a retail buyer, the law you live by is to buy what the customer wants, not what you want. Yet the strengths most store owners will look for in a top-notch retail buyer are predominantly more organizational and financial than customer-empathetic: Behind the scenes retail is a detail business, and a buyer's day-to-day interactions usually involve relationships with multiple wholesale purveyors on the supply side. They struggle to find time to connect with the very customer they are buying for. Thus they depend on the feedback they need to buy the right thing from the sales staff that are on the shop floor on a daily basis: This is the actual end-user relationship they invest in.

In the golf operation of Hualalai, we had The Club Shop, a store with a dual purpose: high-quality resort retail, and golf central for the tee-time reservations on the Jack Nicklaus Signature golf course of the resort. We counted on the staff we selected to work in The Club Shop to be our customer connections. Most of them would not buy for themselves the majority of the retail product our customers adored. Some of them didn't even golf. Yet they were Mea Ho'okipa through and through: They loved our customers and knew exactly what to do to keep them happy. In turn, our customers loved them. Customers told them exactly what they thought about every shirt, dress and pair of socks we sold, and they didn't hesitate to ask for what they wanted. This created a veritable goldmine of information the retail buyer could tap into, and did.

Within their 'Imi ola (mission), The Club Shop staff adopted a motto to live by: "We don't sell; we help our guest buy." In making this motto their reality, they actually sold an awful lot of merchandise! They knew our customers so well, that they'd put new arrivals on hold for them fresh out of the shipment boxes, and call them to come by when they could. This was another deposit into the guest relationship they were cultivating, for they knew what they wanted; to these Mea Ho'okipa it was *not* a sales call. Nine times out of 10 they were precisely right in their picks. Our customers trusted their opinion: One afternoon I walked in The Club Shop to find a guest showing one of the staff a blouse she'd received as a gift on Mother's Day from another store. I overheard her say, "I really do love it, but with this color and print I don't trust myself to wear it well, I just knew that you'd be the one to help me turn it into a couple of outfits. What can I buy to go with it?" She assumed the choices would be right, the price would be right, and the quality would be good: The *Aloha* of the Mea Ho'okipa she was talking to was her guarantee. When she wore the outfit that Mea Ho'okipa had sold her, she literally became a walking billboard of the amount of trust in their relationship!

A common sight in The Club Shop was of husbands and sons sitting in the overstuffed arm chairs we had near the shop windows that overlooked the 18th green: They were waiting for the women in their lives to shop. They weren't buyers, and the staff instinctively knew they didn't want to be "sold," but to our Mea Ho'okipa, they were guests, and all guests needed to have every single comfort they could give them. It might be they needed small talk; it might be they'd prefer the morning paper and some coffee; it might be they'd just arrived and

could use some inside-knowledge on the rest of the resort ...
whatever it was, they got it, yet they had almost never asked
for it—they'd expected to impatiently sit and be bored.

As you can imagine their wives were thrilled with the
attention paid to their men, for they could now shop in peace,
and without much guilt; their purchase dollar increased. Those
who were golfers were introduced to our golf professionals
simply for the pleasure of good conversation. Perhaps they
were given a putter and sleeve of balls to practice their short
game and just kill time, and we booked more lessons. And
guess what else happened? These were the men who would
come back before Valentine's Day or Christmas, walk up to the
person who had helped their wives, and say, "Do you remember
me? Would you help me find a gift for my wife?"

Most retail shops really need to figure this out: You have
to invest in the customer relationship when you have the
chance, not just when you're pretty sure your prospect is ready
to buy! When I first learned the retail business, I was employed
by a large hotel chain, and I was amazed at the general
managers and controllers I'd meet who thought of the retail
shops in their hotels as just convenience stores or places to idly
window shop if it was raining outside. To them retail wasn't
much more than a way to keep people on property until the
sun broke out and they could go back to the beach, or until
their table was ready in the hotel restaurant. A captive audience completely wasted, customer feedback totally ignored.
Lost opportunity, lost dollars.

In contrast, The Ritz-Carlton Hotel Company has a
Guest Recognition Program wherein all staff in contact with
guests are enlisted to write down customer feedback, no matter
how unrelated it may be to their own department. Ritz-
Carlton knows that the server at breakfast will be the one to
hear about a glitch in the system retrieving cars that had been
valet parked. A banquet porter helping the meeting planner
with boxes will be the one to learn about the interference in
guest room data lines. You know this is true: Customers talk to
your staff more than they talk to you, and they are more
truthful with your staff.

What's the moral of these stories? Put your Mea Ho'okipa

together with your guests, and you will find out what your customer wants you to deliver. Talk to your staff often, and thank them for their feedback. The dynamics of Ho'okipa, the hospitality of complete giving, will define the achievement you must seek to cultivate loyal customers.

Ho'okipa is the day-to-day hospitality of complete giving

Let's look at some other lessons taught by Ho'okipa, with their counterpart lessons in the modern business environment. Try to recognize the *feeling* that can be created by Ho'okipa, a summit of hospitality defined as complete giving. Think about your own business as we proceed and ask yourself how you may rate in these areas.

Ho'okipa: When you greet guests in your home, you extend a warm and gracious welcome, and you make them as comfortable as you can.

Customer Service: Greet each and every guest who arrives. Make eye contact. Say, "Good afternoon, how can I help you?" not, "Who's next in line?"

The feelings are: warm, gracious, welcoming, and comfortable. People are individuals and they are your personal guests, not simply another customer or maybe prospect.

–––

Ho'okipa: When your guests arrive, you are there for them. There is nothing else more important than being Mea Ho'okipa for them, and sharing your *Aloha* with them.

Customer Service: The customer is our reason for being in business. When they enter our store, they need to be the focus, and the other things can wait. It's a cardinal sin if they have to look for an attendant or ask to be served. Engage with them. Be in their moment.

Customers feel: they are everything to you. It's not just your goal, it's their reality. You like them! You appreciate them!

–––

Ho'okipa: When you are in my home, you are safe. I will care for you, I will ease any burden you carry, and I will protect you from harm.

Customer Service: Our customers must never be exposed to any danger or risk accidents. They should not be embarrassed in any way. We offer options instead of saying no. Safety briefings are non-negotiable, for we are responsible for them.

Customers feel: safe, comfortable and cared for. They trust in us, and they trust us to do what's best for them.

Ho'okipa: What's mine is yours. I only have these things to make you more comfortable, and I enjoy being able to give.

Customer Service: If it's on the menu, we had better be able to serve it. If they came to buy it, we had better have it in stock. If they purchase it, it had better work and exceed their expectations.

The feelings are: confidence in us, and in our ability to deliver exactly what and when they need us to. What we have is good, and how we offer it is great.

Ho'okipa: I will anticipate your needs to the best of my ability, and I will be ready for you whenever that need must be fulfilled. You need not ask, for I will already have given.

Customer Service: Ask open-ended questions. Reading body language is a part of good listening. Open early, close late. Prepare your work station and keep it organized so you are always ready for the customer. If they have to ask, we delivered too late.

Customers feel: We know them, and respond to them as good friends. We do extra for them, only as friends do.

Ho'okipa: I will give you my complete and unconditional *Aloha*. It is who I am. It would hurt me deeply if I failed to please you, and I will continue my efforts until you feel *Aloha* and well-being.

Customer Service: If you are not serving the customer, you should be serving the person who is. If we cannot satisfy the customer, or they have a complaint, we must discover what can be done to make things right.

The feelings are: unselfishness, and a sense of purpose. Our customers feel we are in business for the right reasons. They become loyal, for they want us to always be there for them.

Hoʻokipa is a gift for customer and employee alike

You can go back through this exercise and simply substitute "customer" for "employee" when reflecting on your management style. The good feelings we want to experience in our interactions with others are largely universal and familiar. How do your employees *feel* about the way they are treated, and the way they are managed by you? Great managers understand they serve others, and *Hoʻokipa* is the value that helps them do so.

> *Hoʻokipa* is to welcome guests, customers and even strangers with your spirit of *Aloha*, transcending the norm in serving others.
>
> *Hoʻokipa* is the hospitality of complete giving. It defines a true art of unselfishly extending to others the best that we have to give.
>
> When we serve others in a way that is genuine, gracious and satisfying, others are drawn to us for the experience we offer; They feel they have discovered the true art of *Hoʻokipa*, an unequalled hospitality infused with *Aloha*.
>
> In sharing our *Hoʻokipa* with others, we gain our own joy and we invest in our own well-being.

7

ʻOhana

Those who are family, and those you choose to call your family
ʻOhana is a human circle of complete Aloha

> ʻOhana is family. Our ʻOhana includes those we have always known as our family, surrounding us with love at the time of our birth.
>
> However ʻOhana also includes those we *choose* to call our family, for the connection we share with them enriches our life.
>
> ʻOhana becomes a sacred form for sharing our lives with *Aloha*, for it gives us the unconditional gifts of love, understanding, forgiving, and acceptance.
>
> ʻOhana is the most secure and comfort-filled support we have for facing truth, for ʻOhana never loses hope.
>
> The bonds of ʻOhana are strong yet supple: They flex with giving and with the love and acceptance of *Aloha*, yet they are made rigidly secure by those same supports. These bonds may be tested, but they cannot be broken.
>
> ʻOhana is a human circle of complete *Aloha*.

ʻOhana is family

ʻOhana is the word for family in Hawaii. From culture to culture we share the commonality of being human beings, and humans need to be in family groups of other human beings: The history of humankind repeatedly has shown us that we were not intended to be alone. We need connection to each other, it nurtures and sustains us.

Families can take on different forms, and they can embrace whomever they wish to include in their circle. The Hawaiian culture is one of those in which family may have nothing to do with bloodlines; If you are considered part of one's 'Ohana you are their family, plain and simple. Since 'Ohana does not necessarily include birthright, you can easily belong to more than one 'Ohana, and many people do. 'Ohana gives us a feeling of belonging. And that's something we all need.

'Ohana is form for the sharing of one's life

As a cultural value, 'Ohana is form for the sharing of one's life. Our 'Ohana includes those we have always known as our family, surrounding us with *Aloha* (love and the sharing of spirit) at the time of our birth: Although we did not choose them, early in our lives we naturally come to love these people unconditionally. However as we grow and associate with others, 'Ohana begins to include those we *choose* to call our family, for the connection we share with them enriches our life. We find they also sustain us, and we want to keep them close.

However, choosing to call someone part of your 'Ohana is no small decision; it is not a choice to be taken lightly. 'Ohana is never a word carelessly spoken. As in many other cultures, 'Ohana is considered the strongest bond someone has, no other earthly connection is more vital than that of family. The bonds of 'Ohana are strong yet supple: They flex with giving and with the love and acceptance of *Aloha*, yet they are made rigidly secure by those same supports. These bonds may be tested, but they cannot be broken. 'Ohana is a human circle of complete *Aloha*.

Other than the spiritual, no other connection is so necessary for the best sustenance of one's life than family, thus *'Imi ola* (seeking life in its best possible form) embraces 'Ohana. People feel safe, secure and protected when in the arms of their family. 'Ohana means comfort and security; it's an anchor in rushing waters and a solid rock on shifting earth. It's the sheltered harbor in the raging storm. With 'Ohana, you needn't carry the solitary burden of being completely strong on your own.

Acceptance in 'Ohana is unconditional

Like birthright, when you are in an 'Ohana your acceptance is unconditional. Understanding and forgiveness are both immediate and unconditionally given as well. Whatever baggage you come with becomes the burden of the entire family. You alone may have caused it to appear, but you will not shoulder it alone. The belief is that many hands will make it a lighter load. The joint life force of Aloha will deal with it in the best possible way.

'Ohana is the most secure and comfort-filled support we have for facing the truth that can sometimes dare us to give it attention, for 'Ohana seeks to give understanding, and it never loses hope. In the Hawaiian culture there is an open discussion process called ho'oponopono which deals with unpleasant situations and seeks to make things right, to bring them to Pono (rightness and balance). When trouble rears its ugly head the 'Ohana will surely and swiftly deal with whatever it is, but there is no reason to waste precious time and energy on blame, excuses or whining. Acceptance is practiced in another subtle way: You identify the root cause of something, for it is too foolish and unsettling to ignore it, but you do not dwell on it any longer than is needed to deal with it.

The character of Aloha permeates everything in an 'Ohana for 'Ohana seeks the best possible way to share the outpouring of one's spirit in a way that is intimate and life-giving. There is little hidden in 'Ohana because there is no need to hide anything from the very people who offer you the ultimate in love, support and understanding.

Now this acceptance goes both ways; thou shall give as well as receive. Being part of an 'Ohana requires much of you, for it requires—and thus teaches—you to give Aloha, understanding, support and forgiveness to others unconditionally as well. And 'Ohana requires this of us all, whether we were born Mea Ho'okipa naturally or are those who intentionally must work at practicing selfless giving. You grow in your acceptance of responsibility, understanding how your choices affect others in the family.

'Ohana is all-inclusive

In your own birth family, you experience inclusiveness without giving it much thought: Everyone participates, and everyone shares whatever can be shared, and that's just the way it is. In counting heads you count every single member: No one is left out. As Lilo would repeatedly say in the Disney movie *Lilo and Stitch*, "'Ohana means family, and no one is forgotten or left behind." You cannot imagine it being any other way. That is the feeling of 'Ohana. You live in a sort of syncopated harmony and in unity: In many ways 'Ohana is a single unit despite the number of those within the family.

'Ohana is all-inclusive, and there are no divisions within it. In Hawaii 'Ohana is considered a more sacred and much higher form than team. If you have 'Ohana, and the 'Ohana is strong, supportive and vibrant, teams are simply not necessary. In fact, a separate team within an 'Ohana may cause suspicion and fear that there is a lack of unity (*Lōkahi*): Why on earth do they separate themselves from the family? With certainty, the sudden presence of some group within the 'Ohana would have many say it was time for *ho'oponopono*, and the process would begin.

The best human circle you can bring to business

With belief in the teachings of 'Ohana as a value, there is a very natural progression toward the concept of an 'Ohana in business. As we have seen in the earlier chapters, employees become business partners. They have joined your family because they identified their Ho'ohana, and wish to work with purpose and intent *with* you. 'Imi ola: they write mission statements with you and set goals. They share in your problem solving (*ho'oponopono*), they give you the feedback needed to make better decisions, they take care of your workplace assets, they propose change and initiatives. They are respected for their intelligence and their full involvement is expected. As business partners do, they share in the work it takes to make your business successful.

In a birth family the elders strengthen the 'Ohana bonds by teaching values to their youth; you are actually told what to believe in. Similar to this, businesses teach new hires about the values of their company: Managers strengthen those bonds for their employees with Ho'ohana and 'Imi ola, grooming the personal connections of professional mission statements.

I believe that work is personal for people, and 'Ohana is an immensely personal form for sharing one's best life with Aloha. Work consumes a lot of time and energy in our lives, and it ebbs in and out of our personal lives whether we like it or not. Back in the introduction I'd talked about what managers should be, what their role is, and I'd said, "Your place in the continuum is to create a work environment in which [employees] thrive, so that when they return home they are in a great state of mind, ready to openly share the positive energy they had gained at work and brought home with them. You are one who can demonstrate values and character traits such as treating others with honesty and respect, with dignity and Aloha." These things get personal, and such personal interactions are dealt with best within the human circle of Aloha that defines what an 'Ohana is.

In the chapter on 'Imi ola we talked about staying in the professional realm with mission statements. Yet this will still become personal for you and for your employees: When someone shares their mission with you they openly put their heart on their sleeve. You asked them about their passion! 'Ohana is the best form you can bring to this environment, for it extends the arms of Aloha recognized as support. When they make a mistake on the journey—when they Kūlia i ka nu'u and stumble in their mountain climbing, 'Ohana flexes with Aloha, braces for any fall, and rigidly supports them. As their manager you may be the patriarch or matriarch of this 'Ohana, but your department is unified in their support: No one goes it alone. Not you, not the employee.

In short, when you adopt 'Ohana as the form for your business, you commit yourself and your entire team to treating each other like family. You grow together as families do, and you deal with change together, as families do.

Now in a business, termination of employment will happen. Remember that we *choose* to belong in an *'Ohana* in business, we enlist. When an employee is terminated, either verbally or through their actions they have made a different choice: For some reason the *'Ohana* in business they were in ceased to nurture and sustain them. Resignations and terminations also happen because values have changed, either on the part of the employee or with the vision of the company. In contrast an *'Ohana* is a human circle wherein values are shared.

Work is personal: a story

While at the Hualalai Resort as vice president of operations, I participated in an open forum discussion our leadership team had with groups of employees that we called "Let's Talk Story." At the time we were feeling threatened by a neighboring resort that we felt openly sought to steal both our employees and our customers. The carrot they dangled was this: "We have an *'Ohana* here too, one that will welcome you in just as warmly." Our counter campaign was this: "You cannot create an *'Ohana* in business purely by saying you have one, you *become* one as we have here. We will respect your right to make a choice, however, consider carefully before you give up what you already have." We were counting on the considerable history that most families have.

In those Let's Talk Story meetings, we asked our employees, "What does our *'Ohana* mean to you?" We knew that learning of their answer was critically important: It would shine a bright light on the crucial components of *'Ohana* we needed to sustain for them, somehow infusing these benefits with more vitality, more dynamic connection. I took careful notes during those sessions, and what they said would prove to inspire and sustain me over and over again as I sought to be a good manager and leader for them.

These were some of their responses:

- When you are part of this *'Ohana* you honor everyone else in it, by conducting yourself with *Aloha*, dignity, and respect. So when I work here, I can practice being

97

a good role model for my children.

- 'Ohana is teamwork, but in the context of our Hawaiian cultural values, because it's more than that.
- When you are away from your own family at home, it's nice to find the same values at work; it feels right.
- With 'Ohana, you get the opportunity to have a stronger relationship with people than would normally happen in a business setting: you care about each other.
- Here, even though our origins and ancestry may be different we can still come together as an 'Ohana. The differences go away, they're just not as important.
- We willingly say we love each other, and we demonstrate it.
- In 'Ohana you lift each other to higher ground, you expect more from each other. You expect more from yourself.
- Acceptance for who you are is huge in 'Ohana, and when you get it you give it, and you give it to everyone, even the customer who's grouchy or complains.
- 'Ohana is more intimate than team, and more inclusive than department. It takes more truth and honesty. You can't hide things, but you also don't need to.
- 'Ohana was the most unselfish gift we could give to the new residents that would help us build this community. It was also the first thing we had to be sure to teach them, for they have to participate.
- Ho'okipa (the hospitality of complete giving) demands 'Ohana, and it must be Kākou (all of us), where it is done by every one of us together, not just a few.

Bringing the customer into your 'Ohana

These last two comments did not surprise us, for at Hualalai our 'Ohana had evolved over the years to include employees, resort residents, resort hotel guests of The Four Seasons, the personal families of our employees, and even the vendors and suppliers within the island community we did business with. Believe it or not, all these people were invited to our annual 'Ohana picnic called the Ho'olaule'a (celebration), and we'd grown so that the only place we could hold it was on the driving range of our golf course.

And here was a unique tenet: If our customers and guests were part of the 'Ohana, they had to conduct themselves accordingly. In other words, they had to give those within the 'Ohana who served them the same degree of Aloha, dignity and respect they received. Our employees were taught to teach these things by demonstrating it with their own behavior. And it was okay to speak of it freely if customers, visitors and guests asked for their help in understanding our belief.

Now you may decide that level of intimate discussion between customer and employee is not okay in your company. Fine. However, you do want to define this for yourself: What is the relationship you want to have with your customers? As it was for Hualalai, the issue ultimately is who *you* are within your character, and not who the customer may be. The customer attracted to your business because you supply what they want and are looking for, is attracted by who you *are*. Hualalai found this worked for them because they knew their employees to be Mea Ho'okipa and they trusted them to speak the language of Aloha. They knew that their 'Ohana in business was 'Ohana: a complete circle of human Aloha.

Bringing community into 'Ohana

If the customer relationship chosen is 'Ohana, there is an even larger circle of inclusiveness to consider. Like 'Ohana, community is a sacred concept in Hawaii. Many believe that a community cannot be created without the foundation of a strong 'Ohana to support it. Likewise an 'Ohana can only get stronger when its connections include the embrace of the community that surrounds it. 'Ohana and community are considered intertwined.

History helps us understand this, for Hawaiian families traditionally belonged to an *ahupua'a*, a land division that was more than town or village. The *ahupua'a* extended from the mountains to the sea, for in our volcanic island environment, different types of sustenance came from these varied elevations. Your 'Ohana was responsible for stewardship of the land you occupied, and thus the entire 'Ohana was bonded in work as well: Yours was a family of fishermen, or farmers or tradesmen. You were expected to share the bounty of your harvest or craft with all in the *ahupua'a*, as they would share theirs with you, making the entire community healthy and strong. The community needed the *'Ohana* to care for the land that sustained them; the *'Ohana* needed the community's reach over the entire *ahupua'a* if they were to enjoy the best possible life.

There is so much good business sense in making community connections. For one thing, its terrific marketing. Let's face it—customers are more inclined to spend a buck with you if they feel you are caring, and often the best way to demonstrate your caring is via community involvement. As a business we must promote and support the volunteerism of our employees within the community as Little League coaches, soccer moms, soup kitchen volunteers, companions for the elderly—wherever their own values drive them to be giving. As Mea Ho'okipa they thrive with these additional expressions of their *Aloha* for others.

Often there are many rewards we gain back indirectly, such as their continuing education, their recognition of good service practices in other organizations, or their participation in fun and social outlets that de-stress and energize them. We may also gain the opportunity to lead and influence community changes that are healthy for both the community itself and thus for our business climate as a whole. This is all part of *'Ohana*, the human circle of complete *Aloha*.

'Ohana helps us see the tremendous worth held within community. A business cannot be all things to all people, and community is there to fill the *pukas* (the holes, the opportunity) and bridge the gaps. Community involvement promotes inclusiveness, open-mindedness and the willingness to seek a better way to live with each other harmoniously, teachings that are all promoted by an *'Ohana*. Establishing healthy community networks that include your business concerns can counteract the fear of evolutionary change that neighborhoods are destined to go through. *'Ohana* is the most secure and comfortable support we have for facing truth, for *'Ohana* never loses hope. And with community involvement in particular,

the lines between benchmarking new ideas, networking with divergent groups and education in general can become very pleasantly blurry; they all seek more knowledge. Knowledge brings hope, and 'Ohana promotes it.

Community involvement also gives prospective candidates the opportunity to interact with your employees in a neutral environment. The reality of any job market is that the employees you really want to work with you are probably already employed. You need not resort to tactics aimed at stealing them away when *they* initiate the effort to seek *you* out because you have offered evidence to them that you can deliver great job satisfaction. The evidence? Your present employee, the one active in the community who is happy and speaks well of you and your business goals and ethics. Are you taking the same risk by exposing your staff to other companies in your support of their volunteerism? Only if your own house is not in order. Only if your own company is not a healthy 'Ohana in business. If it is, what they will see is how good they have it working with you; all they will feel is your support, your *Aloha*. They won't give that up.

I wouldn't be surprised if there is already some reference to 'Ohana or family in your company right now, somewhere within words that are already written down as your mission statement or within your company values, or perhaps in the employee handbook. Universally, businesses do try to name the form they choose for their association of owners, managers, employees and customers. But before we leave this chapter, let's bring it back to you, the manager aspiring to be a truly great manager. What is within *your* human circle, and your own circle of influence?

Managers create their own 'Ohana

Well, you have to name the form for your own culture, too, and what I'm proposing is that the inclusiveness, acceptance, and other unconditional qualities of this value of 'Ohana can get you started and lead you in the right direction. Understand that you can influence quite a bit, no matter how small or seemingly insignificant you may feel your one small department is in the big parent company. I first heard this—really heard and understood this—when said by Marcus Buckingham, co-author of *First, Break all the Rules, What the World's Greatest Managers do Differently*. He spoke at a conference I attended in May 2002. This is what he said: "Companies don't have one culture. They have as many as they have supervisors or managers. You want to build a strong culture? Hold every manager accountable for the culture that he or she builds." When I looked back on my own history, I found it to be so true.

When I was a restaurant manager, reporting to one food and beverage director in a hotel with three other restaurants besides mine, my restaurant did indeed have it's own personality—it's own culture, it's own '*Ohana*. And that personality or culture came from the direction *within* the restaurant that came from me, my assistant managers and our shared values. Whether we were aware of it or not, the distinction of the restaurant, successful or unsuccessful, came from us much more than our theme, the food we served or the prices we charged. And you, my dear manager, have the same capacity to share: You are much more influential than you realize.

As you can imagine, my '*Ohana* in business with the Alaka'i Nalu of Hualalai was dramatically different in character than the one I had with my restaurant crew. Within the very same time frame of my work with the Alaka'i Nalu, my '*Ohana* in business with all the management in my operations division differed as well. The character of your '*Ohana* will depend on the values you share and the mission you aspire to. Yet regardless of those differences, '*Ohana* will furnish you with the form of unconditional caring, acceptance, and support. Every family has a patriarch or matriarch, and in an '*Ohana* in business that person is the manager.

So choose your influence by choosing your form. And my pitch to you is that family or '*Ohana* would be a choice that can serve you well. Work is personal in our world today, and family is personal; it gives you the ability to relate to your employees in a universally comforting and secure way. You probably already realize that as a manager you are a team builder: Seek to be an '*Ohana* builder. You will be thrilled and amazed with the character of respect and support that pervades your team.

Who are those *you* choose to call 'Ohana?

Work will be personal, because the relationships that thrive within the work environment are personal. How will you choose to share your life there? As a manager, how will you choose to affect the working lives of others?

An *'Ohana* is the best human circle you can bring to a business. The work teams that can give unconditional *Aloha*, acceptance, understanding, support and forgiveness to each member have a better chance of perpetuating an inclusive, pervasive atmosphere of *Aloha* that will spill over to the customer.

Great managers are those who create an *'Ohana* in business with their employees, with understanding for their humanity and respect for their intelligence as business partners. *'Ohana* will provide a manager with the very best way to communicate openly and honestly, for *'Ohana* is the most secure and comfort-filled support we have for facing truth. *'Ohana* never loses hope. *'Ohana* nurtures and sustains us. *'Ohana* is our rock and our anchor.

'Ohana is family. *'Ohana* includes those we *choose* to call our family, for the connection we share with them enriches our life.

'Ohana becomes a sacred form for sharing our lives with *Aloha*, for it gives us the unconditional gifts of love, understanding, forgiving, and acceptance.

'Ohana is the most secure and comfort-filled support we have for facing truth, for *'Ohana* never loses hope.

The bonds of *'Ohana* are strong yet supple: They flex with giving and with the love and acceptance of *Aloha*, yet they are made rigidly secure by those same supports. These bonds may be tested, but they cannot be broken.

'Ohana is a human circle of complete *Aloha*.

8

Lōkahi

Collaboration and cooperation
Harmony and unity
People who work together can achieve more

> *Lōkahi* seeks the harmony of bringing people to agreement.
> It is the value of cooperation, collaboration, and unity.
> Therefore *Lōkahi* brings these values to teamwork, defining
> how those who work within an *'Ohana* in business can
> be most effective in their collaborative efforts.
> *Lōkahi* gives us a demeanor to strive for in working with our
> peers in the best possible way. We want their help: many
> hands *(laulima)* make the work more pleasant *('olu'olu)*
> and they move it along faster. With *Lōkahi* we can achieve
> more by working together in harmony with others.
> *Lōkahi* is the value of teamwork in pursuit of synergy.

Early impressions

When I lived on O'ahu we bought a 21-foot boat to use
for fishing. As much as I grew up the local girl who adored
going fishing, my preferences were standing thigh deep at a
shoreline *'oama* run with a bamboo pole, or whipping for *pāpio*
from the rocks with rod and reel. Never having been much of
a swimmer, I had my reservations about that boat, for 21 feet
of floating fiberglass is nowhere near substantial enough for me
when bobbing up and down rolling swells in the Pacific Ocean.

So to secure my buy-in and get me to feel more comfortable with it, my family said I should name the boat, giving her a name with the *kaona*, or deeper meaning, that would make me feel I could enjoy her in harmony with the ocean.

The word harmony was one that appealed to me, for never would I hope to have a greater power than that of the sea. Never would I dare to think that I could somehow control her; I just wanted it to be okay with her that I was part of some pirate crew using this boat to steal her fish. We weren't there to struggle with the ocean or dishonor her; we just wanted to respectfully ask her for some food and go get it without disturbing anything else in her domain. We wanted to coexist.

The harmony of being in agreement

I named the boat *Lōkahi*, learning at the time that *Lōkahi* meant the harmony of being in agreement. On my quest for this name I was taught that *mana'o lōkahi* meant unanimous, and *ho'olōkahi* meant to bring about unity, to make things peaceful and harmonious. I decided that if I would always have a demeanor of *ho'olōkahi* while in our boat the ocean would sense my *mana'o*, my respect, and seek to be peaceful for me. She would believe my intent to only fish for what we needed and no more. I suppose you could call it the power of belief, for from the time of her christening forward I always felt completely safe on that boat; I always felt she protected me, and she did. We were a team—me, *Lōkahi*, and the ocean.

The dynamics of teamwork

Our fishing boat has long since been retired, after helping us bring much fresh fish to our table. However *Lōkahi* is still with me, and still all about harmony, and bringing things and people to agreement. And I've learned even more about *Lōkahi* as a value that can drive people to better performance. More hands make the work more pleasant and they move it along faster. *Lōkahi* teaches us to cooperate with each other, to strive together until we become one in our efforts; it helps us understand that work is always better when we do it together. *Lōkahi* is the value of teamwork in pursuit of synergy. For now, I'll hold off on synergy until we reach the next chapter on *Kākou.* Let's consider teamwork first.

You may be thinking, hey hold on—you just got us to think *'Ohana,* not team! Way to pay attention! Here's the difference: Team is a noun, a thing, and should you choose it, *'Ohana* can be a higher evolution of a team for you, a concept of more intimacy and greater expectations. With *Lōkahi* we think of teamwork as the verb, and the behavior of those within the *'Ohana*—specifically, how do they interact, how do they work together to effectively get things done? Striving for the *Lōkahi* of harmony becomes the lesson, with the basic premise that groups of people who work together will achieve far more if they seek collaboration and cooperation, agreement and ultimately unity. Just as I wasn't about to struggle against the greater power of the ocean, there cannot be any power struggle when it comes to great teamwork.

The positive found in power

Now that being said, I do think that the word *power* gets a bum rap sometimes. Harnessed power can be a pretty wonderful thing—a good force. For example, think about the generative power of medicine and the healing arts. Think about the bountiful electrical power entire cities receive, harnessed from the immense power of the water flowing through the Hoover Dam. In Hawaii, we revere the power of the volcano, and we are thankful that *Pele's* eruptions create more land for us. (*Pele* is goddess of fire and the volcano).

When it comes to people, we are better off thinking of power as influence and effectiveness, and how you harness it for good results in productivity, or in searching for the best solution of several options presented in problem solving. By virtue of the inherent goodness in universal values that appeal to the humanity of our kind, *Lōkahi* becomes a wonderful tenet for the managers who seek to coach their performers to their best achievement within the framework of any *'Ohana* in business. *Lōkahi* sets a proper climate and tone for the expectations of teamwork, for it teaches those involved to pursue the cumulative effect they can have when they harness their individual power and join forces. It teaches them that collaboration, cooperation and alignment are more effective than individual spurts of power.

The role of the individual

Most of the Hawaiian values really speak to personal endeavors, and the concept that all starts from within you. We are responsible for our own attitudes, our own choices, our own happiness and our own success. While *Lōkahi* speaks to the behavior of people within a group, its core assumption is that the group's effectiveness comes from the choices made by the individuals within it.

Lōkahi asks these questions: Are you a bystander or are you truly engaged? Does your reach include the entire team, and are you being cooperative? Do you seek to understand everyone's opinion while sharing your own? Are you looking for mutually beneficial agreement or are you settling for negotiation or compromise? Do you understand the role of every person, and are you respectful of their participation and involvement? Are you fulfilling your own role and responsibility, so that you make the contribution that is expected of you? Are you supportive and positive?

In a subtle way, *Lōkahi* helps managers immensely when incorporated in the language of their *'Ohana*, for it is a value driving cooperative behavior while assuming that individual members of the *'Ohana* fully assume their responsibility. *Lōkahi* helps the manager foster accountability in employees at the same time those employees expect the manager to take responsibility for the harmonious working climate that exists between them and their peers.

The Lōkahi challenge for managers

Lōkahi challenges managers to be the best possible project leaders of group endeavors in a couple of different ways. It affords the manager checklists on group assembly and assignment, on the health of the mission and clarity of desired outcomes, and on just-right pace and momentum. All these things are crucial to maintaining the *Lōkahi* of harmony within the *'Ohana.*

- First, *Lōkahi* requires managers select and train responsibly.

Are you selecting the right participants when you put a group together and give them a project to work on? When you consider that a project is a smaller component of the overall initiatives of your business, a group's assembly is just as critical as the recruitment, selection, interview and hiring you do for the company itself. Your "interview questions" become those you largely ask yourself, to be sure you have selected the right people for the right job, and that they are trained well and have open capacity for the project at hand. You choose those who have passion for it and are committed to its success. Best case scenario, the project you assign serves up a triple-whammy: *Ho'ohana*—it is conducive to helping the participants involved achieve a personal goal in their professional mission statement at the same time they work on attaining the desired project result itself. They are excited about it, they are self-motivated, and they will likely dish up success beyond your hopes and dreams.

- Second, *Lōkahi* requires managers to have their act together.

Ultimately the manager retains ownership of the business plan. You must speak often and passionately of your vision so that it is clear enough and your *'Ohana* can easily see how their project is critical to the company mission (*Kūlia i ka nu'u* and mountain climbing); they understand its worth, and the work they invest in it becomes important and worthwhile (*'Imi ola*). You've taken the time and care necessary to paint a picture of the best possible outcome for them so they are clear on the final result that is expected. You have given them the tools they need to work on the project for you, while trusting them to get it done with full ownership of the steps they take and the decisions they make along the way. Yet you have guided them in planning, and you have made any structure of responsibility and accountability clear. You have set the critical timing parameters, so they can feel the euphoria of delivering just-in-time results for your company. You are ready with whatever support is needed, both to help them learn from mistakes that may occur, and to reward and celebrate wildly when they succeed and deliver *(Aloha)*.

- Third, *Lōkahi* requires a manager's involvement to be consistent and constructive.

Do you remain engaged in the pace and momentum of the *'Ohana* along the way, and do you intercept if any individual parts become disconnected? When the core needs are taken care of, *Lōkahi* transcends behavior, and it becomes a descriptive statement of the overall state of affairs of the *'Ohana*. To ask "are we *Lōkahi?*" is to ask are we all engaged connected and in sync—do we have rhythm and focus; are we all moving forward together? Great managers are always well aware of the pace and momentum of their staff, realizing that pace can vary as may be required. Consider Lance Armstrong's amazing performances in the Tour de France as a great example of pace. He's "pacing" during most of it, conserving the energy he'll need to release later. He wins it by taking the lead where his strength is keenest, up in the mountain tracks.

I doubt that Lance Armstrong looks over his shoulder very much: He understands that he must focus on his own efforts first and foremost. Managers find their involvement is needed—and wanted—because the majority of their employees do not possess this same discipline and maturity, they look over their shoulders more often. However, those employees expect that their manager will be the one to accept responsibility for keeping everyone on pace—they expect their manager to keep things harmonious.

Pace and momentum

Your employees will undoubtedly shift gears often. As a manager, you are helping ensure they are in the right gear at the right time. It can be a daunting task to keep all these individuals within a group in alignment and on pace together. Think of your car; the similarities of human performance are strikingly similar.

I cannot take full credit for the analogy I'm about to share with you. It came from an exercise I had done with a manager of a very troubled team I had encountered in my earlier years at Hualalai. This manager would call his employees "my young bucks," for they were in entry level positions, not one older than 30, the majority single and free of much personal responsibility. Their manager had reached a point where he wanted to get rid of all of them and start over; there was so much dissention in the group.

Talking it through with him, there were two things that stuck out for me. First, he said he felt most frustrated because they never seemed to be in sync. "It's so maddening when I think we're making progress and I've still got one or two stuck in first gear!" A sentence or two later he continued, "The only time I've seen them pretty animated lately is talking about their new cars," for coincidentally three of them had just gotten new wheels, and their peers enviously had the same goal. They happened to be in an age group where a new car was their first major purchase.

We decided to hold a couple of team-building sessions, and play around with a car theme in a manner that would teach them the concepts of *Lōkahi* in their current language of choice. His "young bucks" were the real authors of what we ended up with. They totally enjoyed the gatherings in which they came up with this, their team manifesto—in fact, we all did. For the first one, we chose a late hour so it wouldn't be too hot as we huddled in the staff parking lot, surrounded by their new cars for visual inspiration - sort of like pioneers within the circle of their covered wagons.

The manager started by explaining that we wanted to talk about teamwork, and figure out what it is that makes the difference between when an *'Ohana* works well together and when members struggle because they're out of rhythm. He said, "It's like these cars: If they are to drive at their peak performance, a couple of things have to happen. What are those things?" Everyone jumped into the analogy quickly, and this is what they came up with:

Preparation: You can't even engage first gear if all systems aren't a go, tuned up and ready for you. There's got to be enough gas in the tank and air in the tires. There's that magic sweet spot in timing where you release the clutch and pedal to the metal the car moves forward. *Lōkahi* encourages the individual within a group to be responsible for the level of preparation they bring to the table when the group comes together. If they are not there, and they are not ready with their contribution, the "magic sweet spot" where all gears interlock, where all players engage, will not happen.

Acceleration: Those low gears require the most fuel, and you can hear and feel the roaring surge in power that results if you don't shift soon enough. You reach a point where more gas is simply wasteful and you're revving an impatient engine; you've got to shift. *Lōkahi* recognizes that the talents within a group can vary, their readiness can vary, but no one need be held back waiting if they are ready to surge forward; The others will look for the collaboration that is necessary to propel themselves forward, as well. Cooperation is the sharing of an energy that begs to be shared, and shared energy begets more energy.

Transition: Second gear has the shortest lifespan, and you're never in it that long, but you can't ignore it or skip it, for you can't get to third gear without it. Second gear is the transition that is both sequential and consequential. If the car could talk it'd be screaming, "Let's change it up!" *Lōkahi* helps us understand that every player is important, everyone can participate and make a contribution, everyone can learn and progress together. If we are all seeking cooperation and collaboration, we will not ignore or forget a missing part that may later prove to be critical to our success. We will not hesitate to change course and try something different if we need to, for we are confident the others in the *'Ohana* will be there to sense what we may not sense if we were on our own. The work is better when done together.

Efficiency: The higher gears are more fuel-efficient, and if there isn't much wind resistance your car will give you maximum thrust and optimal performance in fourth gear. The sound of the engine changes; like a pressure cooker that's found its release, there's smooth impetus. *Lōkahi* is equally as satisfying when a group feels they really gel together. There is the sense that things are happening so quickly you can barely keep up, but it's *all good*. You trust more, and you look over your shoulder less, for in your time together thus far your co-workers have earned your confidence. The bonds of the *'Ohana* are further strengthened.

Control: You stay alert and pay attention, both hands on the wheel. When you want to stop in a way that is better for the car racing downhill you don't brake hard, you downshift. Remember what I said a few pages earlier about power? When it comes to people, we are better off thinking of power as influence and effectiveness, and how you harness it for good results. The *Lōkahi* concept of control is *staying in control* and being alert, and as such having the optimal amount of influence and effectiveness when you work in collaboration with others. You are always conscious of your approachability and your overall demeanor.

Reward: Throw it into fifth when the momentum is right and you are truly enjoying the ride, taking in the scenery and singing along with the radio. You, the car, the ride, you are all *Lōkahi*, in harmony cruising down the highway. Groups of people who have achieved *Lōkahi* together truly enjoy their journey, they can think of no better *'Ohana* to be associated with and they will eagerly pack for travel to the next destination with their peers.

Basically, this *'Ohana* in business came up with new vocabulary they could use to encourage each other. It was themed by their cars, but the message was all about *Lōkahi*. When someone said, "I think I'm stuck in second gear," his peers—and perhaps most importantly his manager—knew what he meant, and how he needed some help. But first he was thanked for recognizing where he was on the journey, and for his honesty and willingness to "get a fill-up."

What did the manager do?

The manager's role in the discussion had been to keep *Lōkahi* in the analogy as well, reminding everyone we were in alignment with a central value of our company, one that taught us to seek the harmony of agreement and work in collaboration and cooperation with each other. He wanted to keep his *'Ohana* intact, and not allow individuals to offer scenarios where they'd be working independently of the rest of the group.

In this particular case, the manager came away with an increased level of optimism, energy and excitement, for within these discussions he realized that his *'Ohana* was unified in their understanding of the job at hand, and they were passionate about their mission—there was no problem with Ho'ohana or with *'Imi ola*. They simply had to spend more time and energy on the how they got there, enlisting *Lōkahi* for help in recognizing their individual responsibility and smoothing their pace as a better functioning group of people.

Let's look again at the "*Lōkahi* challenge" for the manager: I'll tell you more about how he took the driver's seat and met that challenge.

First: *group assembly and assignment.* He made sure that he had the right team dynamics in place, carefully considering the individual assignments he'd made within the *'Ohana*. A few minor changes were made before the discussion was held to better match person to role and assignment, to their capacity for assuming responsibility. He had reviewed their professional mission statements and had more confidence in the "fit" of the assignments he made.

Second: *health of the mission and clarity of desired outcomes.* He pursued absolute clarity in the job at hand with every project. He spoke of vision and mission more often than he had before, and he spoke of *Kūlia i ka nu'u* (strive to the highest summit), so the final desired outcome would be clear. He made sure everyone had the tools they needed and felt confident in their training. He treated them like business partners, evaluating results to business plan along the way, asking for feedback and celebrating successes.

Third: *just-right pace and momentum*. He maintained visible involvement in his *'Ohana's* pursuit of their goals, accepting his own responsibility to inspire, engage and energize them. He learned to respect someone's ownership when they were fully engaged in their work, and he learned to intercept when someone's pace faltered and they became disconnected from the efforts of their peers. He never lost sight of their momentum. As a result he drove the car as a finely tuned vehicle of optimal performance.

With every group of people you assemble and lead, and with every group you may individually participate in, allow *Lōkahi* to guide you. When you are the manager, get in the driver's seat.

Ho'olōkahi

When you *ho'olōkahi*, you seek to incorporate the value of *Lōkahi* into the *'Ohana* in business which you lead as manager. By incorporating *Lōkahi* you seek to gain the agreement of everyone involved, you look for their individual readiness and their collaboration and cooperation with others. As manager you are the one to look for alignment in their efforts, and harmony in their pace; you take responsibility for their momentum. Ultimately *Lōkahi* will help you achieve agreement in purpose and the unity of common intent, delivering the best results in productivity.

Lōkahi. Collaboration and cooperation. Harmony and unity. People who work together can achieve more.
Lōkahi is the value of teamwork in pursuit of synergy. We strive together until we become one.
Lōkahi is the attitude and demeanor great managers expect, from employees who strive to work with their peers in the best possible way.

9

Kākou

All of us
We are in this together
Learn to speak the language of we

> *Kākou.* All of us together.
>
> *Kākou* is the language of the *'Ohana,* for it is the language of "we," and we are in this together. Together we are stronger. We are better.
>
> Managers depend on other people, both peers and employees, to gain their results most effectively, and *Kākou* teaches us inclusiveness. When we inculcate *Kākou* into our language we bring life and reality to the words we speak.
>
> We. All of us in the *'Ohana.* We are in this *Kākou,* together. We have an *'Ohana* in business, wherein the whole is greater than the sum of its parts.
>
> No burden, no task, no goal, no mission will be too great when we are *Kākou.*

Inclusiveness

How do you feel when someone tells you, "We're in this together."

How do you feel when someone says, "No one will be left out or left behind."

How do you feel when someone tells you, "Come, take my hand."

How do you feel when someone says, "I couldn't have done

this without you."

You feel good. You feel included. You feel *Kākou*.

Kākou is about inclusiveness. At its elemental core, the spirit of *Kākou* acknowledges that we are not on this Earth alone, and as the human race we seem to survive better—we thrive—in each other's company, sharing the ups and downs of our day-to-day existence. *Kākou* is less intimate than *'Ohana*, for it applies to everyone that surrounds you in the consciousness of some particular striving or effort or task. For instance, when I address a group of people, large or small, I normally start with the words *"Aloha mai kākou,"* meaning that I offer my *Aloha* to everyone there. *Mai kākou* includes me as the speaker, and it's my way of asking permission to be included in their conversation, in their attentions.

Kākou promotes sharing, and making the effort to promote the well-being that is felt with inclusiveness. When we teach the value of *Kākou* to our *'Ohana* in business, we coach them to involve and include their peers in all they do, promoting *Lōkahi* and the harmony that comes from togetherness. *Ka'ana like* was a phrase we would use at Hualalai, meaning "we share in the work, and we share in the joy" of whatever that had been done, of all achievement large and small. We worked and celebrated together, *Kākou*, all of us.

The language of we

Kākou is the language of "we." And the language of we stimulates ownership and personal responsibility in the all-encompassing initiatives of a company. If you hear your employees talk about *"our* company" versus *"the* company" you know you're on the right track. They feel they have a stake in what you do, and they take actions they believe are important and worthwhile. They are your partners, and these words of inclusiveness imply that they feel their voices and opinions are considered carefully in the decisions you make. The language of we is one of collaboration and partnership, and it also implies agreement and support of your vision. These are the words, the empowering force, and the strength of mind of *Kākou*. All of us. *Kākou* serves to give an affirmative voice to the unity you were able to achieve in your efforts with *Lōkahi*.

Personally I believe that every manager in Hawaii needs to respect the needs of our culture here and figure out how to use the word *Kākou* in their own language, in the sentences they say to their staff every day. For the beauty of *Kākou* is that it includes the speaker in whatever is being said, and the message is explicitly clear that you are in it—whatever it is— with them. There is no me versus you, no us versus them, it's all we and us. You may be the boss, but you are one of them. In a company you are all employees, you are all business partners, you are all on a mission. Your staff needs to hear this from you, and they can never hear it enough.

Let language lead to action

This is what happens when you incorporate something into your language, into the words that people hear you speak often: You have to walk the talk to keep your credibility and your integrity. The surest way to change your own behavior for the better is to speak the words that will force you to make it so. And the brave soul who will say to his or her staff with humility and sincerity, "I need you to help me with this," often becomes their champion.

I am totally convinced that this is what had happened for me in my journey with the Alaka'i Nalu. I often asked them to see in me another employee of the company, and I enlisted their help in every goal written into the execution of the department's business plan. Their self-esteem and their involvement grew, for when I said that I couldn't do it without them they believed I spoke the truth as I saw it; I was not patronizing them. It went beyond the obvious fact that I couldn't steer a canoe or swim very well, and they began to understand just how much I needed them. Individually they came to realize that their work was incredibly worthwhile. *Lōkahi* and *Kākou* are both words that became incorporated into their departmental mission statement. Each time they re-read their mission statement they were reminded they had to live up to what those words challenged them to do.

Let it be all of us, together in synergy

When you seek to create a forum for the collective brain-power of your staff to be voiced, you also gain this marvelous realization you can let go more as a leader. There is tremendous relief knowing you don't have to be responsible for everything and be expected to know everything. Prolific leadership author Ken Blanchard has remarked that when he heard this author-unknown quote, "none of us is as smart as all of us," it helped him relax tremendously as a leader. You may never feasibly achieve as much on your own as you will with your *'Ohana* in business, and hey—not only is that okay, it's better. You have harnessed the additional punch of accumulated experience and knowledge.

Kākou suggests that it takes all of us, together. It is better when we achieve it together—whatever *it* is. Said another way, *Kākou* was the value that taught the Hawaiian people what synergy was long before it became a popular buzzword in business-speak. For those of you who may wish a quick review, I offer you the definition of synergy as I first learned it from the 7 Habits guru Stephen Covey: Synergy is the concept that the whole is greater than the sum of its parts. The easy definition is when 1 + 1 equals not 2, but 3. Synergize is Covey's Habit No.6, and he calls it the "habit of creation." This is an excerpt from his book *Living the 7 Habits, The Courage to Change:*

"Synergy is about producing a third alternative—not my way, not your way, but a third way that is better than either of us would come up with individually. It's the fruit of mutual respect—of understanding and even celebrating one another's differences in solving problems and seizing opportunities ... Synergistic teams and families thrive on individual strengths so that the whole becomes greater than the sum of the parts. Such relationships and teams renounce defensive adversarialism $(1+1=\frac{1}{2})$. They don't settle on compromise $(1+1=1\frac{1}{2})$ or merely cooperation $(1+1=2)$. They go for creative cooperation $(1+1=3$ or more$)$."

I love his choice of words, "producing a third alternative." My dad used to teach this concept of creative and collaborative agreement to us when he'd say, "There are actually three things to consider in everything: Your way, my way, and the best way." When he refereed an argument between us kids, the words were slightly different, but gave the same suggestion, "There are three sides to every story: your side, his side and the truth."

Lesson of the Six Seats

Kākou wholeheartedly embraces this "third alternative [of] creative cooperation" that Covey speaks of. Let me explain with another favorite whiteboard lesson of mine, the simple picture of the Hawaiian six-man outrigger canoe. I'm no artist, and the paddlers in my whiteboard canoe are just stick figures, yet I can manage to draw them holding the *hoe* (their paddles) at the very same angle, ready to slice into the *nalu* (the surf), at precisely the same moment. It's a lesson created in my *'Ohana* with the Alaka'i Nalu; one we called the Six Seats.

There is a purpose for each of those six seats, and each is crucial in the canoe. For instance the stroker is the pacesetter who sits in seat one, the one with best view of the swells that are most imminent, the one who will set the rhythm every other paddler follows. Seat two matches the timing of the stroker on the opposite side of the canoe, and he is thought of as an alert communicator, especially when the ocean winds prevent voices from being heard from the last seat to the first. Knowing he has this back-up, the stroker will concentrate on the consistency of his pace. The steersman occupies seat six, the last seat, and is the ultimate decision-maker, however he trusts his stroker to adjust pace as he steers direction.

The steersman is also the captain, and he must know of the individual talent and strength of each and every paddler before he assigns the seat they will occupy. Most watermen will agree that all paddlers must have the common traits of discipline, tenacity, focus and endurance. However there are differences too, and a role for each seat that values these differences; qualities such as physical strength or alertness are valued more so in one seat over another.

Something that sounds as simple as taking one of six available seats is actually an exact science of unifying similarities and combining essential differences in a line-up of the best possible pattern. It takes the harmonious, disciplined stroke of all six together to make the canoe surge forward through the surf with the least amount of effort, reserving the power of each when it is most needed. It takes every element of *Lōkahi* (agreement, cooperation and collaboration), and *Kākou* is achieved when the collaboration has resulted in perfect harmony and unity. They function as one, as the whole that has far greater capacity than the sum of the individual parts. At that moment of *Lōkahi*, of achieved unity, the *ama* (the outrigger float) actually skips over the surface, and the *wa'a* (the canoe) surges forward with incredible speed, momentum, and grace. Those paddlers have achieved *Kākou* in that they have achieved something that was impossible for any of them alone. Theirs was a togetherness that produced that third alternative called synergy. In a canoe, simply being all together (*Kākou*) is not enough; they have to produce and perform together as one (*Lōkahi*). It is *Kākou* that has taught them to value their differences in a way unique to paddlers, where powerful impetus is created.

Value the differences

Business has truly evolved. For today this sounds so very logical, that you put a group of people together in a way that treats them as individuals, but is complementary and harmonious so they can function at their best when they are together. (Is it this way in your company?) Yet this is not the way it always was. We didn't always think of employees as perfectly suited for one of Six Seats, each individually so different yet so crucial.

I can remember when Teamwork Rule 101 for all teams was that every assignment was fair and even. As a manager you dared not be accused of any inequity whatsoever; everyone carried the same weight, and they did so by doing an equal and fair share of the same thing everyone else did when it was their turn. This even-steven approach didn't really accomplish much, and it actually promoted a pervasive attitude that sounded something like, "Aw jeez, I'm better off just doing this myself."

The only teams that rose above this were those that forged their own relationships and mutual agreements to divide and conquer, and they actually broke the rules, teaching their managers "contented avoidance." You've all experienced working with one of those lost souls who will openly admit "heck if I know how they do it, but I know when to leave well enough alone. If it ain't broke I don't need to fix it." These are only words said by a manager without an *'Ohana* in business.

It's not a question of fairness

I clearly remember having a maverick of a boss who made this blunt pronouncement to all of us junior managers one day, "Hey, nobody ever said life was fair. Get over it." At the time we thought he was crazy and couldn't possibly understand the grand injustices of our lives, that he'd become too far removed from the trenches of frontline management to remember what it was like. Today I realize—I know—he was right on the money. However he frustrated us at the time because he didn't offer up the solution—what I know of today as the synergy of creation. He didn't teach us a better way, and he didn't help us value the differences.

If you are obsessed with fairness you are missing the boat. If every paddler paddled on the right side of a canoe to be fair, the canoe would flip over, or at best just travel in a circle, getting nowhere. Learn the lessons of *Lōkahi* and *Kākou* instead. We cannot all achieve the very same result when, as individuals, we are so different. And it is our differences that combine so brilliantly: If not for blue and red coming together there'd be no purple. Ultimately the inclusiveness of *Kākou* is all the fairness you need: Look to involve everyone in your *'Ohana* in business. Expect them to bring their unique strengths into your canoe.

Carry the weight, but not the burden

There is a saying we have in Hawaii that has been attributed to King Kamehameha when he spoke to his warriors before the fierce battles it took to unify his island kingdom. He was urging them to remember that as long as they were *Lōkahi*,

121

they were unified in their cause, and *Kākou*, they remained together as one in the battle, they could not easily be defeated. The saying was this: *Hāpai ka pōhaku aka mai hāpai ke kaumaha.* It means lift the rock, but not the weight; Don't carry the burden. When all of us are together, and all hands grab hold of the rock, it does not take as much individual effort to move it. The weight of the rock is the same, but it is not as heavy. The burden is no longer too great to bear, and no one man alone need do so. We are *Kākou*, we are all together, and we lift together. It is always better together.

This lesson of *Hāpai ka pōhaku aka mai hāpai ke kaumaha* was taught to the management team at Hualalai by our *kahu* (spiritual advisor), Billy Mitchell. It was often repeated as our call to unity, to togetherness, for ironically managers have the tendency to go it alone no matter how many other people surround them. They are team leaders so often that they forget how to be team players. They often feel they are in unique situations and must tough it out on their own, when actually the values-centered management they most effectively can employ should be binding them together, looking for *Kākou*.

Kākou teaches us to communicate well

Now King Kamehameha had the advantage of being the solitary monarch: His word was the only word, and it was the final commanding one. In business today, most employees take their direction from more than one manager, and it can be confusing or even contradictory for them. *Kākou*, the language of we, had taught me well that management teams need to speak to their employees in one unified voice, much as parents need to give their own children an answer that is one and the same, no matter which parent speaks it out loud. For this to happen managers need to communicate with each other often, with diligence and full disclosure, and this takes work. It's not particularly hard work, but unfortunately the efforts to do so are often seen as a luxury when time permits.

As I made my own ascent up the corporate business ladder, the team I would focus most on directing were my department heads and managers, and I had one dictum for them that was not negotiable: their own weekly management team meetings. These were not a luxury for them: they were required. The goal of their weekly powwow was to cultivate the tone of collaboration taught by *Lōkahi* and to instill *Kākou* and the language of we into their vocabulary. Department heads were taught to start with an uncomplicated, straightforward round-table sharing of what each manager felt their most pressing priority was so that *Hāpai ka pōhaku aka mai hāpai ke kaumaha*, their burden could be shared.

In the crunch of everyday operations, managers tend to neglect each other most of all, feeling that their peers "will understand," yet they need to be in sync with each other if they are to effect the performance of their employees in the most productive way. And they cannot assume they will make the same decisions simply by merit of being in the same position or circumstance—we all know that just doesn't happen. Management is situational, and as an art it can take some improvisation. To encourage and support each other through the situations that occur we need to talk to each other, and we can best do this by learning the language of we that *Kākou* teaches us to employ, creating forums for collaboration. The more we collaborate, the more we increase the probability of creating that third alternative—often the best way to proceed.

I knew that the management teams I needed to audit most often were those that I had discovered did not have regularly scheduled management meetings with planned agendas, and a department manager who would tell me, "But I talk to my managers and supervisors every single day!" Patiently I'd talk that department head through the content of exactly what they spoke about "every single day" and we were sure to discover that those on-the-fly conversations were not enough. Conversations in passing between managers are largely directive for the subordinate or informational for the superior; rarely do they turn into discussions. It is the nature of the beast that the tone of those conversations are of operational control and command, not the collaboration and agreement of *Lōkahi* and *Kākou* which seek win-win agreements, and with which senior managers coach junior ones.

Here's a quick exercise for you. For a moment, think of

the last conversation you had with another manager. Were you standing (on-the fly) or sitting (settling in for a discussion)? Were you on the phone (unscheduled, needing a quick answer) or face-to-face (feeling it important you had their full attention and could read body language)? Quite a difference, isn't there.

My own lesson was that I couldn't simply dictate this to my managers: I had to get involved in their meetings to model the behavior that would help them learn to communicate with each other more effectively, and I dared not be guilty of one-directional conversations myself. In my later years at Hualalai, I spent a considerable amount of time mentoring the design of collaborative management meetings, with a comprehensive schedule that kept me seated at the table of countless appointments. They were mutually rewarding, for I learned as I taught; I was coached as I mentored. And after each one I was more convinced that *Kākou* was the value of effective communication.

Truth be told, it was a source of irritation for my own superiors at times, who asked me to work more on "the business" and less with "the managers who should be held accountable for their own performance." Personally I was convinced that the latter was my means to the former, for you need to invest time in coaching managers if you expect them to be the ones who can elicit high performance levels from the staff.

Management is an art, not a scientific formula or repetitive process. And my experience did bear this out: The most harmonious and productive departments at Hualalai were those whose department heads learned to embody the demeanor of *Kākou* in all they said and all they did because they felt supported. They adopted the practices of *Lōkahi*, and they required the same of every assistant manager and supervisor they led, having also learned to model themselves the behavior they wished to see in others. As a result they created networks of managers who felt they had participated in making the best possible departmental decisions. They would have total ownership in the actions that followed.

Bring Kākou to your ʻOhana

Ask employees how they see your management style, and the manner in which you communicate with them will come to mind first and foremost. *Kākou* is the value of effective communication, in that it naturally seeks the decision and action that is created by synergy. It is the style that great managers seek to adopt, as they serve others with *Hoʻokipa*, and manage with *Aloha*.

Let *Kākou* infuse your voice. When we inculcate *Kākou* into our language we bring life and reality to the words we speak.

> *Kākou.* All of us together.
>
> *Kākou* is the language of the *ʻOhana*, for it is the language of "we" and we are in this together. Together we are stronger. We are better.
>
> Managers depend on other people, both peers and employees, to gain their results most effectively, and *Kākou* teaches us inclusiveness.
>
> We. Our *ʻOhana*. We are in this *Kākou*, all together. We are an *ʻOhana* in business, wherein the whole is greater than the sum of its parts.
>
> *Hāpai ka pōhaku aka mai hāpai ke kaumaha.* No burden, no task, no goal, no mission will be too great when we are *Kākou*, together.

10

Kuleana

One's personal sense of responsibility
I accept my responsibilities, and I will be held accountable

> *Kuleana* is the value of responsibility. It drives self-motivation and self-reliance, for the desire to act comes from accepting our responsibility with deliberance and with diligence.
>
> Responsibility seeks opportunity. Opportunity creates energy and excitement. *Kuleana* weaves empowerment and ownership into the opportunity that has been captured.
>
> There is a transformation in *Kuleana*, one that comes from *ho'ohiki*, keeping the promises you make to yourself.

Kākou, all together in our Kuleana

Once a quarter, I would gather all my Hualalai Operations department heads together for a half-day meeting. The purpose was to step back from the day-to-day resort business, entrust the day to their assistants and junior managers, and *Kākou*, all together, take a broader look at the full scope of our operational goals and responsibilities.

Quite honestly, I never planned too far ahead for these quarterly meetings, for inevitably the agenda would present itself, whatever the hot topics of the time. The logistics of getting these managers in the room all at once were already daunting, and I was not about to let go of an opportunity to conveniently deal with issues they felt were immediately at hand. Because the operations were fairly diverse—golf operations and course maintenance, sports club and spa, resort landscape maintenance, retail, food and beverage, natural resources, ocean recreation and safety, accounting and finance—the discussion normally revolved around the best way to manage our people while remaining mission-driven, values-centered and customer-focused, for those were the common threads despite our operational differences.

Lōkahi and *Kākou* were frequently mentioned at the last-quarter *Hālāwai* (meeting), our literal name for this quarterly meeting, in which we prepared criteria that would keep all operations consistent when awarding the year-end incentive bonus. Two weeks before another *Hālāwai*, copies of the book *Raving Fans, A Revolutionary Approach to Customer Service*, written by Ken Blanchard and Sheldon Bowles, were distributed to everyone to read, and in the meeting itself we discussed how we would create raving fans with our own Hualalai service. For at least one *Hālāwai* per year, I would come with no agenda at all, recognizing that silence always begs to be filled, and knowing we weren't leaving the room for five hours, lively discussions would surely get started of their own accord.

It was at one of these no-agenda sessions that I simply started the meeting by asking, "We are very fortunate that we can collect all of you in one room for the afternoon, *Kākou*. Together you represent the collective leadership and managerial brainpower of the operational *'Ohana*. Having your peers here to listen to you, to offer ideas and support you, what would you like to ask them? How can they help you?" My director of golf maintenance spoke up before anyone else had a chance to lift their hand in the air, and he said, "I'd like to have us talk about what it takes to motivate the guy doing routine stuff day in, day out, so that I can hold him 100-percent accountable for the work I need him to produce." He was thinking of his guy that moved bunker to bunker systematically through the entire 18 holes of the golf course each day, and that heavy machine operator who drove stripes up and down the fairways spreading fertilizer. Hualalai had opened its Jack Nicklaus Signature Course nearly two years before the rest of our operations, including the Four Seasons Hotel, and so within the golf maintenance department were our most long-term employees. They had been locked in monotonous routine well before most of us completed our new-hire orientation.

How do you keep your staff motivated? It was a question everyone had, and before we got to any answers for him, several people chimed in with stories of similar concerns in their own departments, sharing how they turned into babysitters reviewing task work more often than they wanted to. At face value, it might seem too big a question to get your arms around: Essentially, how do you motivate people?

There were two main themes of the discussion that ensued. One was the proposition that you cannot expect your employees to be as mission-driven as their leader may be if they haven't bought into the mission and goals of the department in the first place. If they are to *Kūlia i ka nu'u*, and strive for the summit, they must want to reach that summit for themselves; self-motivation largely comes from desire. The second theme revolved around a shared view that motivation essentially comes from within, and if you are knocking yourself out trying to motivate someone, you're wasting your time. You should've hired better or assigned better in the first place, and one of the things you should've selected for was the innate value of *Kuleana*, one's personal sense of responsibility. We couldn't fire everyone and start over, yet it was unanimous among the department heads in the room, that if they had to choose one thing that would make a huge, instantaneous difference in their operations today, it would be having employees who highly valued the reputation they had for taking personal responsibility.

I listened to most of this from sidelines, and when I next added my own voice to the discussion, I offered, "There is no need to hire all over again. I am certain we already have employees with self-motivation within them: We need to draw out what is already there and lying dormant beneath the surface for some reason. You are talking about *Kuleana*, one's personal sense of responsibility, and it is a value most of our employees probably grew up with or can pretty easily relate to. How shall we begin to talk about it with greater frequency and

Aloha so that they remember, and they bring it to the job every day? The core belief in the value of *Kuleana* is this: No one should be expected to hold you accountable—you should hold yourself accountable."

That became our agenda for the *Hālāwai* time that remained that afternoon: creating a game plan that would bring the value of *Kuleana* into focus intensively and consistently throughout the operation in the next 30 days. We would do this with what we said, what we taught and coached, with the progressive discipline we may need to provide, and in how we walked the talk, accepting our own responsibilities in ways that were visible for our staff. Therefore, before we left the room that day, we also talked about our own *Kuleana*, and how managers and management teams have the *responsibility to lead*, to make our statement of what we will and will not tolerate, what we will and will not accept, and what standards we expect to be upheld at minimum and surpassed at best.

The responsibility to lead

Accepting the responsibility for leadership is vital for any organization. And it is best assigned to those with the passion to lead for the good of the cause; position and title are not prerequisites. I recently attended a community health conference on the Big Island, and one of the guest speakers was Art Souza, the newly assigned principal for Honokaʻa High School. He was to report on "educational attainment" as a key priority in community initiatives centered on overall well-being, for in his previous assignment as an elementary school principal in Waikōloa he had earned quite a reputation as an academic leader capable of engendering community involvement and parental ownership of school initiatives.

He immediately captured my rapt attention when he started by saying, "When it comes to caring for the children in our schools, we in this community must assume the responsibility for leadership." He continued by outlining his belief behind this statement, explaining that "kids need hope and optimism about the world they will graduate into ... We must teach creative thinking, not out of the box, but without a box

… then as a supportive community network, we must give kids new opportunity once their lives in school come to a close."

To me, that sounded like a terrific plan for stimulating the self-motivation students could ultimately bring to a prospective employer as their natural sense of responsibility. It also sounded like a great plan for stimulating the development of leaders for the next generation. Give people responsibility early. Give them the opportunity to go out and do things. Trust that they'll go forward and do them. As I listened, I found myself cheering him on, hoping that he'd be successful in bringing his impassioned plan to action. I also realized that this was not only a great plan for educational communities, it was about *Kuleana* as a transformational plan for business.

Seeking empowerment and ownership

Here are other English words for *Kuleana* that were discussed that *Hālāwai* afternoon and in our other managerial forums that followed; you have heard them often. The words are *seeking empowerment* and *ownership*.

For a manager, empowerment should be thought of as the positive case for delegation. When you delegate well, you empower others and allow them entry into your circle of influence. In doing so, you achieve two things: First, you offer your faith, trust and confidence to be placed in someone else, and second, you open up your own capacity to embrace newness or additional growth yourself.

In the coaching that I do, my initial strategy with managers who tell me how busy and overwhelmed they are is not with time-management, it is a strategy of effective delegation. We take a blank sheet of paper and first fold it down the middle to create two columns. In the first column, I have managers write down a simple list of all the things they found themselves doing in their last two or three working days. Once that's done, in the second column I have them write down the names of the people in their department they feel are performing well, and they find they count on the most. This distinction is an important one—I want them to start with people they have a good relationship with. Sometimes their junior managers show up in this column, sometimes they don't: Title and position don't necessarily reveal their performers. The informal leaders they have in the ranks are normally identified for me pretty quickly. I'll stop them at only three or four names.

Together we analyze the tasks in the first column. First, I'll have them circle the one thing they find they enjoy doing most of all—it's a keeper: What you enjoy tends to serve as an energy catalyst for you. Second, I'll have them circle two or three things that they feel are their most important priorities— these things will usually point out for me what they feel to be their *Kuleana*, their personal responsibilities. For everything that's left on their list we draw a line to connect it with a name in the second column—these are the things they will begin to delegate and clean off their plates. The rest of the coaching session will be devoted to a discussion of how they can delegate in an effective way that will bring favorable results for both of them, personalized for whom they've chosen. Future coaching sessions will be devoted to how the manager can best use the time they've freed up for themselves.

We usually spend some time talking about how the tasks they delegate are looked at by their subordinates who accept them. There is a gift you give someone when you delegate worthwhile work. Your "lower priority item" becomes another's opportunity to show you what they can do. Let's look at this from the perspective of the employee.

When you agree to be held accountable for something, you are making a promise to deliver, and there is real self-empowerment simply in making that promise, whether it is to yourself or to someone else. A spoken promise is this wonderful obligation you hang within your own reach, begging to be "made good on." When you make a promise you are putting your good word at stake, and with the actions you then take to deliver on your word you have created your self-worth and your value to others. You have built upon your reputation, coming full circle to growing the credibility of your word when you next speak. You have accepted responsibility, you have been held accountable, and you are transformed, the engineer of your own growth and self-development. Quite an incredible gift, so why don't managers do this more for the people they manage?

A game plan for Kuleana

Where to start? How do you set the stage so that your delegation is not perceived as dumping versus the gift it can be? How do you "talk about *Kuleana*," and the value of taking personal responsibility for one's job with your employees? To return for a moment to the story I'd opened this chapter with, the apprehension a few of my managers had was that their staff would react defensively. They were afraid the staff would assume there was a hidden accusation behind the message, a thinly veiled statement that they presently were not devoting enough attention to the full scope of their job responsibilities.

First of all, that was the case, that's why it was brought up in our manager's *Hālāwai* in the first place, so why not bring it out into the open and talk about it? Second, it should have only been a fear if talking about values was not normally part of their operations, for if values-centered forums were the norm, *Kuleana* would have simply been another value on the list of what the *'Ohana* believed in and committed themselves to. If *that* was not the case, there was probably a larger problem within their department to deal with.

Thus our game plan was to hit attitude head on, and the leading question for the talk-story on *Kuleana* with their staff became this one; "How do you *feel* about the responsibilities that you have here at Hualalai?" We knew that they themselves would ultimately define the responsibilities they had *Kākou*—all of them together, and also individually, simple things like coming to work on time, taking care of personal grooming, being *'eleu* (alert) whenever the guest would possibly need your attention.

"This is my Kuleana."

As we had hoped, the staff would indeed use the words themselves, saying "this is my *Kuleana*," and then explaining their *mana'o* (thoughts and beliefs about it). The managers would later report back their pride in their staff upon hearing some of the things that were said: "Stay healthy, understanding that your contributions to the *'Ohana* are important, and others are counting on you ... Set a good example. Practice

132

what you preach. Keep your promises ... Remember that your actions speak louder than your words ... We are all responsible for the caring of our guests and customers ... Understand that people will give you their respect when you have earned it." Time after time, they found that their employees actually had bigger expectations of themselves and their responsibilities than the managers did: What they wanted most in order to deliver upon them was the manager's act of delegation and statement of faith and trust in them. In some cases, the staff just needed clarity on departmental goals; they needed affirmation and acknowledgement.

Thereafter, *Kuleana* would continue to be the value we would most closely associate with self-motivation, empowerment, and ownership. It became the living, breathing example of a *value that shapes people's behavior*, and one the managers had the biggest desire to drive, so they could free up their own time and not be babysitters. Once again, we saw that defining our values, and reaching agreement on them would help us lead our division strategically, effectively and consistently. We would be able to better communicate expectations and goals because they were in alignment with our values. We would learn to script them for better communication (*Kākou*), so we could reach win-win agreements and act as a cohesive team, pursuing *Lōkahi*.

Once again, working on values had become synonymous with writing the software that drives work processes. In doing so, we had accepted our own *Kuleana*, our own responsibility to lead.

Seek Kuleana, gain transformation

Kuleana is one's personal sense of responsibility. Those who embody the value of *Kuleana* say "I accept my responsibilities, and I will be held accountable." The truth of this statement is seen in their daily actions.

Kuleana is the value which drives self-motivation and self-reliance, for the desire to act comes from accepting our responsibility with deliberance and diligence. When *Kuleana* is a value that drives us, we take initiative and we motivate ourselves; others need not stoke a fire that already burns within us.

Those who accept responsibility will seek the opportunity to do so. Finding this opportunity creates energy and excitement for them. *Kuleana* weaves empowerment and ownership into the opportunity that has been captured. The manager who has learned to delegate well is one who has learned to tap into this natural circle of energy that *Kuleana* has created.

There is a transformation in *Kuleana*, one that comes from *ho'ohiki*, keeping the promises you make to yourself. When you make a promise, you are putting your good word at stake, and with the actions you then take to deliver on your word, you have created both your own self-worth and your value to others.

You have accepted responsibility, you have been held accountable and you are transformed, the engineer of your own growth and self-development. You are living the value of *Kuleana*.

Kuleana. One's personal sense of responsibility. As a great manager, accept and explore the responsibility you have to lead.

With *Kuleana*, managers offer their delegation to others as a gift, one of growth and self-development. There is a transformation that comes from seeking empowerment and taking ownership.

When the value of *Kuleana* is part of the language, you will find employees readily will say, "I accept my responsibilities, and I will be held accountable."

11

'Ike loa

To know well
To seek knowledge and wisdom

> 'Ike loa is the value of learning.
> Seek knowledge, for new knowledge is the food for mind,
> heart and soul.
> Learning inspires us, and with 'Ike loa we constantly give
> birth to new creative possibilities.
> 'Ike loa promotes learning in the 'Ohana; We must incorpo-
> rate the seeking of knowledge and wisdom into our busi-
> ness plan and into our daily practice.
> 'Ike loa is to know well, and knowing others well enhances
> our relationships and broadens our prospects.
> 'Ike loa: pursue wisdom. Learn and know well.

The value of learning

'Ike loa is the value that my managers have told me "turns you into an absolute fanatic" and I suppose that's true. It is one of my favorites, for it is all about learning and seeking more knowledge, something I am very passionate about. Gaining more knowledge equates to having more confidence and belief in one's ability and capacity to learn, and having more of that self-belief empowers you, liberates you and releases a creativity you may not have even realized you possessed. You constantly give birth to new possibilities in this creative process; you create your own destiny seeking your best possible life ('Imi ola).

You are sure to feed your body each day, aren't you? Well, new knowledge is the food for mind, heart and soul. Without it, you are not providing nourishment for your overall well-being. We grow as we learn.

To a business, knowledge is the asset of intellectual capital. Great managers have intellectual capital in good supply, and they work at refreshing it and keeping it well-stocked.

I stand firm and unmoving in my belief that someone who calls themselves a manager of people must be a learner, and they must dedicate themselves to non-stop, sequential and consequential learning. Sequential in that it builds upon previous lessons learned, and it takes you through a process where you question instruction and do not always accept what you are taught at face value; you polish it like a gem in your mind until something about it rings true for you. Consequential in that it is worthwhile stuff; it makes a difference for you, and you aren't simply collecting lessons on some scorecard. There's some personal take-away in it for you. Now that you know it, you're going to use it.

Personally 'Ike loa will naturally come to mind for me whenever I speak with others about Kuleana and one's personal sense of responsibility. I had once seen this quote attributed to Jan Carlzon, former CEO of Scandinavian Airlines Systems: "... an individual who is given information cannot help but take responsibility." It was easy for me to nod in agreement with those words for I've experienced it so many times within my own experience, and as a manager it became an employee ownership strategy for me. The wonderful thing is that with learning you are not just passing out information: You are teaching people how to think.

Learning inspires you

I recently assisted a client with their executive recruitment efforts, and at their request I interviewed a gentleman with years of experience in his field. He had been associated with organizations that I recognized as firms known for their quality standards and highly ethical reputations. He was professional, articulate and charming. Early in our conversation, I could tell his personality was one that would assure him quick acceptance with my client's staff and with their customers, and he revealed substantial character when he spoke about the values he believed in. However, the interview was over for me when I asked him to tell me about something he had read lately, and he responded, "Oh, I don't read much. Just the occasional golf or travel magazine."

You may be thinking that was pretty single-minded of me, however the position this gentleman was applying for required that he exhibit rousing leadership; he would lead other managers and his operation needed to consistently deal with new variables that had emerged in the marketplace within which my client competed. I could not fathom how he would possibly conjure up leadership that would inspire others to follow if he was not linked into learning habits that would inspire *him*. Energy begets energy, and when people are not up for work on any given day, it is the manager who must be the catalyst that energizes them. That's a hefty requirement, and one we need to continually replenish.

If managers are to become truly great managers they must be voracious readers, and they must make pulse-checking connections with some community of learning in their chosen industry. They must benchmark success, and they must network with others who are successful, thus opening themselves to auditory learning as well. They simply must. It is by remaining students that managers become better teachers, and great managers teach and teach constantly.

Learn by reading

At Christmastime, I was usually able to pack the gifts for two dozen managers in just one carrying crate: They all got books. For some of them, it was probably the third or fourth one I'd asked them to read in the past year, and the only surprise in my wrapped but obviously-shaped gift was the title. Magazine and web articles were sent to them frequently as building blocks that took away the intimidation a former non-reader may have once had when presented with a 300-page book. Reading had become part of the culture.

In the days that followed some article's distribution, I could easily pick out those who were the movers and shakers in my operation. They were the ones who always had something to talk about that was different, new, inquisitive and thought-provoking. They were within their creative process. They were polishing gems of new learning in their minds, looking for new insights that would energize and inspire them.

Promoting learning in the 'Ohana

Of course 'Ike loa with the rest of my employees differed. While I could drive and uphold this "reading homework" standard for my managers, other approaches were more effective with the staff.[3] Still the premise and belief was the same, and my conviction was equally unwavering: Knowledge is a key, and learning is vitally important. One phrase they'd hear from me often was that continuous learning was essential to the success of our business, it was not a luxury. As business partners in our 'Ohana in business, we'd learn together so we could succeed together.

Organizations need to embrace learning because it is the excitement about new discoveries that helps them let go of the old sacred cows that may not be working for them anymore: New learning lends objectivity to the emotion that will keep people comfortably tied to their old ways. The pace of change in today's world is amazingly quick, and even the most technologically inclined among us struggle to keep up with it. If we are to stay in the business game, we need to explore the new concepts and ideas that emerge, and we need to embrace varied points of view. Frankly, as managers we must be brave enough to admit we need help in our own game, and then go get it. 'Ike loa is a value that brings that need into our comfort zone, for in applying it we help our staff as much as we help ourselves. Let me share a story with you on how I came to fully

---

[3] This being said, a few of my Alaka'i Nalu eagerly devoured M.J. Harden's book, *Voices of Wisdom*. One of them told me it was the first book he'd read since he got out of high school, and he planned to make up for lost time. It's a matter of matching the right book to the right person. Today, I often recommend managers suggest *The Automatic Millionaire* by David Bach (Broadway Books, New York, New York 2004) to their employees who need help with managing their finances and breaking out of the stress that money can create.

understand this.

The very first position that I held at Hualalai was as retail manager, hired to open three different retail stores. A few years before then, I'd stepped down from the demands of a job that had normally required 60 hours per week from me, for it was too much time to give with two children just 3 and 6 years old. However, I still needed a full-time job, and I still wanted to be a manager. Fortunately for me, retail would reveal itself as my next career. 'Ike loa became my new mantra, for boy did I have a lot to learn: I'd never done any retail before. It was a wonderfully exciting time for me, for I was learning and learning constantly, and I was able to put my new learning into immediate practice.

However, once I arrived at Hualalai my responsibilities became overwhelming; within two years the retail volume I was accustomed to jumped from the thousands of dollars to the millions. I was right back at those 60 hours per week I'd once left behind, and I needed some help.

In creating the Hualalai retail department, there was one thing I was particularly proud of: my crew. We had been able to hire an opening 'Ohana that was very passionate in their Ho'ohana (their work intent), and most were Mea Ho'okipa, exceptionally in tune with the needs of our guests. I admired them and I respected them, and I knew that they were the best ones to give me the help I needed. I was confident that talent surrounded me: I just had to tap into it more effectively.

We started a weekly forum called ShopTalk. For one hour each week, every retail clerk on the resort—which included a modest warehouse staff—would participate in this forum of retail learning. Product knowledge was a staple on the agenda, and my vendors were asked to help me teach it—they were the ones who knew most about their own products (think back to Kuleana and delegation strategy). My shop managers were asked to facilitate forums on store operations, and our warehouse staff covered that operation. For my part, I normally taught and explained our retail business plan, investing more in our relationship as business partners. As retail manager I was also buyer, and I'd attend the instructional seminars given at trade shows as student so I could replenish my own arsenal as teacher: My crew came to think of my post-travel ShopTalks as the trend discussions they could look forward to, linking our local operation with the retail industry as a whole. Soon we found that our ShopTalk students became the teachers too: As Mea Ho'okipa, they were the best qualified to mentor all of us about delivering better service, and maintaining our ever-constant focus on the customer. ShopTalk became both a forum for learning and a celebration of the immense wealth of talent we had and could share with each other.

From ShopTalk evolved our Vendor Partnership Program, an initiative that would serve as a model for our peers in the industry: Word of its effectiveness was lauded by vendors who participated, and they encouraged other retailers to consider it. In this program retail clerks adopted shop vendors they were interested in working with directly because they loved their product. Their goal within the program was to learn and then participate in my buying process while improving our vendor-business relationship. For my part, I fine-tuned our supplier certification and procurement systems so that both vendor and retail clerk had the right tools to work with. When a product line entered a new season, catalogs and promotional mailings went directly to the retail clerk, and no longer were delayed in my inbox. Vendors enrolled in the program made appointments directly with the retail clerk they were assigned to, and they would spend more time in the shop and less playing phone tag with me. Vendor servicing of our account improved, product turn improved, in-shop visual displays improved, new product knowledge was more timely, sales volume in special orders jumped and there was an unbelievable amount of creative energy generated within our entire retail 'Ohana.

Of course for me, this also meant I got the help I had desperately needed. My industry peers were amazed that we were able to run the Hualalai retail operation with only one director who managed the business plan and functioned as buyer and merchandiser, and with a single shop manager in each outlet. I was retail manager, the assumed "expert," yet my retail clerks and warehouse staff did a much better job with their vendors than I possibly could have done. Because the clerks were restricted to working in-shop and could not travel with me, the lines of accountability became pragmatically clear, and I learned to let go in-shop and honor their domain. In turn they celebrated the faith and trust I placed in them; they were encouraged to take bigger risks with the responsibility they assumed. However, I felt connected and in-touch: They were very open in communicating to me what they needed from me as support (*Kākou* and *Lōkahi* were maintained).

Both ShopTalk and the vendor partnership program came from our belief in *'Ike loa*, and what the pursuit of more knowledge could do for us. As they gained more information my retail clerks accepted their *Kuleana* (more responsibility) wholeheartedly; they accepted complete product-line ownership and they became empowered and self-motivated, understanding that ultimately their success was measured by our sales and customer loyalty.

Enter 'Ike loa into your business plan

'Ike loa was guaranteed its place on the very first draft of the business plan I wrote for my own business, Say Leadership Coaching. When tax time came, I entered a parenthesis in the language of my tax accountant: *'Ike loa* (Staff Training and Education). Even starting my business as a one-woman show, I fully realized that if my business was to survive and thrive, it would have to continually invest in my learning and development, and that of every prospective employee to come.

I incorporated what I'd learned as basic good business sense, for I have been blessed and fortunate that this assumption has been in the business plan of every company I have worked for. After living more than 30 years worth of experience seeing the good results of this practice, part of my *mana'o* (deeply held beliefs) is this: Businesses must invest in the training and education of their employees. Safety training alone is an area where on-the-job safety training has direct monetary benefits to your bottom line with savings in medical premiums, loss time prevention and workers compensation. And training need not be very expensive: My only cost for ShopTalk was one hour of labor time per week for each employee, and it more than paid for itself in the concrete sales dollars those employees generated as a direct result.

With managers in particular, I believe that companies must bridge training expenses with travel expenses: We live in an increasingly globally aware society and managers today must enlarge their professional networks. Yes, I absolutely feel that managers must be culturally sensitive and respect the sense of place that resides wherever they manage. However, knowledge has a universal character and is immensely adaptable, and we cannot be too incestuous, blindly feeling we have all the answers in our own school yard. The managers in Hawaii who aspire to greater leadership roles must embrace diversity and be leaders in their chosen fields as a whole: They have to travel out of the islands if they are to pursue *'Ike loa* and their own learning to the fullest. *Kūlia i ka nuʻu*: strive to the summit.

Get the most out of the travel dollar you spend: When managers return, be sure there is a forum wherein they immediately graduate from student to teacher and coach. Knowing that this was the expectation, my own five-hour plane trip from the U.S. West Coast was always well spent designing lesson plans. With ShopTalk, we were very creative and *Kākou* (inclusive) in our reach for discussion facilitators. Our head golf professional would speak on retail trends he'd heard about at the annual PGA show. Our spa director would speak on new developments discussed at the annual ISpa convention, and how these new concepts could possibly translate to different retail product for our customers. They collected sample trade publications that were devoured by the staff, for they'd come home to the energy and excitement that *'Ike loa* naturally engenders.

'Ike loa in daily practice

Everyone has the capacity for learning. This capacity is a gift of our birth, and it is not difficult to begin learning processes within your own company's culture. One way is to simply incorporate it into your daily communication forums: Personally, I have the Ritz-Carlton Hotel Company to thank for teaching this to me so very well with their daily Line-up.

For 10-15 minutes each day Ritz-Carlton managers are required to start their employee work shifts by sharing the information they feel is vital to current daily company and market knowledge. The human resources department in each hotel does most of the work for you, with a daily Line-up sheet distributed to each department manager with the information that is to be consistently shared. My own hotel's general manager figured he'd do the company policy one better: Human resources was given eight minutes and department heads were required to fill the other seven minutes with departmental "learning bites."

When I led the operations team at Hualalai, my Ritz-Carlton daily Line-up evolved to something we called the Daily 'Ohana Mālama (taking care of our 'Ohana in business). The process was pretty much the same, still only 15 minutes per shift. And the theme was still about learning. However, with the Daily 'Ohana Mālama we took care to ensure that 'Ike loa was incorporated into our language. After the success we'd enjoyed with ShopTalk, we confidently delegated facilitation of this daily process well below the supervisory level, and we uncovered another benefit: Employees were much more adept at soliciting feedback from their peers on a daily basis than were the managers—they knew the right questions to ask.

When we spoke of the value of 'Ike loa, we would simply concentrate on the meaning: to know well. What else did we need to know? Managers were encouraged to have question-and-answer discussions within other staff forums that would turn anyone with a possible answer into a teacher and coach for everyone else. For example, these were some of the questions that managers would use to start discussions with their employees: Take notice of Kākou and the language of we.

- What are the things you'd like to learn more about? What kind of knowledge would make it easier for you to practice the art of Ho'okipa with our guests?
- What have you learned about recently? How has this new knowledge helped you—at home, on the job, at play, in any way—and how did you learn it?
- How can we best stay connected with the rest of the company? What are the tools we have to keep needed

information readily at our fingertips?

- Often, our customers are our best teachers in alerting us to how we must deliver exceptional service. What are some examples within our own department in which we've found a better way to practice the art of *Ho'okipa* because a guest clued us in? Going forward, how can we be more open to receiving these lessons our guests offer us?

'Ike loa is to know well, and we'd simply assume there was always more to learn. The more your staff knows about their jobs and why they are important, the more passionate they will be about them, and the more they will experience their own creative transformations in the process. Learning becomes more than their school-days memory; it starts to mean something concrete for them because they gain personal results from it.

Learning is about the student

I've said often within these pages that managers must be mentors, teachers and coaches. However, as ShopTalk taught us, managers needn't be the designated experts; The best teachers are *alaka'i ka 'ike* (guides of learning) who guide their students to the best sources of the learning (*kumu a'o*) they need. In other words, the best teachers are those who understand that learning is about the student and what that student feels they need to learn. The best teaching is highly personal: It doesn't follow a set formula. And the act of learning itself is transformational, just as we had learned happens with *Kuleana*, and accepting responsibility.

One of my employees learned to play slack key guitar after decades of wishing he could, because he'd gained "learning confidence" from some of the programs we had enrolled him in while at Hualalai. What he has learned now overflows to others; the music he creates is hauntingly beautiful, and he adores sharing it. In other words, gaining knowledge also creates an abundance mentality. Once you learn something that excites you, you feel you must share it with others—just as I am hoping to do through this book.

The Daily Five Minutes

Perhaps my most valuable lesson in 'Ike loa was the one born at Hualalai out of our desire to know our *employees* well. We instinctively knew we could manage better the more intimately we knew those we managed. 'Ike loa became the birthplace of a core standard we initiated with all managers called "The Daily Five Minutes." It started as an experiment, and it was so effective that it became non-negotiable as a habit my managers were required to cultivate and practice daily.

It is a simple habit: Each day, without fail, managers are to give five minutes of no-agenda time to at least one of their employees. They'd log the event in a simple checklist of names to ensure they didn't miss anyone, and they'd speak to each employee in turn on a regular basis.

To be honest, my initial goal was actually to give the managers daily practice in the art of listening well, for I was trying to come up with a solution for the common complaint that "my manager doesn't ask for my input and feedback, and if I do give it, he/she doesn't really listen well to what I'm trying to explain to them." I reasoned that if they had no agenda themselves with this Daily Five Minutes, they wouldn't "half-listen" as they mentally prepared what they'd say when they could get a word in. Employees were brought into the plan and openly told about the program: they were asked to prepare something, and be ready to fill the silence when a manager approached them and said, "How about a break from the action here, let's step away and Take 5."

In the beginning, the managers were cautioned to give themselves a good 15 to 30-minute window, for there'd likely be some pent-up stuff that had to come out. However, over time, the managers who kept up the habit discovered their Daily Five Minutes rarely stretched over 10. This is what happened: In the process of developing this habit, they greatly improved their own approachability. They had nurtured a circle of comfort for their employees to step into and talk to them—whenever time presented itself. The Daily Five Minutes itself soon became a more personal thing. Employees started to share their lives with them—what they did over the weekend, how their kids were doing in school, how they felt about a local news story. Managers began to know their employees very well, and their employees began to relate to them more as people and not just as managers. They were practicing the art of *'Ike loa* together.

Knowing well enhances relationships

Benefits from the Daily Five Minutes piled up: Managers ceased to judge employee situations prematurely, for they had built up a relationship that demanded all be allowed to speak first—and they *wanted* to speak with their employees, sure they'd receive more clarity. The Daily Five Minutes became a "safe zone" where employees felt they could talk story with their manager "off the record," and managers learned to ask, "are you venting, or asking for help? Do I keep this in confidence, or do you expect me to take action?" It became clearer who was responsible for following up on things. Managers had less and less of those "if only I had known about this sooner" surprises.

Employees began to initiate the Daily Five Minutes themselves, both with their managers and with other employees they wanted to know better. Everyone learned to say "no" and to be more respectful of time issues, saying scripted sentences that were non-emotional: "Now is not the best time, but I promise to Take 5 with you later." Everyone became much better at reading expressions and body language, a skill that had added benefits when they were dealing with the customers. Cultural barriers started to break down, because managers started to learn the "communication language" they needed to use to relate to each employee as an individual, and they gained better understanding of the "sense of place" of each one.

So you see, *'Ike loa* promotes all types of knowledge, and it is just knowing, and knowing well. When programs like the Daily Five Minutes give it form, even spontaneous unrehearsed conversation can erase confusion, and replace wrong assumptions with the right information. Personally, I have an ongoing and passionate love affair with books and the written word, yet some of my best knowledge has simply come from talking story with my staff: They are exceptionally patient teachers.

Talking Story

This may be the best place to pause, and explain why I refer to "talking story" fairly often. Unfortunately, our Hawaiian ancestors did not pen a written history of our islands. Information was passed generation to generation verbally, with the 'Ōlelo (the language and spoken word) and in storytelling. Today there is much effort in our Hawaiian renaissance to record what we know about our past history before the *kūpuna* (the elders) forget and can no longer tell it to us. Still today, for us to communicate and dialogue is to "talk story." There is so very much I personally have learned from the 'ōlelo form of teaching, perhaps most of all that anyone who speaks has the potential to be my teacher. I only need listen as well as I can, quieting the voices in my own head.

As much as I love reading, you cannot replace the interchange that happens between human beings when you 'ōlelo and talk story with each other. Learning is as much about the questioning, and the requests for clarification and complete understanding. Yes, I am very passionate about 'Ike loa and all kinds of learning: Call it fanaticism if you will.

And as long as you are alive, it is not over for you— 'Ike loa waits for you; it beckons to you. Grab your opportunity to learn, and to know well all you wish to know.

'Ike loa: learn and know well

'Ike loa is a big part of managing with *Aloha*, for the manager who adopts 'Ike loa and incorporates it into his daily practice demonstrates the *Aloha* of good intent. By investing in the learning of his staff, he shows them how much he believes in them and in their capacity for greater things. He shows them he cares.

Learning inspires you, and 'Ike loa encourages us to constantly give birth to new creative possibilities. As your knowledge grows, so does your confidence, and your belief in your own capacity and ability to learn more: Your belief in self will liberate, inspire and energize you.

'Ike loa promotes the building of a learning environment in the 'Ohana, and we must incorporate the seeking of knowledge and wisdom into our business plan and into our daily practice.

'Ike loa is the value of learning.

Seek knowledge, for new knowledge is the food for mind, heart and soul. For a business, knowledge is intellectual capital, a highly sought asset.

The learning of 'Ike loa is about the student, and managers who are the best kumu (teachers) know this: Learning is personal.

'Ike loa is to know well, and knowing well enhances our relationships and broadens our prospects.

'Ike loa: Learn and know well. Seek knowledge and wisdom.

12

Ha'aha'a

Humility
Be humble, be modest, and open your thoughts

Ha'aha'a. Have humility.

Ha'aha'a teaches us to groom our own character with humility in respect for others. There is nothing noble in being superior to someone else; true nobility is in being superior to your previous self.

Ha'aha'a helps us understand that no individual can satisfy every need. All in the 'Ohana are needed. All are to be respected and supported for the talent and uniqueness they offer.

Be humble, be modest, and open your thoughts. This is Ha'aha'a.

The bounty of Ha'aha'a

The seven years that I worked for the Hualalai Resort marked a time of ever-growing success and prosperity for us; it was an energizing time to be part of the staff there. Industry awards and community recognition came often, and as they did we'd be sure to celebrate, reward, and acknowledge the 'Ohana for their achievements. However, with each and every victory we'd take care to assemble our management team together to talk about the value of Ha'aha'a and the importance of remaining humble. There was to be no place for arrogance within our definition of success. With our demeanor thus in check, we'd celebrate our victories with a healthy degree of humility and thankfulness that justly recognized what it took to get us there.

As a Hawaiian value, *Ha'aha'a* does encompass pride in your accomplishments, recognizing that there is merit in feeling proud of the good things you have done; it fuels your self-confidence and the energy that will carry you to future achievements. This is the favorable character of pride we call *ha'aheo*, and *ha'aheo* resides in *Ha'aha'a*. There is another Hawaiian word for the unfavorable pride of arrogance and condescension which is *ho'okano*. To be described as *ho'okano*, one wallows in haughtiness and conceit, and is thought of as insolent, vain and disdainful of others. In contrast, *Ha'aha'a* teaches us to groom our own character with humility and with respect for others. We can cherish what success we achieve with the quiet pride of *ha'aheo*, understanding that if we have achieved this much, we can and should expect ourselves to achieve even more. To *Ho'omau*, to continue. To *Kūlia i ka nu'u*, and strive for the summit of other achievements.

Our talk story with *Ha'aha'a* served as a reality check for us, another view of the vision we had that we were part of something bigger, an entire community. *Ha'aha'a* helped us recognize that whatever success we achieved came with the efforts of many people, *Kākou*, all together, and in every likelihood with the full support of the *'Ohana* and the surrounding community as a whole: Our success was their success. The best emotion we could bask in was the *Ha'aha'a* of humility and thankfulness that recognized all these elements, all these contributions. Having an attitude of humility helps one understand that no individual, and no single company, can satisfy every need—everyone in a community is needed, and they are to be respected and supported for the talents and uniqueness they will offer in turn.

Perhaps the greatest gift of the value of *Ha'aha'a* is open-mindedness. Those who embody *Ha'aha'a* have a genuine desire to uncover what other people can offer. They are intrigued by how others think, and how others feel differently from them. Yet those with *Ha'aha'a* are confident and self-assured, they are not meek and they do not consider themselves lower in stature. They do not require less of themselves within their own *Kuleana*. *Ha'aha'a* has created in them a sort of receptacle open to being filled with the knowledge and opinions of others.

Competition and measurement

To keep our attitude in check at times of great success, *Ha'aha'a* was a word that came up often in our conversations about competition and measurement. In the final analysis, who were we competing against? To truly use all the talents of the *'Ohana* we competed against ourselves, and our ability and capacity to do even more, to be even better. There is nothing noble in being superior to someone else. The true nobility is in being superior to your previous self. Therefore, how did we take stock, how did we measure up? We chose to measure ourselves against our previous selves, not against our peers, our neighbors or our competition.

Taken altogether this demeanor and attitude of *Ha'aha'a* is one of quiet and effective power: It serves as an internal energy source that is self-renewing and self-perpetuating. It grounds you, and gives you a presence that is confident without any arrogance or pretense. It reminds you to know of what you speak. It opens your capacity for *'Ike loa*, for a more complete learning.

The demeanor of humility

To have inner drive, to want to be successful is a good thing (*Kūlia i ka nu'u*). And I believe that part of humility is believing in those possibilities that presently may be larger than life for you. *Ha'aha'a* speaks to the demeanor and attitude you must have as you seek your success, so that your inner drive and desires are in balance with your composure, and the face you display for the rest of the world. One of the best definitions I've ever heard for humility was that "humility is an act of courtesy." You then feel comfortable, that you "rightly fit in" and have your proper place as you *Ho'omau* and strive to persevere and continually improve yourself. You develop a self-managing style, with a discipline that keeps you humble and modest, open-minded and never arrogant. With *Ha'aha'a* you gain a constancy of understanding that you were not put on this earth alone—frankly, others have to live with you—and you must live and work with others to be completely fulfilled (*'Ohana*).

Now, that being said, humility does not require us to underrate ourselves. Sometimes we confuse shyness and even intimidation with humility, and they aren't the same thing. Those who are humble are modest, however they are not meek, afraid or fearful. In Hawaii, it can be frustrating drawing people out of their shells when trying to engage their involvement and energize their performance. For some reason, our island society seems to create a reluctance to shine in people here; they do not wish to step on someone else's toes by assuming their place or by tooting their own horn. This courtesy begins to make them a bit too comfortable staying in the background. They will avoid any chance of embarrassment at all costs, and shyness can dramatically inhibit involvement. To be honest, there isn't much ethnic evidence that this is a Hawaiian trait; history has shown that we're a gregarious bunch, and I've often wondered where it stems from. But whatever the source, it's something that managers in Hawaii will find is maddeningly prevalent among their employees. And this reticence has direct implications on stalling better performance.

In these cases, open discussions about the meaning of *Ha'aha'a* turned out to be a very effective tool for me. We would talk one-on-one and departmentally about the "demeanor of *Ha'aha'a*" to subtly encourage those who were reluctant to step out of the starting gate. We'd acknowledge that we wanted everyone to be comfortable in the work environment, but we'd also openly say that we didn't want them to step back and hide: Not participating was not an option. Together we'd find comfortable ways to have their presence known in our department initiatives so they would slowly but surely become involved and eventually, be fully engaged. In the business environment, you cannot afford bench-warmers: All your players need to be in the game. The score is healthier when they have the exhilaration of playing offense versus the apprehension of playing defense.

As their manager, I would take care to uncover their *Ho'ohana* (their work intent), so I could be sure my own management style was in alignment with the inner passions that drove them: I wanted to stoke those fires! Once certain of this, I would then turn to *Kuleana* (their personal sense of responsibility) and *'Ike loa* (their desire for more knowledge or insight) for the clues I needed on fostering their growth. In these situations, *Lōkahi* and *Kākou* were words I would encourage them to incorporate into their professional mission statements, for I often found they needed to distinguish between when it was more productive for them to work independently (as was probably closer in tune with their nature) and when they should engage with others for far better performance results. The Daily Five Minutes was extremely effective with these employees for follow-up that was highly personal and very timely.

A softness of voice

One of the things I personally sought to learn from *Ha'aha'a*, was to speak softly with a quieter and calmer presence. I knew that I was thought of as an assertive and decisive manager who walked that fine line of intimidating or dismissing others at times. Years climbing the career ladder had produced forceful tendencies I was far better off consciously suppressing as much as I was able to. This was something I just didn't like about myself, and struggled to change.

One of my early observations within the lessons I received from others on *Ha'aha'a*, was that there is something more calming, nurturing, caring and respectful about those in the *'Ohana* who chose to speak softly. Their listeners would tune in carefully, so that they would be sure to hear them. They would more willingly engage and respond, and the soft-speaker's complete message and true intent would be understood. In contrast, I would find I had to repeat myself at times when I was more forceful, for my loudness became the background noise others tuned out. It simply wasn't as pleasant to listen to; *I* wasn't as pleasant to listen to! Once I understood this, there was a time I actually hated the sound of my own voice. *Ha'aha'a* would be a good teacher for me in the art of communication, for I needed to learn more about my own sound; my tone needed to cultivate more respect, and thus more interest.

I'm still on this learning journey. I *am* forceful and decisive, and these are traits that serve me well most of the time; thus *Ha'aha'a* and my timing require constant work. To this day, these two sentences are included in a list of commitments I keep within my personal mission statement: "*Ha'aha'a*: I will listen with humility, and listen more than I speak, understanding that there are lessons and discoveries within the words and voices of others. When I do speak, I will speak softly." I keep them there because I know I must read them often.

Mistakes are cool

Ha'aha'a can also help you enormously when it comes to creating a safe atmosphere in which your employees are not afraid of making mistakes with new challenges. They understand that mistakes happen on every journey. When you think about it, mistakes are wonderful things. Mistakes uncover variables that may otherwise be missed. Mistakes can point you toward investigations of probable solutions that are complete and comprehensive. Mistakes test all the options.

If someone makes a mistake, it leads me to believe that they tried something they hadn't ever tried before; they had a new idea (*'Imi ola*, seeking new life). They were willing to put themselves on the line in testing this thought, this idea (*Ho'ohana*, working with purpose). They were willing to share it. Even if their peers completely changed or destroyed the original thought in the process of consideration, it was their original idea that launched them into the synergy of creation to begin with (*Kākou*). They learned to value different opinions, viewpoints, and perspectives when seeking their own solutions (*Lōkahi*). They were self-motivated to take initiative, be daring and explore their gem of an idea more fully (*Kuleana*). It was the seed of a new beginning, and one that would mulch some very fertile ground in which to germinate even more new ideas (*Ho'omau*, causing the good to last).

Mistakes teach people to be cautious but unafraid. Mistakes stimulate experimentation and exploration. Everything is impossible until the first guy does it. Mistakes point us to better and best. Mistakes are cool.

Haʻahaʻa is healthy

Within the value of *Haʻahaʻa* we learn that humility is *healthy*; humility should never be self-deprecating or negate one's confidence; there should be no damaging hits to one's self-esteem. If you make a mistake along the way, it's not because you aren't good enough or up to the challenge, it's simply because you are still within the learning process, and making mistakes are part of sequential learning. The higher the tolerance for mistakes, the smaller the risk of outright failure. You can stumble, you can fall—it's okay. You only fail when you don't get up again.

The more you speak of *Haʻahaʻa* in your management coaching, those with this "healthy humility" become even quicker to recognize their missteps, and admit to their mistakes when they happen because they are more open to them—they expect them. And that recognition, that admission of a mistake occurring has to happen before they can advance to seeking a better and different course of action. Without the first admission of a mistake being made, the beginning of "let's try again" will not happen. With this first hurdle more easily overcome, people dramatically shorten the time it takes to arrive at the next step—learning from those mistakes and moving on. Fruitless denial has not been an obstacle for them. Thus *Haʻahaʻa* helps you groom an attitude that "hey, that's just part of the process; let's Hoʻomau" —continue and persevere.

Said another way, *Haʻahaʻa* fuels an internal energy source that the brain understands as "I can always learn more and do it differently." It goes hand-in-hand with *ʻIke loa*, to know well by seeking to know more. It goes hand-in-hand with *Kākou*, understanding that you need not go it alone; synergy is created when you seek the involvement of others. It goes hand-in-hand with *Lōkahi*, cooperating with others on your team so efforts are harmoniously in-step. It goes hand-in-hand with

ʻOhana, recognizing the encouragement and self-sustaining support that comes from a community distanced from self-serving competitiveness.

Haʻahaʻa teaches the how

In coaching other managers, I have discovered that grooming humility is the key difference between being tough and tough-minded. Keeping the value of Haʻahaʻa at the forefront of consciousness for managers charged with production helps them strike a balance between getting results and *how* they go about getting them. There's a way to ask tough questions and set challenging expectations without being too hard on people in the process. When their demeanor is colored by the Haʻahaʻa of humility and haʻaheo (favorable pride) managers build Lōkahi and cooperation within the ranks of their staff: They do it together, and they learn from each other along the way. They celebrate victories by giving credit where credit is due. They issue orders less, and they seek answers and ideas from below more often. They look for defects in tools and systems before making the assumption there's a problem with their people. They build an ʻOhana that has the capacity to change when they need to, for they are unafraid. This fearlessness helps banish insecurity and hesitancy: Their employees seek the moment and grab it.

Admittedly, getting to this point can be a frustrating growth process for new managers. When someone is first promoted, they feel the great weight of others expectations on their shoulders, unaware that in fact they may be reading the wrong thing into those expectations: They need not come up with all the decisions. New supervisors and managers have a tendency to direct and control when they should facilitate instead. Haʻahaʻa helps me coach young managers toward a realization that their employees want their attention much more than they want direction. The humility, modesty and lack of arrogance that color Haʻahaʻa can help managers lead by asking questions instead of barking out orders.

In this regard, you can see that as we spoke of with Kākou, Haʻahaʻa is another one of those values that when internalized helps you relax considerably as a leader—you don't have to be the one with all the answers for everyone, fulfilling everybody's needs. In fact, sometimes this knowledge is your best ticket to growing a business that is far better off focusing on what everyone else wants: ask Feargal Quinn.

Assumptions in humility

When we spoke of *'Ike loa,* I encouraged you to take advantage of any opportunity to travel in the quest for more knowledge, learning what you can outside the fences of your own school yard, be it in Hawaii or elsewhere. In May 2002, I had the chance to attend the annual leadership conference sponsored by *Fast Company* magazine in San Diego, and there I had the good fortune to meet Feargal Quinn and hear him speak.

Quinn is founder and executive chairman of a 19-store chain of supermarkets in Ireland called Superquinn, at the time of the conference a business enterprise with estimated sales in excess of $700 million annually. For Quinn, who had also done a 10-year stint as chairman of Ireland's national postal service, customer service innovation and being in public service demand the same defining trait: humility. In his speech, Quinn told the business leaders assembled that they should make only five assumptions, which he calls his five lessons in humility; "My customers know more than I do. My employees know more than I do. Neither my employees nor I can be creative all of the time. What I knew yesterday is not enough for today. I'm not responding fast enough for my customer."

Is the man a leader? Most certainly, and his *Ha'aha'a* philosophy apparently has helped him get there, achieving success and producing results for those who count on him to do so. During his tenure as chairman of Ireland's national postal service, he led the transformation of a money-losing government institution into an innovative semi-profit making business. At the conference, an estimate was shared with us wherein his company Superquinn captured 9% of Ireland's $11 billion grocery business.

Quinn has made his philosophy on humility one of his

greatest strengths, perpetuated by his willingness to admit he doesn't have all the answers, but he will continue to seek them. When he spoke to us, his anecdotes about the lessons he's learned from both his staff and customers had the audience bubbling with laughter. *Ha'aha'a* and humility certainly help us have a sense of humor as well. We can laugh at ourselves and with each other.

Humor and humility

Now here's where I will freely admit to you that I take complete creative license with *Ha'aha'a*: Just look at these words again. Ha'aha'a. Humility. Humor. They've just got to go together.

Humility is healthy: We've already explored that, and I'm totally convinced of how the attitude of humility taught by *Ha'aha'a* helps a business. Humor is healthy: The proposition that humor heals is not a disputed fact for most people. When we can laugh at situations and laugh at ourselves, there is a tremendous amount of stress and pressure that is released, you can almost feel it seeping out of you—and it's great! No mistake, no failure that we could somehow laugh about ever gave us a feeling of impending doom, we just got back our composure and tried again—in a better mood.

Yet laughter is cruel when it takes the form of ridicule, and I've always felt that one of the responsibilities that managers have in creating healthy work environments is to find good and healthy outlets for laughter and for humor. Laughter is one of those things that just has to release once in awhile. When *Ha'aha'a* is incorporated into the language of the *'Ohana* and into the behavior of the culture, it gives you a standard to uphold with humor that will always be welcomed and always remain healthy. You will not err and define *Ha'aha'a* as lowliness or meekness. I'm sure you know what to do in this respect; as Clive James wrote, "Common sense and a sense of humor are the same thing, moving at different speeds. A sense of humor is just common sense, dancing."

The lessons of humility: Haʻahaʻa

I was forever humbled on a day one of my Hualalai employees gave me their definition of humility. We were having a talk story on *Haʻahaʻa* as we wrapped up a staff meeting, and I believe his words can end this chapter far better than mine. This is what he said: "To me, being humble means you have to earn the right to speak, and let your actions do the talking instead of your mouth. And you gotta listen so you can understand the other guy first. When I'm humble, I can remember that my opinion is not the only one that counts."

Let *Haʻahaʻa* groom your demeanor as a manager seeking to facilitate versus direct: Be honest with yourself as you contemplate your management style.

Haʻahaʻa. Have humility.
Haʻahaʻa is the value that teaches us to groom our own character with humility and with respect for others.
There is nothing noble in being superior to someone else.
The true nobility is in being superior to your previous self.
No one individual can satisfy every need. All in the *ʻOhana* are needed.
Be humble, be modest and open your thoughts. This is *Haʻahaʻa.*

13

Hoʻohanohano

Honor the dignity of others
Conduct yourself with distinction,
and cultivate respectfulness

> *Hoʻohanohano.* Honor the dignity of others. Help them find
> their own nobility.
> Treat others well in honor of the health of their spirit.
> Honor the intelligence of others—trust it is there, and they
> are learners.
> Conduct yourself with distinction, by honoring your own
> dignity and self-respect. Act with integrity.
> Cultivate an inclusive attitude, and seek to demonstrate
> your respect for others—always.

When I first learned about *Hoʻohanohano* I would think
about the Golden Rule: "Do unto others, as you would have
them do unto you." However, I came to realize that
Hoʻohanohano wasn't this self-serving; instead it taught you to
treat others well simply in respect for who they are, not just
because you want them to respect you in return.

Respect and honor the spirit within

As a value, *Hoʻohanohano* is respect for the spirit within,
and the recognition that one's inner spirit must be kept
healthy. It comes from a belief that the spiritual will always

manifest itself in the physical realm eventually, and as the keepers of our own spirit, we must hold ourselves accountable for this. When it happens—when the spirit manifests itself in the physical realm—you want that inner spirit to be at its highest possible level, not at a low point. The low points come when you feel you are not treated well—think of a time when you saw someone lash out at someone else. Thus, Ho'ohanohano urges you to treat all in a respectful manner that values who they are, and with the dignity they deserve. Those who feel they have dignity act in a way that befits them.

Therefore, Ho'ohanohano teaches us to take responsibility for the inner spirit that drives us, creates us and moves us toward the actions we choose to take. When we accept this responsibility, incorporating it into our *Kuleana*, we begin to think of ourselves as just the stewards of something greater— we treat everyone with dignity and with respect as a way of appreciating our own dignity as human beings, and in a way, getting our own spirit to be better deserving.

These first paragraphs give you my descriptions of the Hawaiian value of Ho'ohanohano in as straightforward a manner as I can, true to what I was taught about it. However, I'll be honest with you: As a manager, I didn't relish dipping into these spiritual discussions with my staff. These concepts rang true in my own belief system, so it was possible for me to talk about them; however, I felt that spirituality was a very private thing for people, and I shouldn't venture in uninvited. At times speaking of spirituality can close doors with people rather than open them. My own choice was to keep our discussions of Ho'ohanohano simple and true to the definition that crowns this chapter for the words are easily understood: Honor the dignity of others. Conduct yourself with distinction and self-respect. Honor your *own* dignity. Always treat others with dignity and respect—it's the right thing to do.

These reminders probably helped me most when it was time to hand out progressive discipline. No matter what had happened, I could focus on the behavior that resulted from an unfortunate choice, and still recognize that the person in front of me deserved my respect. When our conversation was over, I had to leave them with their dignity intact. The dignity that remained would sustain them, and keep them healthy enough to seek improvement. If I stripped it away, I took away their self-esteem and confidence, I took away hope.

Conduct yourself with distinction

Simply said, Ho'ohanohano is the value of good behavior; it is a benchmark of proper conduct. Dignity is about poise and self-respect, and both qualities are needed if you are to conduct yourself with distinction. Managers must be worthy of the esteem and honor of their position, always conscious of the example they set for others. Both management and leadership are highly visible—your visibility is expected, and this is something a manager must continually be conscious of. What you say must match up to what you do. What you teach must match up to what you demonstrate. What you expect from others must be what you expect from yourself. The bigger one's title, the more behavior must be beyond reproach: It must inspire. Every manager, every employee, must ask themselves how they define acting with honor, with dignity and with integrity, and they must strive to do so daily.

I remember an early Daily Five Minutes I held with one of the Alaka'i Nalu at Hualalai when I first became their manager. I asked him, "What is it that you most expect from me?" and this was his answer, "All I want is to see you keep it real." I interpreted this as meaning sincerity, truth and honesty, candor and lack of pretense. Later, I asked a manager who had been working closely with the group, "What is it that you feel I need to do for the Alaka'i Nalu? His answer was a little different, "I think you need to be someone they can look up to." When you think about it, both answers are all about Ho'ohanohano and really not that different at all: I needed to conduct myself with distinction, it would be the best gift I could give them.

The mantra of dignity and respect

We're all subject to human frailties, so let's be honest: At times it is very difficult to call upon your spirit of *Aloha*, completely willing to share unconditional love and care for others. There are those times the person standing in front of you seems to be, well, undeserving of it. It is at these times that *Hoʻohanohano* has been tremendously helpful in helping me communicate better and communicate *responsibly*. Dignity and respect. Dignity and respect. These two simple words—words that everyone seems to understand and define in the same way—would swirl around in my head whenever I had to tackle a difficult circumstance. As I spoke the words that had to be said, I'd listen to them come out and silently ask myself, "How did that sound? Should I explain better? Does my facial expression convince them of my honesty, my sincerity? How about my body language?" Dignity and respect. Dignity and respect. "Uh oh … how have I made them *feel*? Do they believe that I care about them? Do they feel I've respected their point of view?" Dignity and respect. Dignity and respect. "What else do they need from me? Have I said all they need to hear to be okay with this? Am I leaving them with their dignity intact?"

As I trained myself to do this, guess what happened. *Hoʻohanohano* would open the door to my *Aloha*. Problems and difficult circumstances are by nature emotionally charged for everyone involved, and my self-talk calmed me down and gave calm and a soft tone to my voice. I could naturally honor my own dignity in the process by keeping in control. I discovered that I had to do less explaining and less convincing. People simply believed me more than before. My care and concern with doing right by them became more visible; it almost seemed they could read my thoughts on my face, and they believed my intent was genuine. The good intent inherent in *Aloha* had surfaced.

Did this always happen? No, discipline is an uncomfortable thing; No one likes to talk about things that have gone wrong, especially when they're personally involved. However, it happened with greater frequency. And it became easier for me to tell the truth, completely, openly and honestly—no matter how difficult it was for my employees to hear it. It was *Hoʻohanohano*, part of treating others with dignity and respect, and it was the right thing to do. Plain and simple. Dignity and respect. The right thing to do.

Respect intelligence in everyone

Another element of Ho'ohanohano all managers can learn in their quest to be great managers is this: Part of treating someone with dignity is having *respect for their intelligence*, and demonstrating it. We tend to treat our employees on a need-to-know basis much too often, questioning the wisdom of saying too much, and thinking, "Can they handle it?" As parents, we fall into the same trap with our children. Wake up and smell the coffee … your employees can handle way more than you probably give them credit for. Yes, there are differences between managers and staff, but in their Ho'ohana, *not* in their intelligence and their capacity for learning and reasoning. The more people know, the more they can do, the more effective they can be. Knowledge is an enabler. Remember what we'd spoken of with *Kuleana* and *'Ike loa?* "… an individual who is given information cannot help but take responsibility."

As an example, a demonstration of Ho'ohanohano for all our employees at Hualalai was freely sharing our financial statements with them. We respected their intelligence with the assumption they could understand these statements, and they weren't simply distributed as the meeting hand-outs to be later studied as homework: They were discussed and analyzed together. We needed each other's help as we explored every cause-and-effect dynamic. In doing this, our *'Ohana* in business could quantify their *Kuleana*—their own individual responsibility to achieve the profitability that would sustain us.

Financial statements are an easy example: In what ways do you Ho'ohanohano with respect for the intelligence of your own employees? In retail I learned to take this further by discussing the purchasing plans of my inventory mix with employees to get their feedback. I then discovered we'd all gained the added benefit of more advance notice when merchandising overhauls in-shop would be required, and that execution went more smoothly. Over time the Alaka'i Nalu became very comfortable in talking about the before (the business plan), participating in creating it, as well as analyzing the after (the past month's actual financial statement). In the Spa, my managers learned to explain their reasoning for dropping or discounting treatments in direct discussions with the massage therapists who would be affected before changes were actually made. They did this realizing there was a financial impact on them as commissioned employees, but at times they'd walk away with far different insights about possible solutions for their overall menu of services.

I understand that you are faced with much more difficult choices at times, deliberating how much to share with your staff, and when. Well, consider this: Employees usually find out what you don't tell them anyway. The advice I'd offer you is to tell them what you sense they will inevitably discover in time themselves, and then open your thinking to go another small step further. Wouldn't you prefer that they heard it from you instead of in the locker room or at the water cooler? Why rob yourself of the opportunity to gauge their first reaction, their gut feelings about things? Why abandon them to make rational sense of things they discovered on their own—those things you should have shared with them? Why imply that you don't trust them with knowing something? Personally I have never believed in that old adage that "what they don't know can't hurt them." The rest of the sentence is missing, "... until they hear it from someone other than you."

Respecting a person's intelligence is vital in building trust. You have to place your trust in someone for them to have the opportunity to prove to you just how trustworthy they are.

Neglect is visible

About a year before I left Hualalai, I discovered that as self-defining as dignity and respect seemed to be, I could continually learn about *Ho'ohanohano* and treating people better *with foresight and intention*. It was a very difficult and painful lesson about "unintentional neglect."

An employee became very angry with me for not continuing to involve her in my work, and she became very bitter about the organization as a whole in the process. She felt that I had made her an outcast, because in reassigning her to another manager I severed the line of communication we previously had. As my own job evolved, I found I no longer needed the service she had once provided me with. However,

I recognized her contributions and wanted her to have a new role in our company, and I felt we had agreed upon a reassignment as the best course of action. I truly believed that her new role would be much better for her. I felt that it was expected, understood and fully explained; however I was wrong thinking she was okay with it. I felt all these things, but I hadn't fully considered how she truly felt, and I totally missed seeing the hit to her dignity. One of our issues was that she was unable to communicate with me very well; she was very uncomfortable with open and honest dialogue. The words that were spoken didn't complete a full picture. This became my problem, not hers.

Reassignment complete, the time came to end our professional relationship, and in doing so, she perceived the unfortunate message that I no longer felt she was of any use to me or to the organization at all. She felt alone and isolated because the new manager I assigned her to was junior to me— their own character and personality were irrelevant—and thus she no longer had access to the "confidential information" that was the norm of the day when she previously worked within my circle of influence.

Her actual title and position in the company didn't change. Yet up until then, I didn't fully understand that people feel they are respected more when they are in the "inner circle" of an executive manager. My lesson in this was that as a manager things will get personal for the people you manage, even when you feel you are correctly "maintaining a professional distance." She ended up leaving the company unhappy, angry and disillusioned. I'd explained things to her as best I knew how, and I apologized repeatedly, however the damage had been done. She felt my message was this: She wasn't good enough to work with me.

I really beat myself up for this one, horrified that I had made her feel that way. Then I was faced with others in the company being angry at me for her, and I found my own credibility to be at stake. Many times anger is a sign of misinformation; however, this result seemed to speak for itself. I had to admit to myself that, however unintentional, I had in fact created an outcast. I could not react defensively and do even more damage in this aftermath; thus, this was the time my plan of programmed self-talk began in my head. It helped keep me calm, and helped me feel I still had control of things: I could improve them. Dignity and respect. Dignity and respect. They may be simple concepts, but they need to be kept at the fore-front: One of the hardest things about being a manager is that you are expected to know about all the goings-on around you. This was a situation in which I had totally missed the warning signs until it was too late.

In the days that surrounded this horrible incident, I learned more about *Ho'ohanohano* than I would have imag-ined. I learned that when you do not engage with those who expect to interact with you, your misinterpreted silence can deliver more hurt than words can. I learned that the hierarchy in a company's structure causes people to associate their own influence with yours when you're the leader, looming large in their own dignity. I learned that no matter how I might think about it, no matter how much I may need to maintain my own balance, work is personal for people, it just is, and you need to make allowances to welcome personal interaction. When you are the leader, you affect everyone around you, and you need to understand how, being more in tune to symptoms of discon-tent. I needed to strike "professional distance" from my vocab-ulary, from my train of thought: Prior to this I had only thought of it as a way to maintain my own work balance, insensitive to how my own need for it could become detri-mental to others.

Looking back, there are a number of things I'd do differ-ently. For one, I would have simply made more time for her so that we spoke to each other more often and she felt she had enough of my attention when she needed it (the sharing of *Aloha*). Her reticence had made this difficult, but I could have tried harder and with more deliberate planning. Second I would have reassessed a few of my priorities: I recall this as a time in which I had many balls in the air, my time was crunched and I succumbed to the quick fix of putting tasks ahead of people. I worked on these tasks myself when I should have been a manager that sought to delegate better (*Lōkahi* and *Kākou*), perhaps most of all to her: It would probably have been the morale boost she needed for her own feelings of self-worth. Most of all *Ho'ohanohano*: In cultivating my own respect for her, I would have done more to help her find her own nobility. She was clearly a very intelligent woman, one who potentially could have been a better partner in our *'Ohana* in business.

I now realize I will always have more to learn when it comes to treating other people well, with the highest respect for their dignity, and their feelings of self-worth. They have to feel it themselves before I have the self-righteousness to think that I actually delivered it to them. Personally, I have always been very self-confident, with a more-than-healthy dose of self-assurance, and this was a time in which I learned that a person's dignity is much more fragile than we sometimes imagine it to be. Managers must learn to continually groom the sensitivity they have for the feelings of others, and *Ho'ohanohano* helps us do so.

The conduct of Ho'ohanohano

Allow *Ho'ohanohano* to open the door to your *Aloha* spirit. Others will eagerly and gratefully walk through your portal of integrity, for we all seek dignity and respect.

Managers must be worthy of the esteem and honor of their position, always conscious of the example they set for others. Both management and leadership are highly visible— your visibility is expected, and this is something a manager must continually be conscious of.

Cultivate an inclusive attitude, *Kākou*. Always treat others with dignity and respect, recognizing the fragile nature of a person's self-worth. It's the right thing to do.

> *Ho'ohanohano.* Honor the dignity of others. Help them find their own nobility.
> Treat others well in honor of the health of their spirit.
> Honor the intelligence of others—trust it is there, and they are learners.
> Conduct yourself with distinction, by honoring your own dignity and self-respect.
> *Ho'ohanohano.* Act with integrity.

14

Alaka'i

Leadership
Lead with initiative, and with your good example
You shall be the guide for others
when you have gained their trust and respect

Alaka'i is the value of leadership.

When you are *Alaka'i*, you are one who leads with initiative, and with your good example. You are willing to shoulder the greater responsibility that comes with leading others.

As a person who is *Alaka'i*, you build the strength of character found in initiative and in independence.

As a leader who is *Alaka'i*, you continually seek to gain the trust and the respect of those you lead.

Those who are *Alaka'i* possess a strong belief in their own capacity and in the power of possibility: They are confident optimists, filled with hope.

Those who are *Alaka'i* are the managers and leaders we so greatly need.

The calling of Alaka'i

Leadership is about getting things done with others and through others, and as such, aspiring to leadership is not a goal or quality reserved for those with title, position or power. Conversely, when you have been one to demonstrate your leadership, people take notice you have it, and those promotions of title, position and power will find you.

The value of leadership, *Alaka'i*, is a value for everyone who finds themselves in a position where they need to guide others. It is not surprising that we often cite our parents as our first leaders and role models, and as those we admire, trust and respect. Many of us find we will follow in their footsteps. However who will follow ours?

When you are one who aspires to be a leader, you must constantly ask yourself one central question: Why would anyone choose to follow me? In the business environment, the question becomes: Why would anyone choose to *Ho'ohana* with me? The answer must be because they believe in you and admire the path you have chosen, and they believe you will guide the right way for them as well. You have what it takes to capture their belief, and you deliver what it takes to honor it. You are willing to be an authentic and vulnerable leader, and you eagerly will shoulder the responsibility that comes with leadership.

Alaka'i is a value that challenges managers and leaders to raise the bar on all of the values we have discussed up to now. For example:

- *Alaka'i* seeks to build on *Aloha* and *Ho'ohana* with the central intent of good leadership.
- *Alaka'i* seeks to build on *Kuleana* (one's personal sense of responsibility) by specifically accepting the responsibility to lead others well, and being held accountable for taking care of those who are led (*Mālama*—our next chapter).
- *Alaka'i* seeks to build on *Ho'ohanohano* by raising the bar on the conduct of leadership with the self-talk of integrity.
- *Alaka'i* seeks to build on *Lōkahi*, on *'Ike loa*, and on *'Imi ola* with the understanding that leaders do not create more followers, they create more leaders.

When you are a manager, the lessons taught by *Alaka'i* are incredibly exciting, for they frame the doorway to your growth. For some, *Alaka'i* can clarify if they prefer to focus on management, on leadership or on both.

Management versus leadership

The words "management" and "leadership" have become interchangeable in our common use of them. Personally and practically, I see them as two different things, and *Alaka'i* does embrace both of them. Let's take a look at what Webster says[4]:

Manage v., to bring about or succeed in accomplishing; contrive.

Lead v., to go before or with to show the way; conduct or escort.

In my view these are terrific definitions, concise and simple to remember, and clear in the difference between them. I am one who believes that those in a position of leadership today need to understand both things, and learning to manage well comes first. Managers are charged with delivering results: That's the reality of business. As you work toward producing your expected business results, *Alaka'i* is the personal value that will help you cultivate the qualities which will earn you the trust and respect of others, others who potentially will choose to follow you.

Leaders see great managers as the glue that holds everything together for them, partners they desperately need. Leaders need not be great managers themselves, but they need to enlist the help of those who are, giving them both freedom and space to work, and supporting their efforts in a strong partnership.

The call for leadership

We live in a world that desperately needs good leaders to show us the way. There are so many arenas of opportunity in our civilization that cry for betterment, and we need the visions of insightful leaders to paint better pictures of possibility for us to strive for. Consider our desires for longevity and better health, for saving our natural resources, for educating the next generation and for banishing poverty and homelessness as just a few examples. We need new leaders to inspire us, excite us, energize us toward affirmative action, and secure our commitment to goals that will make a difference for humanity.

---

[4] *Random House Webster's College Dictionary*, Random House New York, 1995 edition.

When I left the Hualalai Resort to be a management coach, my personal desire was to help create better education in the very broad field of management by teaching and coaching prospective business leaders. It is my dream to inspire you to seek, possess and deliver nobility in management, to accept your first responsibility in the principles of honor and integrity, paving a smooth road for leadership initiatives that will make a difference.

It is my belief that teaching to manage well comes first, so that emerging leaders can learn the empathy needed to lead effectively when they have found a new and better way, and they will have earned a circle of influence from which to stage their efforts. A manager's authority is respected when he knows his job, he knows his business, he knows his people and he shows his respect for them; he empathizes with what others must do to make a business successful. The results he has already achieved award him with his credibility.

With management I think of these "O words": others, operations, organization, and optimization. These are words that become associated with the how-to of systems and processes, with directing the efforts of individual people, by managers who wholeheartedly take full responsibility for all of them. As I've said before, you must invest in the basics of being mission-driven, values-centered and customer-focused. However once these things are in place, you will be a manager that only frustrates others if you are one without the talent, skill and knowledge in the how-to. It is the how-to that gets you there as you "bring about or succeed in accomplishing." I had the lofty dreams of all fledgling managers; however, I wasn't going to find my audience for them until I had earned the right to do so with good solid performance.

Alaka'i calls for values-centered leadership

With past success in good performance as your lily pad, you can now leapfrog to leadership: You've mastered the norm and are ready for the innovation and daring of better ideas and the new way. To be *Alaka'i* is to live the value that will prepare you as the one best person for the job. To command the attention of others and gain the trust needed for them to choose to follow you, you must be one who is highly respected. *Alaka'i* is about cultivating the qualities that will earn you that respect. When a leader is respected, he will find that others *want* to be guided, and he's the one they choose to lead the way for them; he's the one that others are naturally *compelled* to follow.

So how do those with the capacity for leadership achieve this? I believe they do so with the soft stuff of good values. When *Alaka'i* is a value that drives you, you are a student of the others. Of *'Ike loa*, to learn more, and to know well. Of *Ho'ohanohano*, to conduct yourself with distinction, and respect the dignity of others. Of *Ha'aha'a*, remaining humble and opening your mind. Of *Kuleana*, accepting your responsibilities completely, and holding yourself accountable first and foremost. Of *Kākou*, and using the language of "we." Of *Aloha*, *Ho'omau*, *Lōkahi*, *Kūlia i ka nu'u* and all the other universal values of business. Everyone has certain values that speak to them more directly than others, and if you are to be a leader of others, you must be able to empathize with the values that may drive them, even if you do not possess them yourself. As Stephen Covey put it so eloquently, you must "seek first to understand, then to be understood."

I listed the "O words" of management for you, now what about leadership? Whereas management is about others, becoming a leader is mostly about you as leader-capable and your vision. Whereas management concentrates on operations, the leadership focus is on the innovation and new ideas that will challenge operational growth to happen. Whereas management sweats the details of organization, leadership embraces the change and evolution that will call for those details of reorganization. Whereas management looks for the optimal and best known way to deal with what's at hand, leadership looks forward with bravery, daring and risk-taking to uncover a way that presently may not exist.

As a manager, you've cut your teeth with systems and processes, so that as a leader you have the instinct to live in the world of better ideas and promising experiments. As a manager you have directed people well; As a leader you understand you must inspire them.

The Ho'ohana of a manager

Will every manager progress to becoming a leader? No. Count me among those who believe that great leaders were born with this inclination. However they do share in part the *Ho'ohana* (the purpose-full work) of natural-born leaders: They realized that discipline, diligence and much determination were needed to groom themselves as "recognizable" leaders who inspire others to follow them. They are managers who have internalized the value of *Alaka'i*. They lead with initiative and with their good example. They seek to gain the trust and respect of those they feel they are destined to lead internally—even if within another leader's greater vision.

Will every leader be a great manager first? As I propose, I sincerely believe it to be a better way, but realistically the answer is no. Managers and leaders are driven by different passions, and this is where their *Ho'ohana* differs. However, *Alaka'i* gives leaders their empathetic understanding of the great managers who support them and will partner with them: The wise leader will fill his ranks with the great managers he needs to work with him, and he will understand what support he must give them so they will be successful.

Alaka'i is not limited in reach

Now I started this chapter with the statement that *Alaka'i* is not a value reserved only for those with title, position or power. When you reflect back on the definition of leadership as "to go before or with to show the way; conduct or escort" you can quickly realize that there are formal (bearing title) and informal leaders (by demonstrated action) all through the different levels of your company, no matter what your chosen business may be. Informal leaders are those who others are naturally compelled to follow because *Alaka'i* is a value that drives them, and thus it is one they seem to embody. If you are a manager who chooses to talk story with values as I have suggested throughout this book, your jumping off point with *Alaka'i* is simple: Encourage potential leaders to show initiative and set a good example for others to follow. Ask them to step forward and accept more responsibility. Encourage them to be trustworthy by entrusting them with more information. Give them guidance in *'Ike loa*, the pursuit of knowledge that will further inspire them.

In my own history within the hospitality industry, *Alaka'i* was a value talked about often with those who were in positions such as guide, host or concierge, and with professionals such as personal trainers, golf and tennis professionals, and recreational instructors. In these professions you need to know your stuff in a transmittable way, and be able to answer all kinds of questions as you teach, coach or guide. You need to cultivate a professional demeanor and stage presence that commands attention and establishes authority. "We will be *Alaka'i*" was a sentence that frequented the departmental mission statements of people in these positions. We'd talk about the very same question I proposed for managers and leaders: Why would anyone choose to follow you? We'd talk about earning trust. Sometimes the question was a little simpler: Why would anyone want to come with me? We'd talk about being pleasant and being an excitement builder, versus being bossy and an excitement drainer. Essentially we talked about the best way to take someone else in hand and make them comfortable.

Alaka'i and 'Imi ola

You will recall that *'Imi ola* is the value that places the ability to achieve your purpose in your own hands, giving you the clear understanding that you have the power to create your own destiny. We have talked about how much you can learn about your staff in coaching them to first write their professional mission statements, and then the goals that will help them achieve their purpose. Challenging employees to specifically focus on *Alaka'i* when they write their goals can be a very revealing exercise for a manager. Employees will often surprise you with their acceptance of leadership responsibility, clearly pointing you in the right direction with your coaching.

When the desire for leadership is revealed to you, employees throw open the doors to welcomed delegation from you. That frees you up to work on other pressing priorities, or set some higher goals for yourself. (Think back to a moment to the discussion we had on delegation, empowerment and ownership in Chapter 10 on *Kuleana*.)

I would especially see this happen time and again with employees who were approaching their two-and three-year marks in tenure. At that point, they've survived the boot camp period of a new job, and they think they know enough about both the position and the company to well assess this question: Do I stay, or do I start looking for the next new thing? Now notice I said "they *think* they know enough." Often they are still dealing with somewhat limited information. This is where the great manager will wisely step into their internal deliberations and offer them some options to consider, often while they remain in the same position. The great manager looks to *Alaka'i* to guide them in more progressive goal-setting and along the way retains seasoned employees who are newly motivated because they have invested in growing their own *Kuleana*.

Similar to a profit-sharing program, Hualalai had an annual incentive program for their *'Ohana* that was directly tied to each employee's goals: The higher the level of achievement, the more they were paid as an incentive bonus. In my final year managing the Alaka'i Nalu I gave them three themes for the goal-setting that was to be measured by this incentive program: They were to write one goal on *Alaka'i*, one on *Ho'okipa* and one on *'Ike loa*. At the time my own job responsibilities were increasing, and I needed them to step forward and accept more departmental ownership so that I could step back. The goal on *Alaka'i* helped me delegate the right responsibility to the person who most had a passion for it. With the goal on *Ho'okipa*, I was ensuring they would maintain a focus on our customers. Often the goal on *'Ike loa* linked back to the first two goals, setting in place the educational plan needed to enhance their knowledge and further inspire them: *They* told *me* what kinds of training they felt they needed to be successful.

I was amazed with the amount of responsibility these line employees willingly took on. They volunteered for jobs I'd never have thought of delegating to them on my own. There were some things that I couldn't say yes to, however, the degree of initiative they'd demonstrated blew the lid off my own limited thinking and other assignments were made that were mutually beneficial for us. The program was a rousing success: Upon my departure several months later, I was extremely confident that my successor would find the Alaka'i Nalu program to be the easiest transition she took on—and she's often voiced that it has been.

The Hualalai incentive program itself had always administratively been considered a department head's responsibility, primarily because of the confidentiality required by their rating system. However, encouraged as I was by the ambitious goal-setting of the Alaka'i Nalu, I decided to delegate the program down to the assistant level in the operations division I led. Reflecting back on *Ho'ohanohano*, I was determined to respect their intelligence, and confident they'd prove to be trustworthy. This group was not assigned value themes for their goals, however "*Alaka'i:* Assuming Responsibility for Leadership" was the theme for the entire program. As I had hoped, the assistants selected rose to the challenge in the goals that they set for themselves, asking for much higher levels of responsibility in each of their departments. In particular I was extremely excited about the leadership I was seeing emerge in the ranks of our landscape maintenance *'Ohana* and under the mentorship of our head golf professional.

I had left Hualalai before seeing the final results of the program that incentive year. Delegating the coaching of those goals to each assistant's department head was one of the items on my final checklist prior to departure. However, working within the potential promised by *Alaka'i* had enabled me to depart with much more hope and excitement about their future success than I had anticipated I would have. I truly felt I'd planted seeds for future succession potential within the capacity of these assistants.

A framework for new managers

As one who managed other managers, I found *Alaka'i* to be extremely valuable in my coaching arsenal for new supervisors and mid-level managers. These individuals are suddenly faced with decision-making and problem-solving at a different level, one with higher expectations than those they easily exceeded when they were informal leaders at the line level. *Alaka'i* gave me a framework within which I could coach them through their progressively increasing responsibilities.

Our talk story would be on diverse topics: How is life at the top? *Ha'aha'a* and humility are important, balance is important, perspective is important when everyone wants to be on the winning team. At the top, you become an easy target, for your visibility has increased. Job pressure and stress will increase; dependability and reliability are givens and work ethic takes on a new dimension. Others expect you will not lose sight of how you got there—the work, the struggle, the routine and monotony at times—but they will not empathize with your new challenges. How do we react to criticism? If we react positively, we continue to win.

Another topic was how to remain approachable. The Daily Five Minutes I described to you in the chapter on *'Ike loa* was a nonnegotiable, so they could build up their comfort level with the one-on-one employee encounters that are the everyday diet of management. It is essential that the leaders of today remain approachable and in touch with those they lead. The days of lofty and detached leadership are over; it is not enough to have people be in awe of you. We live in a generation where people crave connection and expect to give their input to your initiatives. The evidence for this is the established leader who actually leads with bad or faulty ideas: They are successful because they excel in creating and maintaining symbiotic or emotional relationships with their followers. In contrast, when you are *Alaka'i* you are a leader who does not create more followers; you create more leaders.

With this in mind, *Alaka'i* also speaks of having a mind of your own, and of the strength of character to be found in independence. Our talk story would be on self-esteem, confidence and believing in yourself. I have found that those who are good at providing mentorship for emerging leaders are nurturers and maximizers: They thrive on developing the strengths and self-esteem of other people. They teach them to set high standards for themselves, understanding that if you compromise on your internal standards your self esteem will plummet. They teach them independent thinking fortified with *Ha'aha'a*: the humility of open-minded thinking. They nurture fertile ground from which new ideas and new visions will more naturally emerge.

As skills and knowledge get outdated, *who you are* does not: It is your self-image, your values and your ethics that tenaciously persist. Your *mana'o*—that which you believe—is enduring. And I cannot think of anything else as strong as the power of one's belief. Those who are *Alaka'i* possess healthy self-esteem, with a strong belief in their own capacity and in the power of possibility: They are confident optimists. In the world we live in, you must be an optimist, and you must have hope. This is the fundamental requirement I always have for those leaders whom *I* willingly and eagerly choose to follow. They challenge me to be positive, no matter what. The visions they speak of help me see things that are better.

Respect for those you lead

Thus *Alaka'i* can also open the door to discussions about the kind of followers you expect your employees to be. You can be the leader who gives them the permission to openly question direction when they feel they sense a better way. You can be a leader who encourages his staff, by explaining that belief in self means trusting one's instincts when their intention is healthy.

You can be the leader who encourages her staff to speak up and speak freely, welcoming their input, feedback, and ideas.

You can be the leader who expects action and execution with urgency, because he creates an atmosphere where employees feel safe making on-the-spot customer-responsive and mission-driven decisions. You can be the leader who is a change-agent, because she urges her employees to take risks and welcome their mistakes on the path of sequential learning, and they feel safe and secure in the company's embrace.

In other words, you can be *Alaka'i*.

Alakaʻi: Lead with initiative, and with your good example.

You shall be the guide for others when you have gained their trust and their respect.

Those who are *Alakaʻi* possess a strong belief in their own capacity and in the power of possibility: They are confident optimists, filled with hope.

Those who are *Alakaʻi* are the managers and leaders we so greatly need.

15

Mālama

To take care of
To serve and to honor, to protect and care for

> To *Mālama*, is to take care of.
> A manager is a steward of assets and caretaker of people.
> *Mālama* calls upon us to serve, to honor and to protect.
> Acts of caring drive us to high performance levels in our work with others. We give and become unselfish. We accept responsibility unconditionally.
> *Mālama* is warm, and *Mālama* is personal. It comes from heart, and it comes from soul.
> When we *Mālama*, we are better.

To Mālama is to care

The motivation question came up for us earlier when we spoke of *Kuleana*, and one's personal sense of responsibility. There's another far simpler way you can find out what it is that drives your employees, and that's to uncover what they wish to *Mālama*, to take care of. From this value of *Mālama* comes the word *mālamalama*. In their *Hawaiian Dictionary*, Mary Kawena Pukui and Samuel H. Elbert define *mālamalama* as the "light of knowledge, clarity of thinking or explanation, enlightenment" where those things you consider will wonderfully become "shining, radiant [and] clear." Your path is an enlightened one for you when along the way you are taking care of certain things. You serve them, protect them, and honor them, and in doing so you feel better. You become better.

It is those things we deeply care about that are the things most important to us, and thus caring for these things—or these people—can drive us to high performance levels which take the form of unselfishness and accepting responsibility unconditionally. One of the other propositions we just know to be sure, is that everything is "better" when it is healthy in mind, body and spirit. The value of *Mālama* urges us to be the caretaker of good health, caring for ourselves, for others and for those things that somehow cannot care for themselves.

While you can probably read the paragraphs above and find no reason to debate me, it is so seemingly obvious that many of us do not put forth much conscious effort toward this in the business setting. Ask any company, "What are your core values?" and you'll get answers like honesty, integrity, community involvement and innovation. You will rarely get the answer that a basic tenet of who they are is to *Mālama* or simply take care of the health of their business and all it encompasses as they simultaneously drive their business results. Why must it be conscious and purposeful? You don't take care of something else just by being a good and ethical person yourself; it takes focus, and it takes work. It takes premeditated effort.

Caring in business

With *Alaka'i*, we spoke about empathy, and being able to put yourself in someone else's shoes as a means of seeking to understand them. Caring is something both separate and different, for people often care for others or for something emotionally and at gut level without having to completely understand about them. There are those who will say that business needs to be unemotional, and that businesses win more frequently the less the "emotional baggage," and the fewer the personal entanglements, so why is it so important to care?

I've found that pursuing quality in and of itself can be a very cold process, and the true winner is revealed in the combination of a quality product presented by warm and caring people. Consider this for a moment: Have you ever felt you received terrific service from someone who was still in training, or managed to take care of you in a faltering, imperfect, but genuinely sincere way? Ultimately warmth always trumps quality.

Giving care is a fundamental human need; we all want to feel that someone else needs us. In the service industry, addressing this need openly is a direct channel into fostering Ho'okipa, and the ability to serve someone else without any thought of what you may receive in return, giving simply for the pleasure of the giving itself. Mālama also brings an added dimension of warmth to the very noble efforts promoted by Ho'ohanohano, where you honor the dignity of others with respect and with caring.

I believe that one of the most valuable things that I learned from my tenure at the Hualalai Resort was of this value of Mālama, and it was taught to us there by our Kahu Billy Mitchell. Kahu is the word for caretaker in Hawaiian, and in Hawaii today it is a title of respect most commonly associated with someone who is an actual pastor or minister of a church or congregation, as was our Kahu Billy. He became a part-time employee of Hualalai, specifically brought in to work as our non-religious spiritual advisor by Hualalai's first President and CEO, an unconventional move that would prove to have profound effect on the shaping of our company values. Personally, I had always aspired to be thought of as a genuinely caring manager, but learning about Mālama as a value would cause me to be more intentional in my efforts.

Mālama Time

In our second year of operations, Kahu Billy started to hold weekly management meetings for us that were called "Mālama Time." Although some may bristle at the definition, I suppose you could most accurately call these meetings very innovative group therapy. During this one hour each week we came together to talk about how we felt about being managers, specifically at Hualalai and with the challenges she faced, and specifically for the employees we were responsible for. This was a forum in which we could actually question the integrity of our own decisions openly and without judgment. The goal was to explore our own thinking in as complete a way as possible. For me, Mālama Time was about building intellectual honesty.

Management can often make you feel isolated from those you lead, it can be lonely. Mālama Time was the hour each week we devoted to explicitly take care of ourselves and our peers by simply having a safe place to talk and to listen, to empathize, to share, to care. Kahu Billy facilitated it, often by initially posing some philosophical question at the beginning of the session that would evoke revealing responses from us. Mālama Time was not mandatory, but it became something that you never would miss, and we often referred to it as our weekly time to "go to the well" and drink to satisfy our own thirsts. Managers need to be taken care of too.

And of course, there is much that managers must take care of. You must take care of yourself before you can take care of others: Hence, we'd talk about maintaining balance and perspective, or the difference between healthy and unhealthy stress. You must take care of those others: Hence, we'd often talk about the needs of our customers and our employees. We'd teach each other how to keep employees responsible for their own happiness, and we'd talk about how to maintain a customer as a "good one." Managers must take care of all the company assets at their disposal: Hence, we'd talk about retention strategies, supplying our staff with the right tools and equipment, and product quality. Managers must take care of the company's values: Hence, we'd talk about teaching those different values, and then walking the talk, modeling the behavior we wished to evoke in others.

One of our consistent Mālama Time lessons was that you need never go it alone; ask for help and you will receive it. However, asking for help can be a tough thing for managers; they are expected to be "in charge," strong and self-sufficient. Often the executives that support them must be able to ask the right questions so that the managers' needs will be revealed. Safety nets have to be created for them, so they are willing to be authentic—true to themselves, and vulnerable—open and amendable. For us, Mālama Time was the ultimate safety net:

What was said stayed in the room. However what was learned was expected to flow out of it in a way that would serve to *Mālama*, to take care of our business, our *'Ohana* and our community. After all, what good is your new knowledge if you don't do something with it?

A catalyst for soft concepts

This expectation would often separate our management team for me into the "sponges" and the "stampers." The sponges sat through Mālama Time and attentively took it all in, but once they absorbed everything they just kept it inside. The stampers left the room actively looking for where, when and how they could leave an impression of what they'd just learned, and truly make a difference by extending their *Mālama* to another. The people in both groups cared; however, the stampers were driven by caring: *Mālama* was an innate value for them.

There were so many possibilities out there—our *'Ohana*, our business itself, our company assets, the land we occupied, our community. *Mālama* became a sort of catalyst for me: In my position managing the managers, I'd find that my stampers knew what to do and may just need my coaching with timing and with priorities. My sponges needed coaching in translating the soft concepts of people, character, values, relationship, commitment, passion, a cause or a calling into defined tasks they could execute. I began to realize that most of the stampers were my leaders—leaders love the soft stuff.

Mālama in the air and in our veins

I felt very blessed in the last two companies I worked for; I seemed to fortuitously be enjoying a 13-year-long nirvana when it came to the general disposition of the staff as a whole. At both Hualalai Resort and at the Ritz-Carlton, Mauna Lani, I would often have people tell me, "Your employees seem so happy here." This would be said in many interviews, where prospective candidates then continued to tell me they wanted to be part of it, part of this environment they could *feel*.

Mālama was a value shared by both of these companies,

185

and they understood that an employee's happiness is never something to be taken for granted, even when it seems you have a lot of it pretty consistently. To keep it that way you have to diligently work at it. You begin to think of happiness as a way of travel, not a destination. Hualalai began to duplicate Mālama Time, having separate sessions for their administrative professionals, for the supervisory group, and then quarterly for the line staff. The Ritz-Carlton had one of the most far-reaching training and development programs I've ever worked within, but again the difference was their focus on the soft concepts that they were certain engendered rock solid results for the bottom line—it was training in their values. We had training sessions that would talk about only one thing: What did it mean to be the best? How could we become better?

It's not always pleasant

Tough love also is inherent in *Mālama*, for driven by this value you take care to deal with any sticky situations that arise by dealing with them expeditiously. Unpleasant issues must especially be dealt with openly, swiftly and effectively, lest they begin to fester and poison what surrounds them. In particular, *Mālama ka poʻe*, care for the people, is a process that does get harder over time as businesses get older, more established, and more sophisticated. As businesses grow, there are more demands on a manager's time and attention, and it takes more character for them to *Hoʻomau*, to continue to persevere. In directing my own team of managers, I'd often talk to them about the deadly management sin of tacit approval: If you don't deal with it, the message you silently give is that it's okay as long as you don't get caught. Not okay? *Mālama.* The single word meant to deal with issues quickly, but deal with them in complete care.

You must keep your eye on the prize: Managers elicit higher performance levels from employees who trust them and thus are impelled to follow their direction. You know this: Your trusted employees are the ones that take care of themselves and take care of your business when you are not there. They are the ones who understand your values, subscribe to them and will emulate them.

Employees trust more easily and become more trustworthy themselves when they feel their manager cares about them, and they appreciate your honesty even when the message is a hard one for them to hear. For employees, how they are treated—trust, respect, dignity, intelligence, communication, caring—carries much greater weight than the tools of the trade, and even the task at hand. I am absolutely convinced that my successes with the Alaka'i Nalu all primarily blossomed from a single healthy stem: They knew that I genuinely cared about them.

Know well, Mālama well

Mālama ka po'e, care for one's people, requires sensitivity. Managers must learn when it's best to take care of staff issues individually versus collectively at times, treating their staff how they expect to be treated, learning how they define their own personal dignity. This requires that they know their staff well. Thus *Mālama* was a value that would come up often in our discussion of *'Ike loa* and our Daily Five Minutes, for it was usually within this daily ritual that managers would learn about what concerns their staff had, and they were gifted with the timing within which their employees chose to share it. "Listen with *Mālama*" meant to listen with caring, to listen for feelings and for *kaona*—hidden meanings within the words that were actually spoken. When the Daily Five Minutes was diligently programmed employees did not get lost in the shuffle of the day or go unnoticed when they were troubled—the times they need to be cared for most.

Mālama also challenges us to explore the full range of our employee's emotional needs so they are met and not minimized or neglected. For example, do you celebrate success and reward achievement? Understand the need for recognition. Do you have practices that make allowances for loss and grieving? Realize when your understanding is needed. Do you recognize the symptoms of stress and undue pressure? Give time when time is needed.

Take another look at the words crowning this chapter,

and consider the ways in which you "honor," "serve" and "protect" your employees. Chances are you already have several fairly formal company programs that fall into this category—medical leave, disability insurance, workers compensation, and paid time off for bereavement are just a few. Why not put them under a new heading of "Our Mālama Programs" and give them all a value test? Come on, all you human resources managers out there, do it! *Mālama* will guide you if you take some time to consider how you can bring warmth and a more personal touch to them. *Mālama* is warm, and *Mālama* is personal. It comes from heart, and it comes from soul. It is mindful in its caring.

One well-intentioned program I have seldom seen done well is light duty. I can confidently guarantee you that every person presently in some light-duty assignment could use a lot of *Mālama* right now. There is this stigma with light duty that someone is not complete, that they are less than fully functioning—and it doesn't have to be that way! It's not entirely true! Stop thinking that someone on light duty is just taking time to heal—they are working, and you need to think *Ho'ohana*, enabling them to work purposefully and with full passion and intent. Light duty should be an opportunity for a manager to explore the hidden talents someone has. Groom those "secondary inclinations" people have. You could uncover some bonanza—a fertile crop you normally haven't harvested in the confines of that person's "normal job." If you are in any way responsible for someone currently on light duty, please *Mālama* them. It's not that difficult: Close this book and give them your Daily Five Minutes—right now. Listen with *Mālama*. Honor them, and serve them. *Ho'ohanohano*. Give them back their dignity.

Mālama the 'āina

In Hawaii, *Mālama the 'āina* is a *hapa* phrase (part English) you will hear often today. Literally it means take care of the land; more emotionally it means to take care of our sense of place: the land and all it gives life to. We are understanding that our natural resources are not limitless and must be protected; that we have taken advantage of nature's bounty in the past and must now take better care to preserve and maintain it.

In business today, we all have a responsibility to take care of the environment that allows us to survive and to thrive. The effort to *Mālama the 'āina* is often a fertile starting ground for businesses to better interact with the community and with the extended families of their employees. When you adopt a school, a sports team, a park or even a stretch of highway, you are able to forge personal connections that are naturally colored with warmth and caring. Often you are making investments in future employees or unknowingly advertising the fact you exist to potential customers. Use *Mālama* to chart your course: Ask your employees which community or environmental causes they truly care about, and they will get involved with you. You will reap the bonus of strengthening the bonds of *'Ohana*.

Closer to home, *Mālama the 'āina* fosters the responsibility employees have to take care of your business assets, much as we spoke of previously with the value of *Ho'okipa*. Our first director of landscaping, Katy Deshotels-Moore, left behind an incredible legacy for the resort when she championed the creation of our own composting facility. It was a very expensive endeavor in terms of front-end investment in capital equipment, but Hualalai has gained impressive results from her efforts: direct annual savings in land-fill costs, healthier organic environments, a wealth of new knowledge for landscapers incorporating the composting process into existing systems and their horticultural expertise, the assumption of community responsibility for the handling of green waste, and environmentally, the recognition that it is the right thing to do.

Have Mālama be Kākou

Mālama should be for everyone: Think inclusively, think *Kākou*. Within your company, directly ask your employees to *Mālama* the customer, the business and each other. If you have chosen your employees well, chances are they care about many of the same things that you do. For remember, as a manager you need not go it alone.

When you *Mālama* others, you find that they show their own *Mālama* for you. Or as my mom would say when she wanted my brothers and I to treat each other better, "what goes around, comes around." This is the gift you get back from your employees when you are a manager: They begin to know you better than you imagine they do, and when you truly need them they are there for you. Amazingly it comes at times you least expect it and find you need it most. They give you space, they give you understanding, they give you obedience without questions, they give you performance, they give you their own kind of *Aloha*. As I write these words their faces parade through my memory—wonderful stories of giving, from them to me. They are why I am a manager, and love that I am. They are why I learn to *Mālama* them even at the times it is very difficult to do so.

I'll share just one story of how this happened for me, one that proved to be a pretty defining moment in my life. I was working at The Ritz-Carlton, Mauna Lani, and that period of time when I made the job transition from a directorship in catering and conference services to managing a retail operation was preceded by long agonizing months where I felt the emotional weight of neglecting my children. Business was booming, my job was a critical one requiring long hours, and it seemed there was always a client demanding even more of my time. I was torn between family and job in my responsibilities to everyone I knew depended on me. Time for myself? Virtually none.

One night my assistant returned to the office at about 9:30 p.m. after a dinner function, and found me churning out banquet event orders while my 6-year-old daughter drew in a coloring book, and my 3-year-old slept on a doubled-up comforter on the floor next to my chair. My husband sat on another desk, designing a floor plan for one of my client's functions. Without a word of reproach for me, my assistant hunkered down next to my daughter and put her to sleep, knowing that I would not find rest until I'd finished what I was doing; I expected the client in the morning. We all left at about midnight.

The next morning, I walked back into my office and into the arms of an intervention, *Mālama* style. I had three catering managers and three administrative assistants in that office who were just as busy as I was, yet they had commandeered my client files for reassignment. They sat me down, asked me questions on each file they knew would reassure me they could handle everything, and then banished me from the office to go home to my children. The assistant who had walked in on me the night before was in my boss's office, explaining why she'd be taking over for me for a week.

I started to protest, but I quieted with a crushing feeling of guilt—one of the most damaging, useless emotions we fall prey to—when one of my admins said, "You're always the one who takes care of us; why won't you let us take care of you? Trust us." Up until then, I had this self-destructive belief that I was indispensable, and I was blind to the high cost of my job devotion, not only for my family, but for the very ones I believed I served, cared for and protected. I wasn't setting a very good example; I was a leader with a very tentative hold on *Alakaʻi*, working hard, but not working well.

They called me at home every evening those seven days, to fully inform me about every event of the day, but they did it knowing those calls were the connection I still needed: They didn't need my help or advice, the calls came when all the work was already done. They worked like crazy for me, putting in longer hours, and giving their all with exceptionally generous effort. They gave me their complete *Mālama*. A few months later I'd make the job change that was best for me and everyone I cared about. I had discovered what an incredible gift *Mālama* can be. I had discovered *mālamalama*: the "light of knowledge, clarity of thinking or explanation, enlightenment" where those things you consider will wonderfully become "shining, radiant [and] clear." The guilt was gone.

To Mālama is to share Aloha

My staff grew immensely during that time; They had gained their own growth in their acts of giving. *Mālama* should be for everyone, it flows in all directions: Think inclusively, think *Kākou*. Serve all and honor all. Protect them and care for them.

Mālama pono (*pono* is balance): Take care of yourself. We function best by taking care of ourselves first. In doing so we enlarge our capacity to care for others, and share our *Aloha*.

Mālama, to take care of.

A manager is a steward of assets and caretaker of people.

Mālama calls upon us to serve, to honor and to protect.

Acts of caring drive us to high performance levels in our work with others. We give and become unselfish. We accept responsibility unconditionally.

Mālama is warm, and *Mālama* is personal. It comes from heart, and it comes from soul.

When we *Mālama*, we are better.

16

Mahalo

Thank you, as a way of living
Live in thankfulness for the richness
that makes life so precious

> *Mahalo.* Thank you, as a way of living.
>
> With *Mahalo*, we give thanks for every element that enriches our lives by *living in thankfulness* for them. We relish them. We celebrate them joyously. *Mahalo* is the value that gives us an attitude of gratitude, and the pleasure of awe and wonder.
>
> Say "thank you" often; speak of your appreciation and it will soften the tone of your voice, giving it richness, humility and fullness. People need to hear it from you: *Mahalo nui loa.*

What makes you rich?

Ironically, when you live on an island in the middle of the Pacific Ocean, over two thousand miles from the nearest continent, water is rare. You treasure all sources of fresh water and learn to conserve it. So it's no surprise that the Hawaiian word for richness or wealth literally translates to "double water." The word is *waiwai*, for *wai* is the word for water (*kai* is sea water). *Ho'owaiwai* is to enrich, to bring about prosperity and abundance. I share this context with you, for it says much about the simplicity and purity of life's richness that the value of *Mahalo* teaches us to treasure.

Like *Aloha*, *Mahalo* is a word of common use in the Hawaii of today where relatively few Hawaiian words are actually spoken. I lived more than 40 years of my own life in the islands before I came to realize that *Mahalo* was actually a value, one which meant much more than just the polite statement of "Thank you."

When lived to its fuller potential, *Mahalo* is a value that creates habits of thankful living in us. Appreciation and gratefulness stroke deeper color and richer texture into our character. We give thanks by the acts of living thankfully, not simply by saying the words "thank you." When we look around us, we are filled with wonder, and we sense the immense richness that already surrounds us. We do not lament that which we may not have. As we count our many blessings we *Mālama* them and cherish them, we relish the bounty they bring to life, to our life. We celebrate them joyously.

Creating the habit of appreciation

As managers we make a frequent lament about our employees, "Why can't they be more appreciative?" Or perhaps we've said, "Can't they understand just how good they have it?" Sound vaguely familiar? Well consider this: As a manager, appreciation is one of the most generous lessons we can teach and coach. It's also a fairly easy one to incorporate.

I've shared several stories of the Alaka'i Nalu with you, the "leaders of the waves" at the Hualalai Resort. If I had to pick a favorite one, it would be the story of their *"Mahalos"* for I am certain that *Mahalo* gave them a gift of healing.

There was some *pilikia* (trouble) among the ranks at the time this group of athletes became my gift, and it was clear we had to *ho'oponopono*, clear the air and make several things right. So as a way to begin in a small but consistently occurring way, we started a practice of "sharing our *Mahalos*" at the end of each operational weekly meeting. For several months, the only real homework they had for the week was to catch someone else on the team doing a favor for them. They were to say thank you then and there, but they were also to share their *Mahalo* at the next weekly meeting in front of the entire group, adding a few words on why the favor given meant something to them.

One of the first things I discovered was that they didn't know how to graciously accept it when someone said thank you: It was hard for them to just say "you're welcome" and leave it at that—far easier to crack a joke or even look at someone else and say, "Yeah brah, you should do some of that too sometimes." They used sarcasm and humor to build up this defensive wall around them. In those early weeks, I'd have to ask them to just listen quietly and not respond at all other than nodding in acknowledgement that they'd heard all the words spoken.

There were more ground rules that would spontaneously get added as we went, such as picking a different person each week to break down the buddy-to-buddy game playing. With each wisecrack I'd have to say, "Either you start being sincere, or I add another rule you gotta remember." I also learned to start modeling the behavior that I wanted, ending the meeting with my own *Mahalos* for each of them, "Mahea, thank you for taking the initiative to start early today without being asked to: *Hui Wa'a* (the program name given to our Friday community paddle) was easier for all of us because you took the time to reassign last night's late sign-ups. Daniel, thank you for taking care of those kids that got so badly sunburned at King's Pond on Tuesday: I got a call from their parents about how thoughtful and patient you were, and your actions add to the reputation of the entire team" ... and on for each one in turn.

If their names were not spoken, the silent message hung uncomfortably in the room that they had not earned the recognition that week. To make something up was the gravest sin: This was a rule that was never spoken but completely understood by all.

They caught on, and I'd have to say less and less about the ground rules as time went by. In fact, this became the best part of the meeting by far. One week we went overtime on other business, and I nearly got a revolt when I tried to adjourn without giving them the time to speak they expected: Sharing their *Mahalos* had become genuine, generous and candid, and thought-provoking for us all. Thereafter, I was sure I did not commit the cardinal sin of encroaching on their time to acknowledge each other. They loved it when someone new joined the group or I'd invited a guest—they wanted to show off! But here's the thing: They didn't want to show off that they did it, they sincerely wanted more people to hear about how terrific their peers were, and how proud they were to be associated with them. It amazed me how articulate and giving they were when a newcomer was in the room.

They also started to show me how perceptive they were—they caught everything. They learned more about each other because they were understanding more about what someone else appreciated—it differed greatly for each of them individually, and they unknowingly shared intuitive revelations with me that made my own job of managing them far easier: They uncovered all the cause-and-effect relationships of the team for me in a very short amount of time. And over *their* time, the depth of the actions taken by this team was incredible—it became embarrassing to have someone say thank you for something minor or trivial, and hence the assumptions of basic good productivity in the team grew. They tried so much harder, and they were much more aware of how their spoken words of thankfulness affected their peers: I was really proud of them.

There is a word for "thank you" in every culture around the globe. Adopting a practice similar to this one that worked so well for the Alakaʻi Nalu can serve any business well, for there are rewards inherent in it for both the person giving thanks and the one being acknowledged for their good deeds.

Give thanks by living thankfully

As a value in the Hawaiian culture, *Mahalo* digs deeper: It is living within an attitude of gratitude, living each day with a sense of thankfulness for all the elements that make life so precious. It is the fundamental realization of how much you have, simply because you are alive. You begin to relish your present: Both nostalgia for the past and anxiousness for the future lose their grip on your longing. *Mahalo* is living in a way that demonstrates that you are humbled by this gift of the present, and are thankful for it, living your life in a way that celebrates it. When you live *Mahalo* you don't take anything for granted, and you *Mālama* what you have, taking better care of it.

Mahalo is the life perspective of giving thanks for what you have by using your gifts—and using all your gifts—in the best possible way. You draw from *Ho'ohana*, and your inner passions, and live with intention. You begin to realize that it would be wasteful not to use whatever talent you were fortunate enough to be born with; it would be ungrateful and unappreciative. You begin to question what good is destined to emerge from the talent you have, and you explore all possibilities. *Mahalo* goes beyond thinking or saying "thank you" for something you've been given; It is when you give thanks with more giving. You live in a manner that makes you deserving.

Nurses live in thankfulness for their empathy, when they treat patients in ways that are in tune with the nuances of pain, and with heightened perception for the type of care that is needed. Professional athletes live in thankfulness for their physical strength, good health, endurance and stamina when they compete in sports that entertain and inspire millions of spectators. Environmentalists and scientists live in thankfulness for the wonder of creation and beauty of the planet we are so fortunate to call our home, and for their own sensitivity and awareness of the secrets she can reveal to them. Managers live in thankfulness for the privilege and ability they have to affect the optimally rewarding productivity of other human beings.

Like every other normal person on the planet, there is so much that I *want*: I want to be more creative and artistic, I want to know more about the stock market and electronic communications, I want to remodel my kitchen and add a walk-in closet to my bedroom, I want my children to find soul mates and be happy forever, I want an enlightened government, world peace and harmony... my list goes on and on. I will admit that reflecting instead on what I already have and should be more thankful for serves to make me a more reasonable person at times. Does it quell my desire for more? No, for I'm far too human to stop wishing. However, it helps me take stock of the building blocks that are already in place for me to buttress my dream-building on, and I celebrate those things and enjoy them. It helps me shift my focus from the unachievable to the possible, and I get to work at making it happen for me instead of just wishing it were so.

The good fortune of all managers

Every manager has need for better tools of the trade. Every manager yearns for easier and simpler processes, for more generous financial budgets, for more employees, more hours in the day, more customers, more sales opportunities … another endless list. Instead, take stock of what you already have, reflect on what these present assets have already done for you, and what they potentially can *still* do for you: You will then be living the value of *Mahalo*. Most probably you will also be learning to keep things simple and uncomplicated along the way.

One of the most obvious assets all managers have is this: They have employees (think *'Ohana*). If you are a manager who lives within the value of *Mahalo*, being thankful for what you already have, you are one who constantly takes inventory of the strengths of your *'Ohana* and you apply them to the job at hand (*Lōkahi*). The most effective managers are the ones who do not foolishly go it alone: They get everyone involved in ways that are stimulating, challenging, and inclusive (*Kākou*). They trust their people because they know them well (*'Ike loa*), and they dole out in very generous portions meaningful assignments (*Ho'ohana*) and the authority to effectively get them done (*Kuleana*). They give advice vs. approval, forgiveness vs. permission: They have faith in the goodness of people (*Aloha*) and they find that results are achieved faster, in more nimble ways throughout their operations.

Take stock of what you have

So let's do it. Right now. Stop reading, and put this book aside to do a simple exercise. Grab a clean sheet of paper and make a list of those things you have in your job right now—not the things you still want, just those things, situations or people you already have at hand and on your mind. Thinking back to my last assignment managing the Alaka'i Nalu, I'll give you some of my own examples just to get your wheels turning:

- A full crew for the next 42 days: No one is scheduled for vacation for another six weeks.
- In addition I have a new hire in training: He still has another 60 days in his introductory period.
- One of my employees is in training for the Moloka'i to O'ahu race, working out with her paddling club on a very focused competitive practice schedule each day after work.
- The summer season: Weather-wise it's the best time of the year to take our canoes on the water, and all are in repair and ready to go.
- Advance reservations are light, but prospects are high that we'll have potential customers on the resort to sell to.
- Higher residential occupancy in these summer months means many of our residents will want their canoes delivered from our storage facility to their own homes for better daily accessibility.

You can be more basic if you want: Do you have your own office? Write that down. Do you have some budget money to spend before the quarter or fiscal year is over? Write that down. Is there an employee who seems to be bored and needs more responsibility? Write that down. Is there another one on a high right now because you just gave a glowing annual review? Write that down. Is your own boss too busy and preoccupied right now to micromanage you? Write that down, but in a way that is positive, optimistic and not cynical. You get the idea.

When your list is done, the next step will be this: Go back to your list and write a sentence behind each item that describes how you will use what you have in a way that celebrates your thankfulness for having it. Let's go back to my example list for a moment to demonstrate:

- A full crew for the next 42 days: No one is scheduled for vacation for another six weeks. *Time for those back-burner projects, for example Sam can catch up on the wave-*

runner preventive maintenance that should be done.

- In addition I have a new hire in training: He still has another 60 days in his introductory period. *He's an extra body and already doing very well: This gives me the ability to have Sam train someone else to back him up on equipment maintenance when I need him for the Red Cross certification program instead.*

- One of my employees is in training for the Moloka'i to O'ahu race, working out with her paddling club on a very focused competitive practice schedule each day after work. *My own weekly meetings with the group could use a change-up: I'll ask Mahea to do presentations in the next two meetings on what she is learning from their paddling coach (week 1) and on the strategy of the Molokai race in particular (week 2). This third-person teaching will help her own focus, be less physically demanding in light of her schedule, involve and excite her peers and free up some planning time for me.*

- The summer season: Weather-wise it's the best time of the year to take our canoes on the water, and all are in repair and ready to go. *I have a pretty aggressive forecast to meet this month, but the weather is with me, and the crew is healthy and eager to capitalize on it. Ask them to help me figure out how to add some program times to the schedule: We can go for volume vs. variety since these canoe rides are the most highly requested programs we have now anyway. They're the experts and know better than I do how to make this happen. Assign coordinating this to Ikaika and Janelle: It's what they do best.*

- Advance reservations are light, but prospects are high that we'll have potential customers on the resort to sell to. *Since business levels are not as high as I'd like them to be, I'll start a promotional rotation where we double the crew at the afternoon ray feeding and can verbally sell our programs—our prospects will be the lookie-loos who are there at the time. We can also concentrate on involving more parents in our daily keiki (children's) program. Assign coordinating this one to Ed and Daniel; they're really great at these types of things.*

- Higher residential occupancy in these summer months means many of our residents will want their canoes delivered from our storage facility to their own homes for better daily accessibility. *The vacancies in the facility mean less expensive equipment is there to be moved: This is the easiest and best time to give it a spring cleaning top to bottom. However the crew is best assigned to focus on the business at hand—contract the cleaning job out, and let higher business levels serve to cover the expense. Assign this to Puaita—he'll know who to choose for the job, and when to engage with them when needed so the job's explained and done right.*

Your turn. Celebrate what you have by adding similar action-stimulating sentences to your own list. This is *Mahalo* at work for you. Grab a bookmark and finish this chapter when you are done with the list and you have made a few of your own assignments as an effective manager thankful for what you have, and for the employees you manage.

Take another look at my examples and see how much I delegated and how much will be accomplished when everything has been done: The gains in this approach for you as a manager are very clear—what are you waiting for?

The Mālama connection

Mālama and *Mahalo* connect in a very meaningful way. You see, sometimes you need *Mahalo* to open your eyes to your good fortune before you can live thankfully for it, and then take care of it as you should.

One afternoon I had a manager come to see me about one of his employees, intending to just give me a heads up: He was about to embark down the road of progressive discipline with a stage one verbal warning. He felt the employee's work performance was average to marginal, and in the two weeks prior, there had been the warning signs of attendance problems. He concluded by raising a huge red flag for me, saying, "If I just let things go and document it all, he'll hang himself." Listening to his tone, I suspected the problem was the manager, not the employee.

In this particular case, the manager was relatively new to the department, and I knew the person he spoke of to be a longer-term employee that had done very well for us up to that point. This was a situation that didn't make much sense to me. So since he was so willing to invest in documenting something, I asked the manager to instead conduct a small experiment for me, and asked him "have you ever kept a *Mahalo* log?"

I had the manager—let's call him Jake—keep a log for me for a week, where each day he wrote down just one thing he noticed about this employee—let's call him Bruce—that was good; it was something small, but it was good. I told him I expected at least one of those entries to be about a Daily Five Minutes he'd given to Bruce.

Bruce surprised Jake on the very next day. This was his log:

Day 1. Not only did Bruce come to work on time today, he was early. And he didn't just stand around, he started early and on his own time.

Day 2. Bruce got a compliment from one of our guests today. They got lost, and he dropped what he was doing to escort them back to their room.

Day 3. In my Daily Five Minutes, I thanked Bruce for what he did yesterday, and he said he was surprised I actually had noticed it. Ouch.

Day 4. A new employee started today, and Bruce was the one who volunteered to work with him.

Day 5. Bruce skipped his lunch break today. He was getting behind training the new kid, and he didn't want to leave his work for the next shift. The new kid is learning a lot from him.

We had set a follow-up appointment for the end of the week, and Jake showed me his *Mahalo* Log. Without commenting on it, I asked what else they'd talked about in their Daily Five Minutes. He said Bruce told him he quit his other job—a second job Jake hadn't even known he had—because it made him too tired for the job he had with us; That's why he'd overslept so much and come to work late a few times. He said the money had helped though, so would Jake call on him when someone had to work overtime?

Jake found out that Bruce was in his department's circle of

richness, for Bruce brought character and commitment to their department. The *Mahalo* Log became a new habit for Jake each time he suspected he judged someone too quickly. And right after that Daily Five Minutes with Bruce, he started saying thank you to people a little more often.

Give thanks. Live Mahalo

Continue to count your own blessings, and enjoy your own discoveries. Thankfulness is truly a mighty force, and sometimes, like Jake, we may find that it changes us, it helps us become better.

When you teach the value of *Mahalo* to your employees, you help them enjoy the life they have. What a wonderful gift that is!

Mahalo. Thank you, as a way of living.

With *Mahalo*, we give thanks for every element that enriches our lives by living in thankfulness for them. We relish them. We celebrate them joyously.

Mahalo is the value that gives us an attitude of gratitude, and the pleasure of awe and wonder.

Say "thank you" often; speak of your appreciation and it will soften the tone of your voice, giving it richness, humility and fullness. People need to hear it from you: *Mahalo nui loa.*

Mahalo. Live in thankfulness for the richness that makes life so wonderful.

17

Nānā i ke kumu

Look to your source, find your truth

> *Nānā i ke kumu.* Look to your source. Find your truth.
>
> There is an inner wellspring inside all of us, and we will go to this inner well to get healthy. We find reason. We find heart. We find soul.
>
> *Nānā i ke kumu* are words of encouragement, telling us to look inward to this source of well-being as our constant and our truth.
>
> *Nānā i ke kumu.* Look to the source you have revealed, and let it inspire you. Let it energize you. You will not hesitate, and you will not falter.
>
> You will *Ho'omau* with renewed strength. You will be warmed by the *Aloha* of your own spirit. You will continue.

Take a deep breath. Thus far, you have learned of sixteen Hawaiian values, and there is much we have spoken of. In the chapters ahead you will learn of values that can bring more clarity to the others because they seek to make them more personal for you in a wonderful way: They seek to ground you, and to bring you contentment. With *Nānā i ke kumu* we first look to our source, for there is an inner wellspring inside all of us, and we will go to this inner well to get healthy, in body, mind and spirit.

Sense of place

In many ways nature is where it all begins for most islanders, and the Hawaiian people are no different in this regard. We call ourselves *keiki o ka 'āina*, children of the land, understanding that our roots are within the land, and we grow shaped by our environment. In Hawaii the *'āina* is not just soil and sand, lava rock and dirt; The *'āina* is a statement of heart and soul for us. The very word brings forth deep emotion: *Aloha 'āina* are our words for love of the land, for it is with *Aloha* we share the breath of life, understanding it is the land that gives us life and gives us sustenance. In a way, humanity and nature are considered father and mother, brother and sister.

When we opened The Ritz-Carlton, Mauna Lani, I had the privilege of attending classes taught by the late Dr. George Kanahele, a highly respected scholar and civic leader of the Hawaiian renaissance of the 1970's whose *Ho'ohana* at the time of these classes—the early 1990's—was within the field of organizational consulting. The definition he shared with us for sense of place has always struck me as being concisely intuitive: He said that sense of place involves both the feel *of* a place, and the feel *for* a place. In our classes, he taught us that place (*wahi* in Hawaiian) is personally defined for people by their own "locational experiences." He taught us to open the hotel with a spirit of hospitality that would create fertile ground for our guests to have their own place-connected experiences while they were with us, and in that way feel for themselves what the *Aloha* spirit was all about. In my mind, he gave us the key to being "culturally correct" in the way we shared Hawaii with visitors.

The words "sense of place" echo much farther back within my consciousness; I cannot tell you when I first heard them, for it seems they've always been there. Beyond words, they've been more of an assumption for me, something I have—something I need—to help me grow in respect for Hawaii, the land that gave me birth and nurtured me as I grew up. And beyond paying respect, to *Mālama* her, honor and care for her whenever it is in my power to do so. Therefore, when I hear the words *Nānā i ke kumu*, look to your source, it means I need to consider my emotional sense of place as well as my intellectual sense of reason.

Look to your source

When a child is troubled but hesitates to tell her parents just what the problem is, the elders will often say *"Nānā i ke kumu."* They are saying to find a place where you can sit quietly, and look within yourself for the source of what troubles you, for there you will also find strength within your inner spirit with which to deal with the trouble. This was a profound insight for me when I helped the Alaka'i Nalu write their mission statement as a way to help them deal with whatever troubles disturbed them; for them, every source of inner strength they possessed could be traced to the ocean. This is how their mission statement begins:

> "We are the Alaka'i Nalu
> of Hualalai at historic Ka'ūpūlehu.
> It is our mission to help our guests and
> our *'Ohana* see what we see, and feel what we feel
> for the ocean and all she is to us, in honor of our deep love
> and respect for her. We have a strong sense
> of responsibility to teach and to share this,
> our *Aloha 'Āina.* We have a great desire to learn from her,
> and to be *Alaka'i* in all we are, and all we do.
> *Nānā i ke kumu:* we look to the ocean and
> to our history as our source of strength."

For the Alaka'i Nalu their sense of place is their source. At those times they were stuck, unsure of what to do next, I could be the elder who said *"Nānā i ke kumu"* for them, knowing they would look to their own source and figure things out, both emotionally and intellectually. They usually did this while on the water or while washing the canoe in silence on the beach, and not in my office or in any meeting room. I never doubted that the ocean spoke to them in a silent but powerful language.

Find your truth

As my own years in management have gone by, *Nānā i ke kumu* has come to mean what's true for me, my statement of personal truths as my own source to look inward to. My roots are revealed, and I can evaluate for myself just how deep they run within me, and if they still anchor me, or if the need has arisen calling for me to change course. As a calling in my career, my *Nānā i ke kumu* came to mean *Managing with Aloha*.

In Mālama Time at Hualalai, Kahu Billy Mitchell would teach us that *Nānā i ke kumu* meant "Don't forget the ancient ways lest we falter." In my own *mana'o* (i.e. within my intellectual sense of reason) I understood those words to stand for any encouragement I needed to remember my values and the lessons of the past, whether they were to Ho'omau, continue and persevere, to Ho'ohana, work with intent and purpose, to embody Ha'aha'a and speak with the softer voice of humility, or to Ho'ohanohano, conduct myself with distinction and respect the dignity of others in a future decision to be made.

When Hualalai sought authenticity in telling the story of Ka'ūpūlehu, the *ahupua'a* (land division) that is home to Hualalai Resort, they turned to the artist and historian Herb Kane, famous for his Hawaiian historical paintings, rich in their authentic detail. He was commissioned to do 11 paintings that would illustrate the life of our ancestors on our land. These paintings would serve to illustrate the story of Ka'ūpūlehu that was to be showcased in our Interpretive Center for our guests, for our employees and for the entire island community. For Herb Kane, it is vitally important that his paintings be accurate, and I love the way he explains his *mana'o* (thoughts and belief) in these passages from M.J. Harden's wonderful book, *Voices of Wisdom, Hawaiian Elders Speak*:

"My paintings are going to go on speaking to people long after I'm gone, so I feel a certain obligation to make sure that what I say is as truthful as I can find it to be. If my work contributes to our comprehension of Hawaii's past, that will ultimately become the greatest reward. Every culture romanticizes about its past. Hawaiians are no exceptions. You have Hawaiians who talk about the old days as some kind of utopia. What I try to do is avoid that type of thing, because by strip-

207

ping away those layers of fancy that obscure the past, when you get down to what really happened, what people were really thinking about, it's always more interesting. It's always more rewarding, because you know you're getting closer to the kernel of truth that lies in the center of every legend."

"Don't forget the ancient ways lest we falter" is a phrase that urges us to look for this "kernel of truth" that Kane describes, and then apply it to our present endeavors. It does not mean we must return to an old way of our ancestors and do things they way they did, or the way we've always done them in our own more recent past. It means we must tap into our inner wellspring, latch onto what is good and true for us and continue to grow.

Embrace change, embrace growth

In fact, one of the things I've always admired most about my native culture is their embrace of change. *Nānā i ke kumu* teaches us to look to the work we can do on ourselves—repair, maintain, build, grow—so we can better deal with change that is certain to come. Growth may mean that as the leader you must be the one to proactively instigate change that is long overdue. *Nānā i ke kumu* gives us memory, it gives us remembrance that healthy change keeps our sense of place the same; The strengths we have that are rooted in our sense of place will nourish and sustain us. The lesson is not to be a victim of change inflicted upon you: Be the one to instigate the change that is beneficial, the change that holds merit and promise.

Nānā i ke kumu encourages you to begin, as in a way to begin anew, feeling confident that you always have the past to anchor you, to define your roots in their cleanest and purest form, thus giving you a guarantee that you'll never stray too far off course. You can do so secure in the generosity of *Mahalo*, and the certainty of *Aloha*.

Define your essentials

You're nearing the end of my book. How do you incorporate these lessons that I've proposed to you in *Managing with Aloha*? I'm hopeful that you've already started some things, yet whether there are few or many initiatives swirling around you now, *Nānā i ke kumu* is a way to begin anew. For instance it can be the way to tie all those initiatives together for *Lōkahi*, unity and harmony, by looking to your source. What's true for you?

You can do this on your own or with your *'Ohana* by answering these questions: Why was your company started in the first place? Why did you join up? What was your passion then, and what is it now? What are those things connected to your business goals that you fervently believe in? What do you want to bring to the rest of the world?

The Alaka'i Nalu want to bring a love and respect for the ocean to the rest of the world, believing she always has valuable lessons for us. The ocean is their source; she is their truth. I want to bring nobility to the profession of management to the rest of the world. I believe that to be a manager is to touch another's life in a profound way, and managers must accept this certainty with responsibility. *Managing with Aloha* is my source, it is my truth. And I accept it as my responsibility.

What are your values? What is your *mana'o*, what do you believe in? What is the responsibility you wholeheartedly embrace and accept? What will be your gift for the world?

Nānā i ke kumu defines your essentials, your non-negotiables. I've presented to you a list of Hawaiian values that I believe to be universal ones for business as the chapters of this book; however this is not an all-inclusive list. Nor must you adopt them all. However I do maintain that you must be true to the ones you choose. To be more accurate, you must be true to those you discover within you, the ones that have rung true for you as you've read about them, the ones that keep speaking to you when the book is closed. They are *'olu'olu*, comforting in their familiarity, and pleasantly agreeable to you and to your nature. They are *Nānā i ke kumu* for you.

For Hualalai, these were our essentials at the time I was part of her *'Ohana*:

- The Vision: We will practice the art of *Ho'okipa* while we treat each other with *Aloha*, dignity, and respect.
- Being true to our Hawaiian culture. Hawai'i is our sense of place.

- Respect for the land, accepting stewardship for the land we affect.
- Delivering quality and true value to our customers.
- A focus on values-centered management principles.
- A healthy *'Ohana*, one that is an *'Ohana* in business.
- We are a community, and success comes with our self-sustenance. Success without integrity, and without a mutually thriving *'Ohana* is unacceptable.

This list will change for them; it may already be changing as I write this. I agree with all who have said that change is inevitable, and as I've said, I believe change can be healthy. However it is my personal wish for Hualalai that whereas things may be added, nothing will be dropped from this list: I see this as their statement of *Nānā i ke kumu*, the truths they are certain to find when they look to their source. They must *Mālama* them, maintain and take care of them; for thus they will take care of business and honor the expectations of the *'Ohana* they themselves created.

Your philosophy of leadership

In the coaching I do, I have often found that *Nānā i ke kumu* can turn on a light of clarity for managers who want—or need—to articulate their personal leadership philosophy. It certainly did for me. The great manager who aspires to leadership as their next mountaintop (*Kūlia i ka nuʻu*) needs an inspiring vision for those whom they will lead. *Nānā i ke kumu* teaches us to look to our personal truths as where we start from and as the essentials we must maintain if we are to lead with personal integrity. Said another way, you must be true to who you are when you lead—even when no one is looking. There cannot be any duplicity. Just thinking of the words *Nānā i ke kumu* would guarantee I did that.

For me, my source first seemed disjointed and random, thoughts like these: I need to be a role model. The opportunity to lead is an honor. The ability to lead is a gift. When I manage I have the power to touch another life daily. I want to discover all the potential I have within me to inspire others. I can be very creative as a leader. I learn best when I listen and ask questions, and when I read about the experiences of other leaders.

However as I sought to tie them together in my own leadership philosophy I came to realize they were all about managing well, and they started to look like this: *Alaka'i*—I need to be a role model. *Ho'ohanohano*—The opportunity to lead *and to manage* is an honor. *'Imi ola*—The ability to lead *or to manage* is a gift. *Ho'okipa*—When I manage I have the power to touch another life daily, *Kuleana*—I must accept responsibility for that! *Ho'ohana*—I want to discover all the potential I have within me to inspire others. *Aloha*—I can be very creative as a leader, when I manage with good intent. *'Ike loa*—I learn best when I listen and ask questions, and when I read about the experiences of other leaders.

A leader's vision—the core idea that excites and energizes—takes shape from the leadership philosophy that centers leaders and gives them focus. Their passion helps them create a picture of what their success will look like long before they get there. *Managing with Aloha* began to paint this picture for me, of how business would operate, look like and feel like if I could inspire even a single generation of people who managed with *Aloha* pervasively throughout all business enterprise. My quest for *Pono* (rightness, the next chapter) has surrounded this vision I have of a Hawaiian hospitality industry that thrives with the full support of a community who no longer feels violated and exploited by it; they are part of its *'Ohana*.

Go to the well

Hualalai had another definition for *Nānā i ke kumu* as well, mostly referred to within the Mālama Time circle when they felt that their management team was dangerously near burnout, needed to get healthier emotionally as well as physically, and needed some shot of invigoration. At those times *Nānā i ke kumu* was defined as to "return regularly to the wells of life." Managers were encouraged to return to their well, whatever it was, and *Mālama* themselves. We were willing to be vulnerable, honest enough to admit that we weren't of much use to our employees or the company if we weren't in a good place ourselves first and foremost. And the cures we needed didn't take too much creative thought: What we most needed was the permission to pursue them.

How do you "go to the well"? Think of your basic satisfiers. Feel great every time you get some exercise outdoors? Lace up your shoes and take a run. Feel better whenever your desk is cleared? Shut your office door for half a day and deal with the clutter. Love shopping? Whip out that credit card and hit the mall. Need an escape? Choose a new-release fantasy film (there's always one …) and take in a matinee. Need to be newly inspired? Sign up for a conference or leadership seminar. Feel you need to reconnect with your family? Take the day off and spend it with them. *Nānā i ke kumu.* Go to the well: As managers we need to define our range of effectiveness and keep within it.

For the sake of their sanity, managers must realize that they alone need not incur all the responsibility for infusing better health into an organization; However, they do need to be the catalyst who puts up red flags, rekindles signal fires and enlists help where it's most needed. *Nānā i ke kumu*, looking to your source, helps keep you grounded, focused and sure of yourself, your decisions, and the course to be taken. You can then be *Kākou*, speaking the language of we, and tapping into all the talent that surrounds you. You can then *Mālama*, and get help instead of stubbornly going it alone. You can then be *Alakaʻi*, being one who demonstrates leadership and initiative, leading with your good example.

Write and reflect

If you have not yet taken pause, it is time to put my book aside. You need not rush to finish its final pages, for tomorrow will be the dawning of another new day.

There is an inner wellspring inside all of us, and we will go to this inner well to get healthy, in body, mind and spirit. We find reason. We find heart. We find soul. *Nānā i ke kumu.* Go to your well first, and be emotionally healthy. Find your sense of place.

Next look to your source intellectually. Write your list of

essentials and non-negotiables. You will find strength in what you write: There is much power in written words when they are your own. It is a power that fortifies your *mana'o*, your belief. *Nānā i ke kumu* will be your words of encouragement, telling you to look inward to your source of well-being as your constant and your truth.

Nānā i ke kumu. When you look to the source you have revealed, let it inspire you. Let it energize you. You will not hesitate, and you will not falter. Your *Ho'ohana* will become crystal clear. You will understand what you must do to work with purpose—your purpose.

Nānā i ke kumu. These are words of encouragement. They are words of comforting reassurance. They recognize the validity of your *mana'o*.

Nānā i ke kumu. You will *Ho'omau* with renewed strength. You will be warmed by the *Aloha* of your own spirit. You will continue.

18

Pono

Rightness and balance
The feeling of contentment when all is good and all is right

> *Pono* is rightness and balance.
> When you are *Pono*, you have a feeling of contentment, wherein all is good and all is right.
> *Pono* teaches the attitude of positivity. Life itself excites you.
> Those who are *Pono* are optimistic and full of hope. All they see in their future is that things can only get better.
> Keep your life in balance. Do what is right.

Ah, contentment

Are you content? You may feel there is much to be done, however a feeling of contentment is possible when you feel the path ahead is one that is right for you, one where you will enjoy the journey. It may be a difficult journey, but because it's the right one, it's the best one, and you take it willingly, eagerly.

Contentment dishes up feelings of being at peace, of being calm, stress-free and tranquil. For the moment there is no striving.

The feeling and overall image of *Pono* is contentment. When you are *Pono*, all is right for you, and all you juggle in your life is in harmony and in balance. There is no inner conflict and no outside struggles that need be brought to resolution.

Mind, body and spirit

As I have been taught, the Hawaiian culture names three different things that make up the entirety of a human being. They are your *kino*, your physical body and health; your *mana'o*, your mind and beliefs; and your *'uhane*, your soul and spirit. As a value, *Pono* seeks to bring all three of these components to their best health, so they are in balance, and one is not stronger at the expense of the other. The ancient Hawaiians believed that ultimately the spirit will always be stronger, but even the *'uhane*, the soul and spirit, must be good, and it must achieve the rightness and balance of *Pono* to not be hurtful for one's physical well-being, nor overly influence one's mindfulness.

At times I have also heard of a fourth factor in the *'ōlelo* spoken and taught by other *kūpuna* (elders), and it is of *na'au*, one's gut feelings and intuition. Some will teach that the gut is the seat of one's personal wisdom, not the head: They are urging you to listen with your entire being, careful not to dismiss your own intuition too quickly. Intuition is referred to as "emotional intelligence," different from mindfulness, logic and reason.

The mind-body-spirit trilogy can be a bit overwhelming to think about, for each can be daunting in and of themselves. So let me bring you back to the word contentment, and away from self-analysis for a moment. Take notice of your staff, your peers, your leadership team and your family, and ask yourself if *Pono* and the feeling of contentment is the image you see. It should be familiar and recognizable for you. Do you notice that they:

- Have personal control of their lives, easily accepting responsibility?
- Are involved in something meaningful outside of work?
- Are committed to a goal?
- Live within their passion?
- Are healthy, and their lifestyle contributes to their health?
- Don't go it alone; they actively seek the company of others?
- Have a sense of humor, especially with their own blunders?
- Have values that nurture their soul and their spirit?
- Can openly share all these things and talk about them?

You will find that those who score high on this checklist have a great attitude about things in general. They are optimists, and very happily so, feeling very hopeful about what may lie ahead. They are realistic but involved, and engage in life as willing and active participants. They want to be right in the middle of it.

Attitude determines outcome

Thus *Pono* is all about attitude, and how attitude always comes before outcome. Good attitude, good prospects, good outcome. As a manager, I know that attitude is a word, a wish, you are very familiar with. Attitude is that seemingly intangible, frustratingly elusive thing we wish to be found safe within all of our employees, or more concisely, a *positive* attitude, and an eager and optimistic outlook.

Positive versus negative: It's an easy diagnosis when a manager evaluates the health of an employee's attitude. I have found that the most difficult employees I've ever had to manage were pessimistic, those who looked for all the reasons why not, their speech peppered by "yeah but" and "it's not possible." I came to understand that *'Imi ola* was not an inherent value for them, for *'Imi ola* is the value that places the ability to achieve your purpose in your own hands, giving you the clear understanding that you have the power to create your own destiny. In contrast, when you are pessimistic, you more easily fall prey to being a victim of circumstance and happenstance. Personally, I believe that everyone possesses so much more talent and promise than that, they have capacity begging to be filled with more abundance.

Negative employees need a new journey, for happiness is not the destination of a negative outlook. Once I was sure their unhappiness came from inside them and not from other variables I could fix, as their manager, I would normally seek to redirect or recast them. I'd do whatever I could to help them find another position where they would *Ho'ohana*, and work with the pleasurable excitement of purpose-full intention, whether it was inside my own department or elsewhere. Remember, when you manage with *Aloha* you have the belief that people are intrinsically good; what you seek to influence is their behavior.

Pono prepares us for giving

The thinking within *Pono* is that once you are in balance, and all is right with you, one has to give back to others. Thoughts go toward the *'Ohana*, the family, and it is more natural to speak of *Kākou*, in the language of we; you prepare to share your *Aloha*, giving to others unconditionally. And if there is *Pono* within you, whatever you give to others will also be *Pono*; it will be a good and healthy gift. I am perhaps the best example of this: For a long time I wanted so much to share the messages in this book, but it could not be written until I felt *Pono* within myself first. In addition, I wanted to arrive at what was truly right, and any self-righteousness I felt wouldn't necessarily help me.

There are those in Hawaii who define *Pono* as righteousness, and even the motto of our state, *Ua mau ke ea o ka 'āina i ke pono*, is translated as meaning "the life of the land is perpetuated in righteousness." However as a value, think of *Pono* as rightness versus righteousness. *Pono* is goodness, wellness, correctness, and balance. It is not self-righteousness, but self-consciousness, and the keen balance of all those forces that bring you contentment in your life. My experience has been that self-righteous people are not content, for they are resentful or hesitant when it comes to giving their *Aloha* to others: Their *'uhane*, (their spirit) is not *Pono*.

Pono brings rightness to success

In today's common use in Hawaii, *Pono* is a word often associated with being successful. It is significant to notice that although the widely accepted Hawaiian word for success is *holomua*, *Pono* is the word chosen when complete success is acknowledged. To say "we succeeded" one would say *"Ua pono kaua."* To say "we succeeded with our work" one would say *"Ua pono ka kaua hana."* *Holomua* becomes the word of choice for improvement or progress. Complete success is not true success unless it is *Pono*; there is rightness inherent in your achievement, and it has not come at too high a price.

Pono helps us look at the big picture: what is right for a company's present viewpoint may not be right in the grand scheme of things. *Pono* ensures that you at least ask yourself the question. For instance, the long-time struggle in Hawaii's tourism industry is that the success of those within the industry comes at too great an expense for the community as a whole— that it is too exploitive. Retail giant Wal-Mart has been swimming in the controversy that they perhaps can be held singularly responsible for the downfall of independent retailers throughout the country; it is also widely said that the purchasing clout their success has brought them bites the hand that feeds—their wholesalers brace for impending doom should they fall from favor. These are ethical dilemmas without easy answers, but having *Pono* as a value we invest in will ensure that we do not fail to deliberate them at all. At times we can influence more than we realize, moving closer toward that which is right than we otherwise may have done.

Preparing for change

Being *Pono* becomes our best preparedness for the certainty of change. When people are secure in who they are, they do what they do best. They have that positive and optimistic attitude that comes from doing what they love to do in the best way possible. Outside forces do not shake them up too badly. They are centered, they are balanced, and so they are resilient and strong. They confidently know that they can and will survive whatever change may come, and whatever effects that change may bring. *Pono* gives us the understanding that outside pressures will not defeat us as quickly and decisively as inner pressure will.

In a *Mālama* session I'd once conducted with a cross-section of line employees, one of our sports apprentices offered, "To be *Pono* you need to conquer yourself," and I still think this is one of the best insights I've ever heard about it. *Pono* seeks understanding and acceptance for you from you, and when we ourselves are *Pono* the ones around us find we are more positive and more open to meaningful worth-filled relationships.

You are more approachable; your demeanor with others is good because you are coming from a good place where you draw strength from within yourself (*Nānā i ke kumu*).

Finding Pono, finding right

The *Mālama* session I just mentioned came at a time we were on an all-resort campaign to teach and promote three different values to our employees. They were *Lōkahi*, cooperation and unity; *Kākou*, the language of we; and *Pono*, keeping your life in balance and doing what's right. We printed a trio of caps with these values printed on them, *Lōkahi* on a navy one, denim blue for *Kākou*, and a light khaki one for *Pono*, and at the end of the *Mālama* session everyone could choose a cap to take with them. They were to choose the value that meant the most to them, and we also hoped they would explain the value to the guests and residents who asked them what the word meant: Wearing these caps would be the one accepted break from normal uniform.

As did the other managers who taught and shared these sessions, I was able to get one of each cap before the campaign was over. I wore *Lōkahi* and *Kākou* pretty often, but I could not in good conscience wear the cap that was emblazoned with *Pono* and walk my talk. When training the trainers for these sessions, we had been telling our managers these things:

- The reason for our success is deeply imbedded in the belief in our company values.
- If you have never yet talked to your own employees about the values about our culture, start with *Pono*.
- Understand this: To teach it, you must demonstrate it. The teacher must have credibility. The teacher must have integrity.

Finding *Pono* at work, finding rightness, had always been my goal being a manager in Hawaii in my early years, and happily most new managers of our present generation don't encounter the same ethical struggle. When I first entered the hospitality industry in Hawaii, it wasn't thought of as an honorable business to be associated with. The island community largely felt they were held hostage to it: That's where our

219

economy made the money needed, but that money was thought of as soiled and unethically gained. Those of Hawaiian blood and many *kama'āina* (native born, not necessarily of Hawaiian blood) felt the culture was being exploited. *Ho'okipa* had become a forgotten value: Visitors and tourists were not welcomed, and it was believed that those of us who served them were less than honorable too.

Sadly, this attitude still exists, however, I personally don't feel it is as pervasive and widespread. Tourism is now better accepted as vital to the economic survival of the islands and working within the industry is largely without the ethical stigma I had experienced as an employee. However, make no mistake about it: The expectation that we raise the bar on our ethics will always be levelly focused on management, on leadership and on ownership. Today, being a manager here can be the right thing to do, and it can be a noble thing in the hands of the right person. In managing with *Aloha* we accept the challenge, confident we can effect any positive change needed. The leaders of a business must accept their responsibility as stewards of our sense of place, acting as patriarchs of the *'Ohana* in business, in firms responsive to community and cultural concerns.

So let's go back to the question, asking it for all of us today: Is it truly *Pono*, good and right, to work within an industry that exploits our culture? The obvious answer of course, is no. The more accurate challenge is to ascertain the differences between an exploitive business enterprise, and one which is culturally respectful, having something that I now think of as "a Hawaiian sensibility for the way we work." And why limit the discussion to the hospitality industry? For a business that possesses this "Hawaiian sensibility" for the way they work is one that incorporates *Aloha* and the other Hawaiian values into their business environment. The best way to be culturally sensitive is to practice the values of the culture, is it not?

Personally, I'd push the envelope on this and take it a step further: To be *Pono* you work in a way that *shares* our native culture and celebrates it.

I'm fully aware that not everyone will agree with me.

There will be those who ask why we should share it at all. As one who was born and raised here, one who has lived my entire working career here, one spanning over 30 years time, the answer is as clear as it is simple: Because that is who we are. Sharing it is the way we express our gratefulness that we have a rich and unique culture to share at all—sharing it is living the value of *Mahalo*. *Aloha* cannot be separated from our culture, for *Aloha* defines it in all its warmth and graciousness. Living our *Aloha* for our fellow man is the right thing to do, and thus it is *Pono*.

To be Mea Hoʻokipa and in any service business here, we have to be willing to share our culture, giving openly and freely. Keeping what we have for ourselves or a select few may protect it somewhat in the short term, but only sharing it will perpetuate it for generations to come—and surely, perpetuating our culture so it will continue is *Pono*. In the process of doing so we will be better people, for what we share is that which is good: We share our values.

Make it personal

What I found to be true in my own journey was that I didn't understand the inner and personal workings of *Pono*. I would have found it in my industry of choice much faster if I'd better understood this: *Pono* would start and end with me, and within me, *kino* (body), *manaʻo* (mind) and *ʻuhane* (spirit). I could effect whatever change was needed by starting with my own thinking. Among other things, *Haʻahaʻa* had taught me that humility opened more doors to consequential learning for me. *Nānā i ke kumu* grounded me.

So recently, my own personal *Pono* test has been a relatively simple one. When I am faced with a decision to make, especially those difficult ones, and I want it to be the right one, I silently ask myself this question: Will I be able to fall asleep tonight? I give myself credit for ultimately being able to discern the right thing to do. If I feel I may be restless, tossing and turning to get comfortable, or staring at the ceiling in the darkness, I know I have to take more time to seek options before taking action. If the choice is a good one, and my actions have been taken with integrity, being true to my own sense of rightness, I will sleep easily, and sleep well. *Kino:* My body will deliver sleep easily and comfortably. *Manaʻo:* My mind will be at rest, for I have been true to what I believe. *ʻUhane:* My spirit will assure I sleep soundly, preparing me for the next day to come.

Pono brings balance

The lesson on achieving balance proved to be a far more difficult one for me. For so many years I was a person consumed by work. I loved it, and this actually made it worse. I'd convinced myself that I was a far better person, wife and mother, because work satisfied a need in me that couldn't be satisfied in any other way. I was right, and I was wrong. I was right in that the value of *Hoʻohana,* to work with intent and purpose, is a vital driver for me, and it cannot be quieted or denied: It has to be satisfied. I was wrong in that it wasn't complete: It neglected to embrace all my needs, not just the ones connected to work. Taken alone, *Hoʻohana* even with the best of intentions didn't make me a better person. Worse, it kept me off-balance.

After an early promotion in my career, it was my dad who had first told me, "Congratulations, I'm proud of you." Then he added, "Just remember that no job has the ability to love you back." He'd say it again with my next promotion, and again with each one to come. He was effective in his diligence: I'd hear his words in my head several times throughout my work life, and promotions ceased to be the necessary catalyst. Still, I'd rationalize it in some way, or worse, I'd actually tell myself, well, for now the way things are is okay. And when you are young, you don't completely understand how important love is in your life, and how empty time without it can be.

Ironically, I reached the *Pono* I wanted by saying goodbye to the place that had lured me with the promise of it. I found my balance, and I found the *Pono* I'd dreamed of on the day I said goodbye to Hualalai. She'd become an employer that demanded far too much time from me. It was time for more *Aloha* given to my family, and the people who loved me back.

It was time for balance with a change of course in my *Ho'ohana*, by choosing more focused, deliberate work. I had found I needed contentment in all circumstances, and for me, it was *Ka lā hiki ola*, the dawning of a new day.

I've never been happier, and I wear my *Pono* cap all the time.

I have the feeling of contentment one gets when all is good, and all feels right.

I find I have much in me to be given, and my own needs are few.

Life itself excites me. I am optimistic and full of hope. All I see in the future is that things can only get better.

This is my wish for you, for *Pono*.

Find Pono, be Content

Pono is rightness and balance.

When you are *Pono*, you have a feeling of contentment, wherein all is good and all is right.

Pono teaches the attitude of positivity. Life itself excites you.

Those who are *Pono* are optimistic and full of hope. All they see in their future is that things can only get better.

Keep your life in balance. Do what is right.

Epilogue

Ka lā hiki ola
The dawning of a new day

Ka lā hiki ola is a Hawaiian phrase I had only learned of in my recent years living on the Big Island of Hawai'i. I've come to think of it as another Hawaiian value, even though Hualalai is the only place I know of that considers it to be one. *Ka lā hiki ola* translates to the dawning of a new day.

With every sunrise we get another shot, another fresh chance to be all we can possibly be. The sun may rise over some change that has occurred, but it still comes with a fresh new start, and the gift of more time. Therefore for me, *Ka lā hiki ola* has been a value of incredible promise and hope.

The first time I went out on the ocean with the Alaka'i Nalu, I was in seat five of their first and oldest canoe, the seat where the steersman could best keep an eye on me. The canoe was named *Ka lā hiki ola*, the dawning of a new day. My *kaona* (hidden meaning) in that day was that she represented my hope in all we would do together as an *'Ohana* bonded by our *Aloha* and *Mālama* for each other. When I climbed into that canoe, I was making a deliberate choice as to what I was going to give my attentions to. That day figured prominently in my own search for *Pono*, and it would be a turning point in my relationship with the Alaka'i Nalu: They didn't believe I could understand them completely until I had been out on the ocean with them.

Ka lā hiki ola encourages us to make *Pono* today. Let go of yesterday. Give yourself hope for tomorrow. Live again, and live better – start a new chapter going forward. However, knowing that tomorrow will always bring a new day, secure in the certainty of it, I encourage you to live in every moment, and have the attitude that *today* is it. Enjoy your present; relish the now. You will feel more alive. Trust in your instincts, trust in what you know and have learned, and trust in the person you are. Live the day to the fullest, and live it as *your* day.

Kēia manawa is a Hawaiian concept that lives within *Ka lā hiki ola*. It means right now. This is the time. This is it. The here and now. There was a fitting football analogy that Kahu Billy Mitchell would share with us when he felt we needed more trust in ourselves and in the positive certainty of *Ka lā hiki ola*, the dawning of a new day. He'd point out that once the game is in play, it becomes time for everything you've practiced for. It's time to perform. Once the quarterback calls the play in the huddle and you take your place on the line, you had better be ready to go, to perform magnificently. Kahu would open his arms wide and bellow out at us: "The blackboard is not coming on the field!" In the quiet seconds that followed and he leveled his gaze at each of us, we knew the thought of his unspoken words were, so what are you waiting for?

And you don't focus on the obstacles. If you are the running back that gets the handoff you set your sights on the goal line, not on the monster tacklers trying to stop you; you look for an opening. Who they are doesn't matter; who you are does—you have possession of the ball! Everything starts and ends with you. *'Imi ola*: you have choices, and you will be the one to create your own destiny and make it happen. You will be the one to cross the goal line or find you've fallen short.

Ka lā hiki ola places a magic carpet of creativity at the threshold of our new day. Creativity usually finds her opportunity when all the basics are met, but we are still seeking answers, or perhaps need a new energy source to propel us forward. Sometimes it seems that we are the most creative when faced with the new, such as a new business or a new job, because you have to be creative to bring everything together in the way that works well, like the pieces of a puzzle with inter-

changeable parts. But then we find a rhythm and we start plug-
ging away, day in, and day out. Luckily *Ka lā hiki ola* shakes us
out of our reserve and encourages us to be creative again,
asking ourselves how we can live in the present and take
advantage of this dawning of a new day that's been gifted to us
with more joy.

And fortunately, the highest level creativity is inspired by
the new and unknown. With creativity, you can create several
new options to choose from, uncover previously unseen
potential and gain the freedom that comes from having
choices. The excitement you have for the choice that most
appeals to you serves to create new energy, and this new
energy leads to new commitment.

As liberating and hopeful as it can be, it takes an inner
confidence to respond to the challenge set forth by *Ka lā hiki
ola*—to not need that blackboard on the field with you.
Remember the lesson of *Pono*: When people are secure in who
they are, when the needs of their *kino* (physical needs), *mana'o*
(mental needs) and *'uhane* (spiritual needs) are in balance,
outside forces such as change and growth do not shake them up
as badly. When we are calm, ready and at ease, we also find
that others respond to us better—our contentment is very
appealing to them, and they hope it's contagious.

When we are *Pono*, *Ka lā hiki ola* sets the stage for us to
welcome growth. Is there a Phase II or Phase III to your business? Decide on how you'll set the tone for it, and allow the
picture you paint for your staff to color the sunrise in your
dawning of a new day. Start by asking them to help you do
what you do best: Don't dilute your present efforts; reflect on
what you are truly known for and what it is that brought you
to *Pono*. What were those essentials you defined for your
company when we spoke of *Nānā i ke kumu* so you can look to
your own sources of inspiration? How can you raise the bar, or
grab the opportunity to reinvent what may have been started
in Phase I, but can be better?

You have come to the final pages of my book. I wanted to
leave you with *Ka lā hiki ola* because it shares the theme of
going forward with hope, optimism, and confidence. With the
lessons of *Ho'omau* and perseverance in your backpack for the

journey, you also understand that you cannot get complacent; you need to work at it. With *Kūlia i ka nu'u* you are prepared to climb higher than you did before. You must be aware of the sounds of the new morning you are in, allowing it to open your mind and anticipate what lies ahead. You can be excited, rally all your energies to go forward, and thrive in the promise of what's to come. *Ka lā hiki ola*, it is the dawning of a new day; You can live with hope.

My native Hawaiian culture is my product. It's the product that I've shared with you in these collected chapters, my talk story of the values that have made me so hopeful, optimistic and confident about the universal promise of good management. To be true to myself as a saleswoman of this product—and in the service business, as Mea Ho'okipa—I need to be a practitioner of the Hawaiian culture that has made me who I am. I want to promote it, yet portray it accurately: I believe there is such richness here that there is no need to pretend we are something we are not. We just have to get better at living it, and we can: That is my *mana'o*, my deeply held belief.

I have written this book for my fellow managers in the islands. *Nānā i ke kumu*, let us look to our source: In Hawaii we can present our values authentically, accurately and with genuine sincerity. To be Mea Ho'okipa and in the service business here, we have to be willing to share our culture, giving openly and freely. Keeping what we have for ourselves or a select few may protect it somewhat in the short term, but only sharing it will perpetuate it for generations to come: It is right, it is *Pono*. In the process of doing so, we will be better managers, better people. As a community we choose *'Ohana* as the form of our business associations because it is the form in which we naturally relate to each other, the form in which we aspire to treat each other, with *Aloha*, and with *Ho'ohanohano*, with dignity and respect. Let us keep *'Ohana* and the bonds of a strong family inclusive—*Kākou*, for all of us. Not only will we be *Pono* within ourselves, we will achieve *Lōkahi* (harmony and unity) with all we touch.

Hawaii, we are small, but we are mighty! I have also written this book with a strong hope we can inspire the

227

manager that does not live and work here in the islands with us. For all managers, no matter who they are and where they are, no matter what business they are in, touch the lives of others in profound ways. All managers must accept this responsibility with *Mālama*, with caring. They must serve, honor, and protect those they manage and those they lead within the arms of *Aloha*, unconditional love.

You need not remember my Hawaiian words to the point of pronouncing them with perfection. As I have maintained throughout this book, these values are universal, and you may have your own words for them. However select the word or phrase: Be clear when you share them and teach them, and instill the language of values-centered management into your own culture. When you look to my values as a source of inspiration, start with the ones that are *'olu'olu* for you, recognizable, pleasant and agreeable to your nature, for you must live them yourself first and foremost. They will call out to you when you decide you will listen. Use them, practice them, teach them, and they will open the door to the other practices of good management you will discover you must learn. Allow *Ha'aha'a*, the attitude of humility to help you.

I believe in you. You can be a great manager: one who manages with *Aloha*. The world needs you.

Whoever you are, where ever you are, whatever business you are in, *Imua!* (go forward) and start today. I place my hope and my *Aloha* in you.

Ka lā hiki ola. It is the dawning of a new day, and it's your day. Make it your best one ever.

Recommended Reading

'Ike loa: Seek knowledge
New knowledge is the food for mind, heart, and soul

> I have an ongoing love affair with the written word, and these are some of the books I consider my treasures, for in some way they have positively influenced my *mana'o*, my thoughts and beliefs. These are all books to be shared, given to another with your *Aloha* after you have first read them yourself.

Kū Kanaka, Stand Tall, A Search for Hawaiian Values
George Hu'eu Sanford Kanahele, University of Hawaii Press, Honolulu, Hawaii 1986.

I first read Dr. Kanahele's book after I had attended his classes on incorporating *Aloha* and *Ho'okipa* into hotel management in Hawaii. Having had this face time with him, I was a reader completely in awe of his work, accepting everything he wrote as fact. I purposely did not return to *Kū Kanaka* for reference as I wrote *Managing with Aloha*, for I wanted my own book to be based on the learning of my personal experiences. Now that my book is complete, I am currently in a second reading of *Kū Kanaka*, and I am finding comforting affirmation within it. I am also in a renewed admiration for Dr. Kanahele, much more cognizant of the monumental time and effort he had put into this work. His book belongs in the hands of every person who feels the need for insight into the Hawaiian culture.

Nānā i ke kumu, Look to the Source, Volume I and Volume II, Mary Kawena Pukui, E.W. Haertig, M.D. and Catherine A. Lee, Queen Liliʻuokalani Children's Center, Honolulu, Hawaii 1972.

Along with Dr. Kanahele's *Kū Kanaka*, these two volumes would be my recommendations for the reader interested in more fully examining Hawaiian values from the past to present. As explained on their back covers, "In the early 1970's, workers at the Queen Liliʻuokalani Children's Center, to better understand and meet the needs of the Hawaiian families they served, began to research authentic Hawaiian culture." The interviews they reveal as data sources are at once entertaining and enlightening, making these books fascinating reads.

Voices of Wisdom, Hawaiian Elders Speak
M.J. Harden, Aka Press, Kula, Hawaii 1999.

I absolutely love this book. I have encouraged you to seek out your elders, our *kūpuna*, and get them to tell you their stories, and that is exactly what Harden has done in her book. As described on the book itself, "*Voices of Wisdom* is a book that explains Hawaiian culture through the lives of 24 Hawaiians, each an expert in some facet of Hawaiiana. It is not just the stories and personalities of these 24 that are featured; through each individual we learn about a discipline, talent or skill valued in Hawaiian culture. These 24 are leaders of the cultural renaissance that awakened the Hawaiian spirit in recent decades. These are people who have led lives that matter, and what matters most to them is to keep lit the flame of a culture that nearly died." After you meet these elders I can guarantee you will be scouring local bookshelves for more of what they have said or have written.

Harden's writing is exceptional in the way she honors these *kūpuna* and celebrates their *manaʻo*, and the photography done by Steve Brinkman delivers a familiarity and warmth that touches heart and soul: You feel you are with them.

First, Break all the Rules, What the World's Greatest Managers
do Differently
Marcus Buckingham and Curt Coffman, Simon & Schuster,
New York, New York 1999.

Once in awhile, a book will come along that you sense
was written just for you, it would be that important to you.
This was that book for me. I've always been someone drawn to
the strengths of other people, and I've always believed it was a
good thing to "value the differences" inherent in the sea of
humanity, but not until I devoured this book did I put these
two beliefs together into my own day-to-day managing. When
I did, everything seemed to change for me, and change for the
better. I think of this book as my crucible. After I completed it,
I was an addict who desperately needed my next fix; it was
torture waiting for their next book to be published.

In *Managing with Aloha*, I have followed the lead of
Buckingham & Coffman in making a distinction between "good"
managers and "great" managers: what they taught me in their
book has been internalized as my assumptions. For those of you
who may already be Gallup disciples, I bare my soul to you as
more insight into my writing: my own strengths were revealed as
"Deliberative, Focus, Maximizer, Responsibility, and Achiever."

Soar with your Strengths
Donald O. Clifton and Paula Nelson, Dell Publishing, New
York, New York 1996.

I discovered *Soar with your Strengths* on the website of the
Gallup Organization while deep into my obsession with *First
Break all the Rules*. I now think of this easy-to-read paperback
as the best option for managers who are not big readers and
need to ease back into the read-to-learn habit with a book that
will get them excited again.

This book put RORI (Return on Relationship Investment)
into my vocabulary and into my coaching arsenal, with its "Nine
Principles for Managing Relationships." Management is about
people, and a manager's strengths are best built within the relationships they have with others.

Love is the Killer App, How to Win Business and Influence Friends
Tim Sanders, Crown Business New York, New York, New York 2002.

This book is *the* Valentine's Day gift for every single business person you know.

Tim Sanders has a great title: Chief Solutions Officer at Yahoo! This is the "chief solution" his book proposes: If you "want to know how you can maintain and add to your value during these rapidly changing times ... become a lovecat—a nice, smart person who succeeds in business and in life." He explains that you do this by sharing your intangibles: your knowledge, your network, and your compassion. I've long visualized managers as depositories for intellectual capital, and Sanders added the concept of "value currency" to the picture for me—and to my coaching vocabulary.

This book is filled with good stuff, but in particular I loved his approach to sharing the knowledge gained from reading (think *'Ike loa*). Sanders showed me I was a rookie when it came to annotating books, and he turned me into a hardcover junkie. I don't want to detract your attention from the *Aloha* message this book is essentially about; However, the unexpected bonus one gets from *Love is the Killer App* is how to lovingly read and relish books. You will understand why a book is the very best gift you can give, and you will never read them the same way again yourself.

Raving Fans, A Revolutionary Approach to Customer Service
Ken Blanchard and Sheldon Bowles, William Morrow and Company, Inc., New York, New York 1993.

I was introduced to Ken Blanchard when he published his ground-breaking book *The One Minute Manager* with Spencer Johnson in 1982. He has since become a very prolific co-author, mentoring a stable of writing partners as he takes on both management and leadership. Most of his books can be read in less than a day's time, and as a management coach I find that Blanchard supplies me with marvelous textbooks that teach in the simple story form proven to be so effective.

Raving Fans is my top pick of Blanchard's books, for it takes on mediocrity in customer service: "Your customers are only satisfied because their expectations are so low and because no one else is doing any better." I love the clarity the book offers managers on systems versus rules, "Systems give you a floor, not a ceiling."

The One Minute Manager Meets the Monkey
Kenneth Blanchard, William Oncken, Jr. and Hal Burrows, William Morrow and Company, Inc., New York, New York 1989.

This is my second choice from those offered by Ken Blanchard, because I continue to see how challenging effective delegation is for managers. This book is touted as one of the "most liberating books in the extraordinary One Minute Manager Library" for it claims that "one simple idea can set you free: Don't take on a problem if it isn't yours!" I agree, and I've never heard it said better than within the pages of this book.

All managers struggle with something that sounds deceptively straightforward: figuring out who does what and not doing it themselves so they can do what they should be doing in the first place. After I read this book I bought three dozen copies and passed them out to first-time supervisors and their managers. Within days I was delighted to find that monkey mania ran rampant in our language. This is the connection this book has with *Managing with Aloha:* "The more you get rid of your people's monkeys, the more time you have for your people."

The Leadership Engine, How Winning Companies Build Leaders at Every Level
Noel M. Tichy with Eli Cohen, Harper Business Publications, New York, New York 2001.

This was the first book that I "read" on audio cassette, and Tichy hooked me in quickly with his own story-telling style. I listened to those cassettes over and over and still ended up buying his book, for I wanted to be sure that I didn't miss anything.

The book explores the differences between companies that win and those that lose, and essentially this is Tichy's core theory: "Winning companies win because they have good leaders who nurture the development of other leaders at all levels of the organization." Tichy feels that " ... leaders embody their teachable points of view in living stories," because stories "will touch peoples' emotion as well as [their] intellect." He proves his point with the stories he relays of leaders such as Jack Welch of General Electric, Andy Grove of Intel and Roger Enrico of PepsiCo, serving to make the book a bonanza of insider-flavored insight and entertainment.

If a company's success is to be perpetuated, the winning leaders of that company must continually be grooming their successors and the next generation of leaders they will need to carry them forward: It is a strategy for Ho'omau at its finest. Values are part of a four-dimensional formula Tichy presents (he discusses Ideas, Values, Energy, and Edge), and he asserts that having them is not enough—what sets winning companies apart is how vigorously their values are applied to what they do. I heartily concur.

The Little Book of Business Wisdom, Rules of Success from more than 50 Business Legends
Peter Krass, John Wiley & Sons, Inc., New York and Canada 2001.

Peter Krass has some hefty and impressive books to his credit, but what I like best about this one (note the word *"Little"* in the title: He has another out with the same publisher that is larger) is that it's just 5½ by 8 inches in hardcover and fits well in most of my handbags. This is my handy-dandy quick-reading pick-up when I need instant inspiration but not all the answers: This book makes me think for myself, grab a pen, write like mad, and then think some more. I can read the same passages over and over, and find some gem I somehow missed before. Those who are quotation collectors will love it.

As the title promises, Krass "brings together the speeches and writings of more than 50 business giants and presents their ideas and management secrets in their own words." Most business students will recognize the names of those he profiles, however the introductory paragraphs written by Krass telling us exactly who they are and what they're known for are exceptional in and of themselves. Like *Voices of Wisdom*, the pearls we are given in this book serve as quick reference but entice us to search for more from those we feel truly have "spoken" to us.

Living the 7 Habits, The Courage to Change
Stephen R. Covey, Simon & Schuster, New York, New York 2000.

I was very fortunate to have The Ritz-Carlton Hotel Company enroll me in a week-long leadership class on Stephen Covey's first book, *The 7 Habits of Highly Effective People* in its first year of publication. At that time we adopted his philosophy on a corporate level, lock stock and barrel, and terms like "circle of influence," "seek first to understand," and "think win-win" became part of my working vocabulary before I finished reading any of his books. I have counseled dozens of employees with the simple iceberg drawing he did on a flipchart in one of those classes: He called one's personality the part of the iceberg above the water line. The part below the water which you can't see is much more massive, and keeps the entire iceberg afloat, and that part he called one's character. His point was that your character is what you always have when no one is looking.

Covey has been recognized as one of *Time* magazine's 25 most influential Americans, an accolade I can wholeheartedly concur with, for in my opinion he shaped the thinking of the business leaders of our generation. With his 7th Habit on "Sharpen the Saw," he gave managers everywhere the permission to work fewer hours and improve both the quality of their lives *and* their effectiveness at work. *Living the 7 Habits* reveals the depth of influence Covey has had on us: I chose it for my listing of recommendations because this particular book is one that will speak to you even if you have never read any of his other books, and it helps you translate teaching into practice.

Hawaiian society—our culture, our heritage, our tradition—has undergone dramatic change just within my short lifetime. Covey's quote on the back cover was the seed planted in my thinking in regard to universal principles that withstand time, before my cultural training with Dr. Kanahele and my focus on Hawaiian values in particular. His quote: *"To live with change, to optimize change, you need principles that don't change."*

Living the 7 Habits also represents the kind of book I now dream of writing, now that *Managing with Aloha* has been written. However, that largely will depend on you, and if you discover you can manage with *Aloha* too.

'Ike loa, enjoy your reading.

Acknowledgments

Mahalo. Thank you, as a way of living.

With *Mahalo* we give thanks for every element that enriches our lives by living in thankfulness for them. We relish them. We celebrate them joyously.

Mahalo gives us an attitude of gratitude and the pleasure of awe and wonder.

Say "thank you" often.

This is my Mahalo

Managing with Aloha represents a career in management that has been touched in very meaningful ways by others for more than 30 years. I have been greatly blessed to explore my own belief and conviction, my *mana'o*, within the beauty of so many personal relationships in Hawaii's hospitality industry, and I will forever be grateful to the employees who were the bountiful gifts of my management assignments, awakening within me my passion for the art of management. I cannot name all of you here, however you know who you are, and I am deeply grateful to you, *Mahalo nui loa.*

The names that must be recognized here for the ultimate in their generosity, as I have told of in their stories, are those of my Alaka'i Nalu and Ho'okele. Aaron, Daniel, Ed, Ekolu, Ikaika, Janelle, Jerome, Lily, Mahea, Matt, Puaita, Rick, and Sam, you have my *Aloha* and you will be my *'Ohana*— always. You willingly became my living laboratory for

237

Managing with Aloha and gave me your complete trust, and this book could not have been written without all you had taught me, and without your faith in me. You brought me to *Pono*, and I love you.

Toni Howard, I believe there was a place in our Alaka'i Nalu 'Ohana that was meant for you; No one else could have been there in your stead. Because of the person you are, I am certain you will always honor it with *Mālama*. Thank you for being my friend and my comfort throughout the writing of *Managing with Aloha*. Miss Di, Barbara and Violet, I hope we have all made you proud; I could *Ho'omau* because of what you had started, and what you all so unselfishly gave to the Alaka'i Nalu before me.

There is no life without the loving warmth given to that life by family, and I would not have grown to be who I am, capable of the learning that has blessed my life, without my family. Kerwin, Ashley and Zach, you give me so much; I am ready to greet each new day of my life with growing degrees of bravery because of you. You give me the hope and promise of *Ka lā hiki ola*. Marmee and Dad, Jay, Curt, Jeff and Becca there are no words to fully explain what you mean to me. Were it not for all of you, I would be incapable of loving others. Paul, you exemplify what unselfish means, you teach all of us what *Kākou* is when it is unconditional. I am so happy you came to be part of our 'Ohana.

There is strong *mana* (divine power) on the Big Island and I believe that *mana* made it part of my destiny to meet people there who would be incredible teachers for me. Sam Ainslie, I often think you started a new life for me, and I cannot thank you enough. When it comes to sense of place, you are my hero and my mentor, and I am so grateful that you call Hawai'i home. David Chai, I am certain that I did not fully understand *Aloha 'āina* and *Ha'aha'a* until I met you and had the honor of working with you. The depth of your *'Ike loa* humbles me, and you are truly Mea Ho'okipa. Kahu Billy Mitchell, you are an amazingly daring and honest man, willing to speak of what you believe no matter what; both your bravery and your insight inspired me. Thank you for sharing your Hawaiian values with me. All of you challenged me to think *palena 'ole*, without limits, and without boundaries. Because of you I was a local girl bold enough to believe I could explore Hawaiian thought with trust in the *'Ōlelo* shared with me and with the *Aloha* of good intent. Gentlemen, you are my *Kūpuna*.

With so much to learn, I needed friends who would listen to me, and would *Mālama* me at times in ways that my own family could not, for my world of work could become foreign to them. Doreen De Silva and Christine Bean, I think of you both as gifts the Lord decided to give me to keep me reasonable, to keep me sane and to keep me human. *Mahalo* for your love and for your complete honesty with me. Please know I will always be here for you.

In the writing of *Managing with Aloha*, I was to set sail on waters previously unknown to me; it takes so much to publish a book! For this final product you have in your hands, I have so much appreciation for Roger Jellinek and Eden-Lee Murray; you both give of your knowledge so freely, and with such *Aloha*. I could not ask for better steersmen in my canoe. Jocelyn Fujii and Tony McCafferty, thank you for your encouragement— Tony I have so much admiration for you! You are a true friend. And *Mahalo nui loa* to my wonderful crew of proof-readers, taking this journey with me draft after draft after draft: Becca, Curt, Diana, Doreen, Erin, Jeff, Jim, Toni and Tony, you are terrific paddlers!

Imua!

Glossary of Hawaiian Words & Phrases

This glossary was compiled so the reader could have quick alphabetical reference to Hawaiian words and phrases used throughout the book. As it was written, I would continually refer to the *Hawaiian Dictionary, Revised and Enlarged Edition* by Mary Kawena Pukui and Samuel H. Elbert (University of Hawaii Press, Honolulu, Hawaii 1986 edition) to verify the meanings I was familiar with. I believe the Pukui Elbert dictionary, for years considered "the definitive and authoritative work on the Hawaiian language" belongs in the library of every student of the Hawaiian culture. A second recommendation would be *'Ōlelo No'eau, Hawaiian Proverbs & Poetical Sayings*, also by Mary Kawena Pukui (Bishop Museum Press, Honolulu, Hawaii 1983), a wonderful showcase of the beauty and *kaona* (hidden meaning) of the Hawaiian language.

Ahupua'a
A land division that normally extended from the uplands to the sea.

'Āina
Land, earth.

Alaka'i
Leadership. Lead with initiative, and with your good example. You shall be the guide for others when you have gained their trust and respect. Literally a leader or a guide.

Alaka'i ka 'ike
Guides of learning, teachers.

Aloha
The value of unconditional love. The outpouring and receiving of the spirit. Love, affection, compassion, mercy, empathy, kindness.

Aloha 'āina
A very old concept in Hawaii meaning love of the land, and considered to include the whole of our environment, i.e. land, ocean, atmosphere. Also used for the love of one's country and patriotism.

Ama
The outrigger floater of a Hawaiian outrigger canoe.

E komo mai
"Come with me."

'Eleu
Alert.

Ha'aha'a
Humility. Be humble, be modest, and open your thoughts.

Ha'aheo
The more positive character of pride, as in pride for the accomplishments of others. Unselfish pride.

Hālāwai
A meeting.

Hana
Work.

Hapa
A portion, part or fragment of something.

Hāpai
As a verb: to carry or bear, to lift, hold up and support.

Hāpai ka pōhaku aka mai hāpai ke kaumaha
A saying attributed the King Kamehameha meaning lift the rock, but not the weight, and not the burden.

Hoe
Paddle, as those used in the Hawaiian outrigger canoe.

Holomua
Improvement or progress.

Ho'o
Not a word on its own, but a prefix that brings active causation and transition to the base word that follows it.

Ho'ohana
Working with intent and with purpose.

241

Ho'ohanohano

Honor the dignity of others. Conduct yourself with distinction, and cultivate respectfulness.

Ho'ohiki

Keeping promises.

Ho'okano

Negative pride: being haughty and full of conceit and arrogance. Having disdain of others, insolent, vain.

Ho'okipa

Hospitality. Welcome guests and strangers with unconditional Aloha. To entertain, and to treat hospitably.

Ho'olaule'a

Celebration. At the Hualalai Resort it was the name given to the annual 'Ohana picnic.

Ho'olōkahi

To bring about unity, to make things peaceful and harmonious.

Ho'omau

Perseverance. To continue, to perpetuate. Never give up. To persist, to renew, to cause to last. The root word *mau* means always, steady, constant and unceasing.

Ho'oponopono

An open discussion process in the Hawaiian culture that deals with problems and unpleasantness, seeking to make things right.

Ho'owaiwai

To enrich, to bring prosperity.

Hualalai

The name of a resort development on Kona's Gold Coast, on the Big Island of Hawai'i. Also the name of the mountain whose summit marks the highest point of the *ahupua'a* (land division) of Ka'ūpūlehu (place name).

'Ike loa

To know well. To seek knowledge and wisdom.

'Imi

To look for, hunt, search, seek.

'Imi ola

To seek life. Our purpose in life is to seek its highest form.

Imua!

Go forward!

242

Ka'ana like
To share or to divide. At Hualalai the phrase would be used to say, "we share in the work, let's share in the joy." *Like* is alike, same, similar, or mutual.

Kahu
Caretaker. Also a person accepted as a spiritual advisor to others.

Kai
Sea water.

Kai'imiola
The name given to a sailing canoe by the Alaka'i Nalu, the watermen of the Hualalai Resort. *Kai* is a word for sea or sea water, thus the *Kaona* (hidden meaning) for *Kai 'imi ola* was "new life on the sea."

Ka lā hiki ola
It is the dawning of a new day. The word *hiki* refers to ability and possibility, can or may.

Kākou
All of us. We are in this together. Speaking the language of we. Linguistically *kākou* is we inclusive of three or more, *lākou* refers to they or them,

more than two, and *mākou* is also we or us, but exclusive.

Kama'āina
A person who is native born in Hawaii, however not of Hawaiian blood. Literally the words translate to land child.

Kaona
Hidden meaning, or concealed reference. Most commonly used in poetry and in language.

Kaumaha
Weight, heaviness.

Kēia lā
Today.

Kēia manawa
In this present time.

Keiki o ka 'āina
Children or descendants of the land.

Kino
One's physical body and health.

Kuleana
One's personal sense of responsibility. I accept my responsibilities, and I will be held accountable.

Kūlia
To try, to strive.

Kūlia i ka nuʻu
Achievement. Strive to reach the summit. Pursue personal excellence.

Kumu
Teachers.

Kumu aʻo
Source of learning.

Kupuna
An elder.

Kūpuna
The plural form of *Kupuna*.

Laulima
Many hands. A word often used when discussing cooperation and *Lōkahi*. Joint action.

Lōkahi
Cooperation and unity. Harmony. Striving together until we become one. Collaboration as opposed to negotiation; *Lōkahi* seeks win-win agreements.

Lūʻau
Taro tops. Also a Hawaiian feast, so named for the taro tops that were traditionally served.

Mahalo
Thank you, as a life concept. Live in thankfulness for the elements that make life so precious.

Mahalo nui loa
Said to mean "Thank you very much." *Nui* is big, large, or grand, and loa is the word for long.

Mālama
To take care of. To serve and to honor, to protect and care for.

Mālamalama
Light of knowledge, clarity of thinking or explanation, enlightenment; shining, radiant, clear.

Mālama ka poʻe
Care for one's people.

Mālama the ʻāina
Take care of the land, i.e. take care of one's sense of place.

Manaʻo
One's thoughts and beliefs that have become what is true for them, serving to empower them and give them certainty and conviction.

Mana'o lōkahi
Unanimous.

Mauna
Mountain. *Mauna Kea* (name) is White Mountain, so named for the snow that normally crowns her highest summit, and *Mauna Loa* (name) is Long Mountain, named for her gracefully sloping profile.

Mea Ho'okipa
Host or hostess. A person offering the utmost in hospitality.

Na'au
The *na'au* are guts, the intestines, and the word is also used for one's gut feelings and intuition. Instinct.

Nānā i ke kumu
Look to your source, find your truth. Don't forget the ancient ways lest we falter. *Nānā* means to look, and *kumu* gives fundamental or hereditary basis to the phrase.

Nalu
Surf, the waves of the ocean.

Nu'u
Height, high place, summit.

O'ahu
Name of the most densely populated island in the Hawaiian chain, where the capital city of Honolulu is found. The name itself has no literal meaning.

'Oama
The young fish of the *weke*, or goatfish.

'Ohana
Family. The sacred form of sharing this life with *Aloha*.

Ola
Life, health, well-being.

'Ōlelo
Language, speech, spoken word. To talk.

'Olu'olu
Pleasant and nice, agreeable, gracious.

'Opihi
Limpets similar to abalone but much smaller.

Pāpio
The young fish of the *ulua*, a type of fish.

Pau
Finished.

245

Pele
In Hawaiian lore, *Pele* is goddess of fire and the volcano.

Pilikia
Trouble of any kind, large or small.

Pōhaku
A rock or stone.

Pono
Rightness and balance. The feeling of contentment when all is good and all is right. Pono is thought of as goodness, uprightness, and morality. Well-being and prosperity.

Puka
A hole or opening.

Ua mau ke ea o ka 'āina i ke pono
The motto of the State of Hawaii, translated as meaning "the life of the land is perpetuated in right-eousness."

Ua pono kaua
We succeeded.

Ua pono ka kaua hana
We succeeded with our work.

'Uhane
One's soul or spirit.

Wa'a
Canoe. Also used as the name for the hull of the canoe, as separate from the *ama*, the outrigger.

Wahi
Place or location, setting.

Wai
Water. Also liquid of any kind except sea water (kai).

Waiwai
Richness or wealth. An abundance of goods, prosperity.

Index

A

Accountability. *See Kuleana,*
126
in environment of *Lōkahi,*
107
Achievement. *See Kūlia i ka*
nuʻu, 67
to satisfy guests, *Hoʻokipa,*
79, 80, 85
Action
clarity, from leadership
philosophy, 62
from mission, 20
language as catalyst, 117
per plan, per mission, 74
rightness, spiritual, 69
Adversity. *See Hoʻomau,* 65
Agreement
collaborative, with synergy,
118
in *Lōkahi,* for harmony, 105
with vision, implied by
Kākou, 116
Ainslie, Sam, 3, 4
Alakaʻi
coaching employees, 175
coaching new managers, 177
destiny, *ʻImi ola,* 175
guide and host, concierge
and professional, 175

leadership, call for, 171
leadership, focus of, 173
leadership, formal versus
informal, 174
leadership, values-centered,
172
leadership, versus title, 169
management versus leader-
ship, 171
managers' *Hoʻohana,* 174
respect for those you lead,
179
value defined, 169
value-building, 170
Alakaʻi Nalu
asset inventory, 217
Daily Five Minutes, 162
goal-setting, 46, 176
ʻImi ola, seeking new life,
50, 53
inclusiveness of *Kākou,* 117
introduced, 44
lesson of the Six Seats, 119
mission statement, 51, 117,
206
mountain climbing, *Kūlia i*
ka nuʻu, 74
Nānā i ke kumu, 206, 209
reputation, 52, 53, 74, 75
sailing canoe *Kaiʻimiola,* 50
sense of place, 52, 206

Notes

Notes

Notes

Notes

Notes